CISTERCIAN STUDIES SERIES: NUMBER THIRTY-THREE

DOROTHEOS OF GAZA
DISCOURSES AND SAYINGS

A translation of
ΤΟΥ ΟΣΙΟΥ ΠΑΤΡΟΣ ΗΜΩΝ ΔΩΡΟΘΕΟΥ ΔΙΔΑΣΚΑΛΙΑΙ
ΔΙΑΦΟΡΟΙ ΠΡΟΣ ΤΟΥΣ ΕΑΥΤΟΥ ΜΑΘΗΤΑΣ

cistercian publications
Editorial Offices
The Institute of Cistercian Studies
Western Michigan University
Kalamazoo, Michigan 49008-5415

The work of Cistercian Publications is made possible in part
by support from Western Michigan University to
The Institute of Cistercian Studies.

CUSTOMER SERVICE:

The United States: Liturgical Press
Saint John's Abbey   Collegeville, MN 56321-7500
sales@litpress.org

The United Kingdom and Europe: Alban Books Ltd
14 Belford Road   West End
Edinburgh   EH4 3BL
sales@albanbooks.com

Canada: Bayard Books
49 Front Street East, Second Floor
Toronto Ontario M5E 1B3
cservice@novalis-inc.com

ISBN 0 87907 933 9

Typeset by the Contemplative Sisters of the Precious Blood
Cloister Printery, New Riegel, Ohio

Printed in the United States of America

CISTERCIAN STUDIES SERIES: NUMBER THIRTY-THREE

DOROTHEOS OF GAZA
DISCOURSES and SAYINGS

Translated, with an introduction, by

Eric P. Wheeler

Cistercian Publications

Kalamazoo, Michigan

1977

This translation is dedicated

to

Dom Leo Williamson OSB

without whose help I should never

have had enough Greek to do it.

ABBREVIATIONS

Antioche   A.J. Festugière, *Antioche païenne et chrétienne: Libanius, Chrysostome et les moines de Syrie.* Paris: Bocard, 1959.

Apo   *Apophthegmata patrum*

Biblos   Βίβλος ψυχωφελεστάτη...Βαρσανουφίου και Ἰωάννου (The Letters of Barsanuphius and John by Nicodemos the Hagorite). 2nd edition. Volos, 1960.

Bousset   W. Bousset, *Apophtegmata.* Tübingen, 1921.

Conf.   The *Conferences* of Cassian

DS   *Dictionnaire de Spiritualité.* Paris, 1932—

EAO   *Etudes d'Archéologie* II. Paris, 1896.

GCS   *Die grieschen christlichen Schriftsteller.* Leipzig & Berlin, 1897—

Inst.   The *Institutes* of Cassian

MSG   *Maîtres Spirituels au Desert de Gaza.* Solesmes, 1967—

OC   *Orientalia christiana.* Rome.

PE   Paul Evergetinos, ed. Συναγωγὴ τῶν Θεοφθόγγων ῥημάτων καὶ διδασκαλιῶν... Πατέρων. Constantinople, 1861.

PG   Migne, *Patrologia Graeca*, Paris, 1857-66.

PL   Migne, *Patrologia Latina*, Paris, 1844-64.

PO   *Patrologia Orientalia*

ROC   *Revue de l'Orient chrétien.*

TUGL   *Texte und Untersuchungen zur Geschichte der altchristlichen Literatur.* Leipzig & Berlin.

CSEL   *Corpus scriptorum ecclesiasticorum latinorum*

TABLE OF CONTENTS

Preface   9

A Letter to my Readers   13

Introduction

The Text   19

The Life of Dorotheos   23

The Monastery at Thawatha   29

Dorotheos at Thawatha   35

Mystical Experiences   51

The Turning-point   55

Death   67

Part One: Discourses

  I.   On Renunciation   77

 II.   On Humility   94

III.   On Conscience   104

 IV.   On the Fear of God   109

  V.   On the Need for Consultation   122

 VI.   On Refusal to Judge our Neighbor   131

VII.   On Self-accusation   140

VIII. On Rancor or Animosity   149

 IX.   On Falsehood   156

  X.   On Travelling the Way of God
       with Vigilance and Sobriety   163

 XI.   On Cutting off Passionate Desires Before
       They Become Rooted Habits of Mind   172

XII.   On the Fear of Punishment to Come
       and the Need for Never Neglecting
       One's Salvation   182

XIII. On Accepting Temptations Calmly
and with Gratitude   192

XIV. On Building up Virtues and their Harmony   201

Part Two: The Paschal Mystery

XV. On the Lenten Fast   215

XVI. Commentary on an Easter Hymn
of St Gregory Nazianzen   220

XVII. Commentary on a Hymn for the
Feasts of Martyrs by the Same   227

Part Three: Dialogues and Maxims

XVIII. How the President should Conduct Himself
Towards the Brethren and They Subject
Themselves to Him   237

XIX. Dialogue with the Cellerar   241

XX. Reply to Some Hermits who Asked Him
About Holding Meetings   244

XXI. On the Insensibility of Soul and
the Flight of Love   249

XXII. Maxims of Dorotheos of Gaza   251

PREFACE

There is something extraordinary (and comforting) about any spiritual writer who can begin an Instruction *On Fear of the Punishment to Come* with the candid admission that his current bout with rheumatism of the feet was probably occasioned by too much convivial cheer in the guest-house refectory. But this is Dorotheos.

Dorotheos of Gaza has something for almost everyone. What is more, he has so genial a way of saying it that we find ourselves not only listening, but listening with genuine enjoyment—and profit. This is all the more remarkable in that, were we to draw up an inventory of Dorotheos' favorite topics—and such an inventory would perforce include humility, fear of the Lord, renunciation, self-contempt—the cumulative effect would doubtless spell discouragement for even the more earnest prospective reader. Indeed, it might have been in the interests of sales-promotion to have omitted the individual titles of Dorotheos' *Instructions* from the Table of Contents, for there are only two categories of persons likely to feel attracted, on the strength of such titles, to read farther: first, the starry-eyed mere beginner in the spiritual life; and second, the person, who through long years of ascetic effort and growth in prayer and charity, has come to love and to appreciate 'from within', so to speak, the wisdom of the desert.

It would be unfortunate, however, were the prospective reader to be put off by the *prima facie* uninviting ring of the Table of Contents; for to miss reading this Grand Old Man of Gaza is to miss out on a deeply rewarding experience. In some respect, Dorotheos may be compared to the incomparable J. S. Bach. Most of us, for instance, will not feel deeply moved by the lugubrious opening lines of the traditional chorale *Valet will ich dir geben:*

> Farewell I gladly bid thee,
> False, evil world, farewell!
> Thy life is dark and sinful,
> With thee I would not dwell...

Catherine Winkworth's translation is grim enough, but no more grim than the original German, the spirit of which she captures with depressing fidelity. Yet, with so improbably a text as his starting-point, Bach takes flight in his fantasia-like organ setting, and has us rising with him through ascending terraces of triplet-spurts of sheer joy, bounding and soaring as in some great cosmic dance in celebration of a life now freed from all constraint and limitation. Is Bach, then, unfaithful to the opening lines of his hymn-text? Not at all. He has simply experienced them within the context of a deeper vision and a more total understanding of what the death of a Christian really means; so that, through his genius for expression through the medium of sound, he helps us better understand and appreciate the riches inherent in the classical, speciously uninviting *contemptus mundi* theme. In much the same way Dorotheos addresses himself to matters likely to frighten off the uninitiated. But as he begins quietly talking about humility, detachment, renunciation, we begin to feel more comfortable; and, if we are not careful, we end by wanting to share and enter into something of Dorotheos' own experience of the Mystery of Christ.

Dorotheos is wonderfully anecdotal. Further, much of his charm comes from the fact that he is drawing on, not just written sources and oral tradition, but his own experience of day to day life with the brethren. And the brethren include, not only the saintly Abba Seridos, the two recluses Barsanuphius and John, and the model-monk Dositheus, but monks of a more earthy—disconcertingly earthy—stamp. Dorotheos is a shrewd observer, a master psychologist, an accomplished *raconteur*. He is also a learned man, with a prodigious capacity for assimilating in an organic harmony the wisdom of his predecessors in the life of the Spirit; but he is much more interested in humbly serving the brethren than in discoursing about the more recondite aspects of the hesychast experience. The specialist possibly has grounds for complaint that there is not a great deal demonstrably *original* in Dorotheos' teaching. Granted. But for many of us, Dorotheos' 'lack of originality' turns to our advantage. Representing as he does a point of convergence for so many strands of tradition, Dorotheos becomes the ideal spiritual master to introduce us into the rich spiritual universe peopled by the denizens of the deserts of Egypt, Palestine, and Syria. Most of us will be able to approach Evagrius, Cassian, and the Old Men of the *Apophthegmata*, with all the greater love and insight, for having first made the genial acquaintance of Dorotheos of Gaza.

Chrysogonus Waddell

Abbey of Gethsemani

TO MY READERS

Dear Friends,

This is not a work of erudition. I am fitted for that neither by temperament nor training. I am not a Greek scholar, only a labourer sent into the vineyard at the ninth, if not at the eleventh hour. Naturally, I am well pleased with my 'denarius', so pleased, that I am delighted to share it with you and with anyone who understands the English language.

Shall I tell you how it came about? Towards the end of my school days I changed my school. In other subjects I was moderately proficient but I had done no Greek. I was dumped into a class to start learning it with a two year handicap, and listened to the other chaps rattling off their irregular verbs or construing their set book—Lucan, if I remember rightly—and wondering about the chaps who got drunk by eating the fish out of the river that flowed with wine. I was fascinated, but completely frustrated in my attempts to emulate them. I left with a nodding acquaintance with λυω, λυειν, with aorests and duals and the middle voice and a few such oddities. There is might have ended but for St Paul and his Epistles, with whom I had to make a more intimate acquaintance in the course of my monastic studies. I resolved to have another go at Greek, a little at grammar and syntax and much with the text of the Apostle and a dictionary. After a few months I gave it up in despair. There were many things I *had* to do, and others that I *could* do with profit and much less labour. Many years passed, full of occupations, varied and absorbing. Then one day I learned, in reading the life of Lord Melbourne, Queen Victoria's first and best loved Prime Minister, that his favourite reading was the Works of St John Chrysostom—and I kept on wondering, why?

Some little time before this I had made the acquaintance of the Loeb translations of the Classics, and been rather fascinated with Aeschylus and Sophocles, Homer, and especially Aristophanes. Then I began on St John Chrysostom's sermon in the Latin translations. Thus was born the ambition to read Chrysostom in the original Greek, and I went back to school and began at the beginning, starting with alpha, beta, gamma, etc. I was fortunate in having a confrère who was intimately connected both with Greek and the art of teaching, and, thanks to him, after a regular 'task' executed daily for about a year, I was able to make out slowly the sense of what Chrysostom was talking about—still with a rather vigilant eye on the latin 'crib'.

Then I came across the Russian Pilgrim[1], who in his search for the way to fulfill St Paul's injunction to 'pray without ceasing' comes to a monastery and meets a venerable staretz who tells him about the 'Prayer of Jesus', teaches him how to acquire it, and introduces him to a precious book called the *Philocalia*, which appeared to be a compendium of the spirituality of the Fathers of the Desert as continued and developed in the Eastern Churches and especially in Russia. One of the personalities who was quoted from time to time was the Abbot Dorotheos. About this time I was on a tour of Northern France on a Moped and stayed at a small and very poor and austere little monastery not long founded near Poix; there on their book stall I found the 'Maîtres Spirituels du desert de Gaza' produced by the Monks of Solesmes. On flicking through the pages I found several letters of Abbot Dorotheos to St Barsanufius regarding his vocation and spiritual life, and the replies thereto. Needless to say this tied up with my existing curiosity about Abbot Dorotheos and I bought the book for consumption later at my leisure. On returning home I began a little research into the Greek Patrology, to try and find some of the authors quoted in the *Philocalia*, and thus I came on the text I present to you now, in English dress.

Why did I choose Dorotheos for translation as a vehicle for improving my Greek and furthering my resolution to gain enough Greek to read Chrysostom in the original? There were many authors quoted in the *Philocalia* of whom I found writings in the Greek Patrology, like Mark the Hermit, St Nilus, St Theodore the studite and many others. Samples taken from the Latin translations were interesting enough but often very copious, unmanagable quantities. And Chrysostom himself? Well, he wrote or spoke a whole library himself and his vocabulary is extremely extensive. I started translating a few samples of his earlier writings but the state of my knowledge then made it rather too laborious and progress was very slow, whereas the corpus of Dorotheos' works was of reasonable proportions. There were several other factors which influenced my choice. The first was that he was a near contemporary of our own Saint Benedict, and much of what Abbot Dorotheos had to say tied up neatly with what our Holy Founder laid down in his Holy Rule. In fact, on many points, Abbot Dorotheos might have been giving a commentary on the spiritual doctrine of St Benedict. I thought, therefore, that Abbot Dorotheos would provide excellent *lectio divina*; especially as his remarks were based on Holy Scripture, with particular reference to Gospel. Secondly, Abbot Dorotheos was steeped in the lore of the Fathers of the Desert[2] and illustrated his discourses with their sayings and their way of life. Writers nowadays are inclined to play down the importance of the lives and teaching of the Fathers of the Desert. There are writers, even modern monastic writers, who are inclined to dismiss them summarily as a lot of eccentric self torturers. This way of treating them did not coincide with the impression their lives and apophthegmeta made on me. It is true that a good deal is said about their austerities and their apparently merciless treatment of 'brother ass'. But to my mind there was more to it than that. Apart from their sly and charming humour—which may have led to some misunderstanding—there was a flood of pure scriptural Christianity in what they had to say and do. I, therefore, thought it profitable to see how their traditions developed in the generations which followed the fourth and fifth centuries, which had witnessed the stampede into the desert that ensued upon the baptism of Constantine and the end of the era of martyrdom.

The Decrees of the II Vatican Council laid stress on returning to the sources and adapting the lives of religious to the conditions of the modern world: In other words a return to the Gospels and Holy Scripture in general and to the authentic spirit of their Founders. St Benedict in the West summed up and adapted the ideals of monastic life to his day, but he drew the bulk of his teaching from the monastic tradition of the East—from Egypt and the Desert, and he imprinted on it the spirit and genius of Rome and the West. I very soon perceived that Dorotheos was very nearly in the same position in the East as Benedict was in the West and very nearly so in time. His method was different, but his teaching was parallel and complementary. It is true that later the Rule found its way into Greek but it is very doubtful whether it was translated during St Benedict's lifetime or for a century or so after. I should be extremely surprised if either St Benedict or Abbot Dorotheos were acquainted with the work of the other.

Finally, and perhaps most importantly, I translated, and offer in English to anyone who cares to read them, Abbot Dorotheos and his Discourses because of his humanity, his psychological insights and understanding of the foibles and weaknesses of men. Combined with understanding goes a large-hearted compassion which will appeal to men of this age, whether they are religious or not; whether they believe in Christ or not. St Dorotheos was not producing a literary work, but speaking from the heart, to men who were sincerely working to make their Christianity a living reality in their lives, and thereby to become human in its fullest and truest sense.

True humanity is much talked about and universally sought after in these days, though often in strange and surprising ways, but it will never be attained if one of its essentials is left out of count. I mean a personal relationship with God through Christ.

I shall make no attempt to analyse the teaching of Dorotheos, which is pure Christianity; the text literally speaks for itself. I would only point to the almost existential approach: what is, is, and is to be accepted without suspecting or judging our neighbour or allowing ourselves to be upset by his failings. God ultimately has the guiding hand over all things and allows evils or even calamities to arrive only for our greater good—and we can still thank him for all things, and feel gratitude to our neighbour as a benefactor, under God, when his actions cause us suffering.

These discourses have a rugged eloquence about them; they are often hard-hitting and direct; they are often repetitive and call for a little perseverance, but they are spoken with skill. Their simplicity is sometimes deceiving, but the illustrative stories are telling and often enchanting. I make no attempt to mould them into a more literary form, but present them, to the best of my ability, in all their spoken vivacity, with their roughness, even their crudity and repetitions. Do not let yourself be deceived by the blemishes. I would say to you what St Barsanufius said to Dorotheos in one of his letters: 'For those capable of understanding these words and keeping them, there is joy and great profit.'[3] Having lived with Dorotheos for nigh on a couple of years, I can testify that this is no less than the truth.

I am quite conscious that much of what I have written in this introduction is conjectural, and many of the points that I would have liked to verify at their sources I have not been able to, either for lack of the means to do so or for lack of time. Also as I write many more questions arise in my mind, and if I waited until I had means and opportunity to answer them, I, too, should be in my tomb before this translation appeared in print. However, my appetite is whetted and my studies continue. Nevertheless, as I feel confident that what Dorotheos has to say can be of considerable help to many of you, my readers. I send my work to press in spite of the inadequacies, the mistakes, even the stupidities I have committed. For these I hope you will forgive me and give your attention to the great man, whose doctrine I have tried to present to you in readable form. Though I may have erred in detail, I do not think I have substantially misrepresented him. May he intercede for us all from his place near the Throne of him whom he loved, and whose commandments he tried so hard to teach men to keep.

Eric P. Wheeler

1 February 1973

INTRODUCTION

THE TEXT

OF SOMETHING LIKE two hundred Greek manuscripts of Dorotheos' works which have been produced over the centuries, the earliest dates back to the tenth century. There are also twenty-five or more manuscripts of an Arabic translation going back possibly to the ninth century and about one-third that number in Georgian, the earliest is of the ninth Century. Latin translation appeared in manuscript from the eleventh century onwards. Since the invention of printing there have been several editions in Latin and Greek. A French translation appeared in 1597, followed by others up to the famous 'Les instructions de Saint Dorothée', Paris 1686, by the Abbé de Rancé, the energetic founder of the Trappists. The Cistercians, the Benedictines and, strangely enough, the Jesuits have during the past centuries found spiritual nourishment in the works of Dorotheos.

Translations were made into modern Greek and various Slavonic languages from 1676 onwards. Add to this Spanish, Dutch, and German translations and the few extracts in English which appeared in G. Palmer's *Early Fathers from the Philocalia*, London 1964, and you have some idea of the fecundity of Dorotheos' life and teaching. My intention is to give a complete rendering of St Dorotheos' *teaching*, rather than translate every word of his that we have.

The text I used was that of the Greek Patrology (Migne)[4] and it was not until my work was all but finished that I had in my hands the new edition and French translation of Dom L. Regnault and Dom J. de Préville, monks of Solesmes, for which I am very grateful.[5] Ideally I should go over the whole thing again with the new text, but with my present commitments I would run the risk of expiring before it was completed.   However, the analysis of Dorotheos' teaching coincides so nearly with my own impression of it that, in spite of the detailed amendments they claim to have made, I do not think they made a substantial alteration to the instruction given by Dorotheos. I, therefore, think it useful to publish the translation as it stands, apart from a few minor corrections, and to refer those with a more scientific need and outlook to the above named work. One thing I have done is to adopt the modified order of the two sermons on texts of St Gregory Nazianzan and place them directly after the discourse on the Lenten fast. The discipline of Lent is so bound up with the Paschal Mystery—with preparation for celebrating the Passion, Death and Resurrection of Our Lord—that to follow Lent by a sermon on the Resurrection forms a natural sequence. That on the martyrs, the first ones to follow Our Lord to death and to the glory of the Resurrection, complete the sequence; more than this, it seems to have been preached on the octave of Easter. Certainly the two latter were actually delivered during the liturgy of Eastertide. The one on Lent appears to be composite, as the beginning seems to accord with the beginning of Lent and the last paragraph with Palm Sunday. It appears likely that the whole is made up from matters spoken of during the liturgy of the season of Lent.   The whole sequence emphasizes the patent fact that in the eyes of those ancient monks the eucharistic Sacrifice was the focal point of their spiritual life; and, as St Chrysostom points out in one of his sermons, whenever the Holy Sacrifice is offered the Paschal Mystery is re-enacted. The reform of the liturgy which is

going on at present is bringing into clearer focus this ancient
view of things. Hence I have entitled the second part of my
work 'The Paschal Mystery': it comprises *Discourses* 15 to
17. The remainder of the matter contained in the Migne
edition, with the exception of the series of questions and
answers exchanged between St Barsanufius and Dorotheos
which are left out, all comes under the heading of letters in
the next text. I have preferred to entitle this third section,
'Dialogues and Replies', Chps. 18-21. In the final Chapter 22
is the collection of Dorotheos' sayings under the title
'Maxims'.

Dialogue about spiritual and ecclesiastical matters is very
much in the air at the present time, but it is not a new idea;
it is a very old one and it is quite evident from the works of
Dorotheos himself that it was very much alive in monastic
circles in his day. Even the hermits who would normally
come together once a week to celebrate the Eucharist would
come together from time to time to take a meal in common
(*agape*) and to discuss various topics concerned with the
spiritual life. This is where the 'Dialogue' went on and it is
in evidence in much of the monastic writing that has
survived. It is true that among the ancients the dialogue was
a favourite literary form, but there is plenty of evidence that
many of them are basically reports of discussions that actually
took place. As you will see in one of the Discourses (II)
Dorotheos mentions one which took place at which the old
man, Zosimos, was asked by a certain sophist how it was that
he, who had followed the monastic way of life so strictly for
so long and kept the Commandments so faithfully, could still
consider himself a sinner? At this discussion not only monks
were present, but also laymen. He gives also at least two
other hints about 'dialogue' at his conferences; one where he
states that two or three hours had passed since the brethren
he was talking to had assembled; the other when he says that
St Paul gave his instructions by way of precept, while he
himself had to enquire of his hearers, 'What would you like
me to talk about today? Shall I say something about...?' For

this reason I have entitled the last few *Discourses* 'Dialogues
and Replies'. They are much more fragmentary, shorter and
less systematic. They could, of course, have been letters, but
equally they could have been Dorotheos' contributions to
certain discussions. Since the collector of Dorotheos'
teachings says that he has found only a small part of
Dorotheos' output, and at least one of the *Discourses* is in the
form of a dialogue with the cellarer, I am inclined to think the
last few *Discourses* were in fact his contributions to such discussions which monastery stenographers had taken down in
shorthand and conserved. These were the fragments which
were later to be searched out and collected from the different
monasteries by the writer of the dedicatory letter which
accompanied the original manuscript to the confrère who had
asked for it. This letter has been transcribed ever since as a
preface to Dorotheos' work. In the following century another
preface was added in front of it, evidently by a Studite monk;
besides testifying to his orthodoxy, it distinguishes both
Barsanufius and Dorotheos from men who bore the same
name but held diverse opinions.

The collector's letter not only praises Dorotheos' virtues
and summarises his doctrine, but calls him 'our Holy Father'
and mentions his correspondent's great love for him. From
the way he speaks it seems to me that both he and his
correspondent knew Dorotheos in the flesh. Although these
two prefaces are ancient I shall not give a translation in full,
though I shall make use of them. What they praise in
Dorotheos speaks for itself in the *Discourses.*

It only remains to say something of a few short letters
which appear in the new Greek text. They repeat in slightly
different form things which are already included in substance
in the *Discourses*; or if a sentence or two appeared especially
striking it has been added to the Maxims.

THE LIFE OF DOROTHEOS

Who then was this Dorotheos? [6] The Bollandists in the *Acta Sanctorum* give him the title, Dorotheos the Archimandrite of Gaza. The section in the Greek Patrology devoted to the *Discourses* also give the title the *Archimandrite* to St Dorotheos. The *Discourses* themselves are headed literally, 'Teachings of our Holy Father Dorotheos profitable for the soul'. In the monastic milieu of those early centuries there were several interesting and distinguished characters bearing the name of Dorotheos. Although separated in time and place there was a tendency among early hagiographers to identify one with another. [7] The one with whom we are concerned became the *quondam* disciple of Abbat Seridos, and the two famous old men, Barsanufius, the Ancient par excellence, and John, the Prophet, his disciple and alter ego. They flourished at the monastery at Thawatha, a few miles away from Gaza, towards the sea coast.

Historical documents dealing with his life are tantalizingly scanty, but in the *Discourses* and letters are many scattered autobiographical details, from which a lively picture of the man emerges; and I have no doubt that a competent historian, from a complete analysis of them, could draw a competent 'life' of the holy man. For although, according to the Bollandists, no official cultus was accorded him, his evident sincerity and spiritual drive towards christian perfection mark him out as one of God's chosen ones. Born at Antioch in Syria, very early in the sixth century, possibly 506 to 508, his education began very early. He reminisces in one of the *Discourses* that when he was learning to read he approached a book as though he were going up to stroke a wild animal—this 'towards the end of his childhood'. Evidently he came of fairly wealthy and probably christian family—though what sort of Christians we have no means of knowing. The fact that he became a monk and had a brother who was a friend of the monks, if he too did not become a monk, would argue a solid christian home life. Though the picture of rich, pleasure loving Antioch which St John Chrysostom draws roughly a century earlier shows that depths of christian faith in the inhabitants varied markedly. They were an excitable people, not particularly loyal to the Empire. There was a strong Jewish colony there and a good proportion remained pagan. They were as ready to flock to the races and pagan entertainments as to the Christian Mysteries to hear St John speak. There was rioting between Jews and Christians, besides fraternisation. There was a judaizing element in the christian population against which St John preached several sermons. They were not during his time noted for learning, and the teaching profession was largely dominated by pagan sophists, most of them not of very high repute, though there were a few exceptions. Of Dorotheos' family life at home we know nothing except what he tells us about 'learning to read when quite young'. In those days this would connote a wealthy household. Judging from the fact that later in life his brother was a benefactor to the community of monks where Dorotheos was living, one would assume that the two boys were bosom companions and shared the services of a private tutor.

Childhood impressions, especially pleasurable ones, usually give colour to the topics and imagery of our adult conversations and often provide illustrative material for those who become involved in teaching. In the *Discourses* Dorotheos often refers to water, water sports, and sea phenomena, even to a storm at sea. From the expert knowledge of swimming in the sea and fishing with a rod and line for large and lively fish he displays in his conferences, it seems that these were among his favourite boyhood occupations. Anyone who has had the experience of swimming from a shelving beach as large waves are crashing on the shore feels his own experience coming to life as he reads Dorotheos 'talking' of the expert swimmer, or of the angler technique of landing a big fish.

Another topic on which he discourses with a facility that

suggests knowledge gained by personal experience is the cultivation of the land. These two topics lead us to suspect that his parents owned a villa close to the Mediterranean coast at which the two boys would spend at least their holidays. The farm—for such it would inevitably be—seems to have been engaged in the production of corn and possibly swine, for the only animal he mentions—apart from a dog—is the pig. He comments on the pig's excellent constitution, which enables him to turn a disgusting diet of date-stones and mud into healthy flesh.

Further hints about his early life can perhaps be deduced from the fact that, whereas he avoids almost entirely the topic of women and motherhood, he willingly dilates on the Fathers and always shows a touching devotion to his spiritual Fathers. He is conversant with the medical theories of his day, and medical terms can be found scattered about his pages as well as an accurate description of the treatment of wounds and ulcers. Was he in fact the son of a well-to-do doctor and very much his father's boy? Or did his mother die during his infancy or early childhood? [8]

In one of the *Discourses* he gives a description of the distress felt by passengers on a storm-tossed ship in danger of ship-wreck and the enjoyment that everyone had in talking it over when the danger had passed. This would evidently have been a later experience; perhaps when he made the voyage from Antioch to Maiuma, the Port of Gaza, when about to embark on his career. From his description of his life as a student, it seems clear that he was not at home, for he tells us that the companion with whom he was living did all the chores, while he himself got on with his reading. Such was his passion for study, he tells us, that he was obliged to go to the baths every day to restore his played-out body. The Roman baths, of course, were like modern Turkish baths, and not a bit like the little room where we spend some time daily. It implied a good steaming and was followed by massage and gentle exercise. The spur that urged him on to study so hard was, on his own admission,[9] his ambition to become a master of eloquence.

Who could his obliging companion have been?   Could it
have been that same brother who also became a friend of the
monks and was later to furnish the finances for building the
infirmary at the monastery of Thawatha?   He could have
studied at Alexandria, which was the most famous place of
learning of the time; but all the indications point in the
direction of Gaza.   There was certainly a flourishing christian
school of rhetoric there, and to this day the name of
Dorotheos is coupled with Gaza.   In all probability his
teacher, and later his elder colleague, was Procopius of Gaza,
who has left us a thick volume of writings, chiefly commen-
taries on Holy Scripture compiled from the writings of the
Fathers.   There is also a small collection of letters, mostly
letters to friends.   Their contents are not very important, but
their style is considered excellent.   There is also a panegyric
on the death of the Emperor Anastasius (†518 AD) which is
historically important, a discourse to celebrate the completion
of Sancta Sophia, 537, and a lament on its partial collapse
twenty years later in the earthquake.   Among the letters is a
series to a much-loved friend by the name of Dorotheos.
Whether they were written to our Dorotheos, we cannot be
quite sure from the contents, except perhaps the last one,
which was evidently written to a monk who was a man of
influence.   He wrote: 'Here once more is an opportunity for
devotedness and for recourse to your wisdom!   One of the
men consecrated to God, and known for his pursuit of the
monastic ideal has, as a result of false and slanderous
accusations it would appear, fallen under the displeasure of a
judge who is much incensed against him for raising an
unfriendly hand against those whose duty it is to see that the
laws are obeyed.   Those who laid the information attributed
the alleged wrong-doing of others to this good man.   The
judge has cited him to appear and pay the penalty. Now is
the time, if there is one, to seek clemency. Show yourself
therefore and say something in defence of your own men [or
way of life] so as to calm the anger of the judge.... If nothing

else you will have honoured the monastic habit which he wears. Make your appearance with many others, who are apt for the defence, but preferably you [should speak] before the others.' [10]

In one of his *Discourses*, Dorotheos tells of a certain christian sophist who, seeking better to understand the matter under discussion, posed some questions. Unfortunately he is not named, but all the same it does seem likely that it was in fact his old friend and teacher, Procopius of Gaza.

If Dorotheos not only taught, but had previously done his studies at Gaza, we have a reasonable hypothesis as to why he chose to take up his monastic life at Thawatha, which was a little over two miles away. We can well imagine a cultural contact between the monastery and the christian academy at Gaza; and equally well a young and enthusiastic student, in search of piety and learning, paying a visit to a neighbouring monastery. This would provide an occasion for getting to know Abbat Seridos and the two wise old hermits, Barsanufius and John, with whom Dorotheos continued in correspondence both before and after his entry into monastic life. Evidence of this is provided by the large number of letters which passed between them, and which actually exist to this day. But, like so many of the facts we know about Dorotheos, the indications of time and place are all but wanting. These letters are all taken up with matters of the soul—and the soul has no time or place, so such details were left aside as superfluous.

When Dorotheos left his home at Antioch we do not know, but we do know that there was a disastrous earthquake there in 526 which did much harm to life and property. Could this have been the year that Dorotheos installed himself at Gaza? It is possible that the family home fell victim to the earthquake and the parents perished with it. If we guess the date of his birth at 506 to 508, Dorotheos would have been 20 to 22, a proper age for higher studies and sufficient for him to be able to fend for himself. It is tempting to visualise the two young men, Dorotheos and his brother, having lost their home, going off to Gaza in search of learning and adventure. Dorotheos did not enjoy very robust health, a fact that he refers to in several of his letters to Barsanufius:[11] 'As I have sinned much, I want to do penance, but because of my bodily weakness, I cannot keep up all the austerities practised by the Fathers here.' He has to be encouraged by Barsanufius to make up for his lack of physical prowess by concentrating on humility and obedience and the service of his brethren. During his Discourses he refers, as you will see, to his more serious illnesses. The writer of the commendatory letter mentions that he ran straight up the narrow and precipitous path of monastic life 'contrary to the expectations of all'. And Barsanufius, in reproving him for some fault, has to remind him, evidently some considerable time after his entry into monastic life, that he would not have been able to persevere in it for even one whole year, had it not been for the prayers and assistance of the Fathers living there.   Evidently this constant ill health took its toll on him and he did not live to a great age, for the collector of the *Discourses* specifically says of him that having fulfilled the Lord's command to leave all things and follow Christ, '*in a short time*, with the help of God, he was made perfect, and filled a long time'.

   The fact that Dorotheos' name has come down to us connected with the city of Gaza seems to me to indicate that, even if he did not complete his studies there, he acquired a certain celebrity there, and his own affirmation that he studied with fury to become a master of eloquence, invites the conclusion that he established himself there for a considerable time as a professor of rhetoric.

   This conclusion is consonant with the fact that when he entered the monastery he wrote to the two Ancients about the disposal of his property. He mentions specifically some land, a number of books, which in those days—being manuscripts—represented considerable wealth, and clothes. When one reads the list of garments which John, the other Ancient, allowed him to keep for the needs of his feeble body both summer and winter, and which seems quite ample for a monk, one is tempted to think he must have had a lot of clothes when he was in the world and to wonder if he was not somewhat fond of adorning himself with fine clothing before he came to renounce the world. [12]

However that may be, when we come to read the *Discourses*, we can see for ourselves how well he had profited from his studies and the exercise of his profession. His knowledge is extensive both in sacred and profane learning. He is able to draw on the wisdom of pre-christian sages, notably Aristotle and Epicletus, as well as on the Holy Scriptures and notable christian writers, e.g. St Gregory, St Basil, Evagrius, and the apophthegmata of the Desert Fathers. He is conversant with the medical theory of his day; he discourses on the construction of houses and gives a very complete picture of the agricultural process. Besides this, judge for yourself how expert he was in interesting his hearers: apt illustrations of his matter, anecdotes of the Fathers, his own experiences are all expressed simply, yet with a certain rugged art which was artful enough to conceal itself.

The length of the period of his stay at Gaza is nowhere mentioned; if I were to hazard a guess I would say about ten years. Sometime during that period he came in contact with Abbat Seridos and the two Ancients who lived their lives some two or three miles away at Thawatha, towards the sea coast (somewhat southwest of Gaza). But to complete the background of his life I must at least say something about the place and the monastery and its constitution and the personalities, Barsanufius, John, and Abbat Seridos of whom I have already made mention several times befcre.

THE MONASTERY AT THAWATHA

Long before the monastery to which Dorotheos went to take up monastic life, some kind of monastic settlement had been at Thawatha. The village was the birthplace of St

Hilarion in 291 AD; he studied at Alexandria and after a lengthy stay in the Thebaid, returned to live as a hermit in the neighbourhood of his birthplace. Naturally his fame attracted disciples, and undoubtedly a colony of hermits grew up around him; how many we do not know—certainly too many for his liking, for he fled. Everywhere he went, he remained long enough to collect more disciples than he could cope with. Finally we find him in Cyprus. His example seems to have planted a very vigorous aspiration toward the eremitical life in the whole area. There were single cells or group cells scattered over the whole area which was well watered and fertile. The village of Thawatha was twenty stades, i.e. about 2¼ miles, to the south west of Gaza, situated near the top of a broad valley through which ran what was, normally, a small stream, but which during the rains swelled up and became a deep, swift-flowing river. Descending the stream Thawatha was on the left—somewhere in the area of the present Tel et Tineh. It has not yet been identified, but according to M. Clermont-Garneau [13] we should expect to find the buried remains of it near Choubana.

The geographical situation we know from the story Dorotheos tells of the obedient monk who jumped into the river in flood to go in the direction of Ascalon. John Rufus also tells the story, adding the detail that the monk had been sent to fetch a parchment from Abbat Seridos. [14] After the Mazices' inroads into Upper Egypt under Arcadius, November, 409, many of the monks fled. Among them was Peter, an Iberian, who settled at Thawatha for three years. Not far away was Beit Daliha where Abba Esaias had his cell. He had been trained in a cenobium, then had gone into the inner desert of Scete, and between the Councils of Ephesus and Chalcedon had arrived in Palestine. He died 11 August 489 AD, and seems to have been the spiritual ancestor of the way of life which Dorotheos was to know at Thawatha. Esaias led a completely enclosed life; all communication with him was through his Egyptian disciple Peter. There was a collection of hermits cells not far from him, and actually attached to his hermitage was a colony of cenobites, some of whom eventually graduated to the eremitical life.

Seridos, Barsanufius and John

Seridos is reported to have started his *cenobium* (a monastery where monks lived a close community life) about 500 AD in the neighbourhood of some hermits' cells. One of the hermits can be identified with a certain Euthymius, to whom St Barsanufius was writing some thirty years later and of whom he spoke as a Saint when he died. The young cenobium seems to have gone along slowly for the next thirteen or fourteen years, gradually taking shape but making do with makeshift buildings. Then Barsanufius arrived, and both the cenobium and the colony of hermits began to develop. This was in the last years of the Emperor Anastasius or the first of Justin (514-527). Professor Chitty, in his chapter 'After Three Generations', explains that there was a flow of monks from Upper Egypt into Palestine and reasons that the great growth of Pachomian monasticism resulted in large agglomerations of monks leading a sort of community life, a situation which inevitably led to the acquisition of large tracts of land which were exploited profitably by the monks, the consequent acquisition of riches, commercial enterprise, a large amount of coming and going, a lessening of the idea of solitude, and some relaxation of the ascetic life. Further there was a constant flow of visitors to famous ascetics. Some came genuinely in search of spiritual help and guidance; others came with less worthy motives— tourism, idle curiosity. Added to this there were the incursions of the barbarians who invaded the monastic colonies, maltreated the monks and went off with all they could lay their hands on.

There was another attraction that fostered the flow of ascetics into Palestine; it was Our Lord's own country and hallowed by the lives of the patriarchs and the holy men of Israel. Certainly solitary places in the mountains of Judea and

the desert plains of Palestine were not wanting. Gerara and
the parts around the Wadi of Gaza were associated with and
sanctified by the life of Abraham.   St Barsanufius bears
witness to this in one of his letters to Dorotheos. It is even
possible that the monastic complex at Thawatha was
dedicated to Holy Abraham.

Barsanufius was an Egyptian who had spent many years
in the deserts of Upper Egypt and had acquired enough fame
to be much sought after. Perhaps too he was saddened by
the increasing wealth and growing softness of some of the
communities there, for signs of a slackening of the monastic
ideal were not wanting.   Desiring to escape the flow of
visitors of all sorts who began to beseige him, and to pursue
a life of even greater solitude and severity, he fled to
Palestine.

We have no documentation about his reasons for leaving
Egypt or parting from his cell mate and *alter ego,* John the
Prophet. We can only presume from the intensity of the
spiritual life manifested in his correspondence that it had
something to do with his entering into a new and deeper state
of solitude and prayer and his separation from his faithful
companion, John, which had been agreed between them
before he went. When John finally arrived at Thawatha some
ten years later, Barsanufius gave up his own cell to him and
took a different one. They both took up the kind of life which
Barsanufius had adopted from the beginning, following the
pattern established by Esaias and his disciple, viz. complete
and permanent enclosure, with no communication with the
outside world except by the written word communicated
through a secretary.   For Barsanufius this service was
reformed by Seridos, the *hegumen* of the cenobium, and for
John, by first another, un-named, monk, and later when the
latter fell ill by Dorotheos himself for nine years. The extraordinary thing about this relationship was that, although John
was himself a highly charismatic person, he always wrote of
Barsanufius as his spiritual Father and Master, whereas
Barsanufius always referred to John as his *alter ego* and

powerful ally in the spiritual combat; yet they never saw one another, and never corresponded with one another. John was often asked to explain some of the things which Barsanufius had written to a correspondent—and he did so to perfection, while some of Barsanufius' correspondents who had consulted John (and not mentioned the fact) were told summarily to do what Brother John had told them.

No sooner had Barsanufius arrived at Thawatha than Seridos put himself under his direction. He was subjected to a hard course of spiritual training by Barsanufius who was already an old man. We have few personal details about Seridos except that he was Greek-speaking and probably of Syrian descent. From childhood he had been Christian; he was chaste and temperate. The first buildings of the cenobium and some of the anchorite cells were probably built with his patrimony. He was given to such excessive austerity in his ascetical life that Barsanufius had to put a check on him after he had made himself ill. He became Barsanufius' spiritual son and enjoyed his complete confidence. Except for one occasion (mentioned below) his was the only face that Barsanufius saw for forty years or so. He was also endowed with a share of Barsanufius' supernatural gifts. He shows this in an aside in one of his early letters to John of Berosaba. He revealed that while Barsanufius was telling him what to say—and there was plenty—he became disturbed, wanting to go and fetch his writing material so that he could take it down word for word. Barsanufius read his thoughts, encouraged him and told him that the Holy Spirit would call to his mind what had been said so he would not be able to add or take away one word of it. So strict was Barsanufius' rule about not seeing anyone that some of the monks, one of whose name was Theodore, began to be skeptical about the existence of Barsanufius—this was probably before the arrival of John the Prophet. They taxed Seridos about this Barsanufius he talked about and brought letters from, saying that he was merely the product of Seridos' own mind and a cunning trick he was playing on

them. When he heard this, Barsanufius made an exception.
He told Seridos to bring the doubters to him—and he washed
their feet. On another occasion one of his own race, named
Abraham, wrote to him in Coptic, but he replied in Greek,
because Seridos could not write Coptic. Even so he did not
agree to make an exception to his rule and allow Abraham to
come and see him.

Although his rule about not seeing anyone but Seridos
was strict, he exercised—and exercises to this day—a powerful influence on the world around him. He dictated
thousands of letters of spiritual direction to people of all
classes, to monks, bishops, priests, lay men and women.
Many hundreds of them still exist. On his arrival, John the
Prophet began to live the same kind of life and to share this
ministry. Through their written communications and the
excellence of their teaching and spiritual direction they drew
numbers of would-be disciples to the monastery of Seridos.
Such was the case of John of Berosaba to whom Barsanufius
admitted that two years previously he had had a revelation
that he, John, and others, would join the monastic colony at
Thawatha.

Growth

Both Barsanufius and John were too experienced in the
spiritual life and combat to allow a loose agglomeration of
untrained ascetics to lead the eremitical life in their vicinity,
so they brought them into the cenobium under the direction
of Seridos. Of set purpose I use the word 'cenobium' in its
strict sense: it is a monastery where the brethren lived their
lives in common, chanting their Divine Office in common,
sharing the common table, sleeping in the common
dormitory, attending the same instructions and owing
obedience to the same superior. In fact, they were fully in
accord with the opinion of St Benedict who, while manifesting
high admiration of the eremitical life, says that those who
undertake the hermit's life ought not to be in the flush of

novitiate fervour, but to have learned by long testing in a monastery by the help and support of a community of brethren, to fight the Devil before they enter on the single combat with him and the vices of the flesh and the mind, in the solitude of the desert.

We have some evidence that John and Seridos died between the years 540 and 543 AD, and that John lived at Thawatha eighteen years. So he must have arrived at Thawatha around 522/525, and it was about that time that the cenobitic section of the monastic colony began to flourish. Somewhere, not too distant from the cells of John and Barsanufius, was the cenobium proper, with the community church which had to be completely rebuilt by Seridos on account of the growing numbers. In close proximity were the rest of the communal buildings: the dormitory, bakehouse, refectory, workrooms, and the garden and orchard with the land they cultivated for food. Further out, at varying distances, would be the separate cells of those who had graduated in varying degrees to the life of solitaries. Later on, as we shall see, there was a guest house for the reception of wayfarers and pilgrims, and still later an infirmary for sick monks and possibly strangers. By the time the colony had reached its full development, the number of cenobites and hermits in the colony and the area covered must have been considerable, for in one of his discourses Dorotheos says that it was not convenient for the watcher to stop beside the heavy sleepers and see that they got up—presumably because of the distance he would have had to cover.

DOROTHEOS AT THAWATHA

This was the monastic milieu in which Dorotheos made up his mind to settle. He had known the two old men and Abbot Seridos for some considerable time and had had frequent correspondence with them on the affairs of the soul. His spiritual friendship with them had started in his days at Gaza. It developed no doubt because of his docility and obedience, and his willingness to seek their guidance and to follow their counsel—a fact testified by the number of letters he exchanged with both Barsanufius and John. Their training was very frank and searching, as the letters testify, not free from deserved reproof, but abounding in good advice and encouragement. He became, evidently, a favourite disciple of theirs, so much so that when the personal minister of John fell ill, it was Dorotheos who was appointed to succeed him, a fact that led to a certain amount of jealousy and persecution on the part of some of the brethren, who were anxious for the privilege, he relates in one of his Discourses. This service to Abbot John continued for nine years, in spite of the other duties that were imposed on him. At one time or another he was Guest-master and Chief-Infirmarian. The persecution continued for some time, for when it began he was still in the communal part of the monastery and sleeping in the common dormitory, but it continued even after he had graduated to one of the nearby separate cells. For some of the brethren took to shaking their mats and dumping their rubbish outside his cell, until it was infested with flies and stinging insects. They were so many that he could not hope to kill them all before he lay down to sleep, and wearied from his work he would fall asleep as soon as he lay down. In the morning, or when he was awakened for night Vigils, he would be covered with insect bites, which tormented him, but he bore it patiently without complaining or saying to his brethren, 'Why do you keep on doing this?'

Infirmarian

When the growing number of sick and ailing brethren inspired Barsanufius to suggest the building of a proper infirmary, Dorotheos' own brother came forward with an offer to provide the means to build it, and Dorotheos was entrusted with the building of it. When it was completed he was immediately appointed the Chief Infirmarian and he was expected to use his initiative to see that it was well organised and competently run. His brother evidently had ample means, and had already proved himself a good friend and benefactor of the Community. I would hazard a guess that he was an eldest brother who had already entered into the family inheritance.

The colony was evidently growing rather large and the number of sick proportionate; he had need of several assistants, and even then work was so heavy that he could barely cope with it. Besides this, he hankered for a more contemplative form of life and had to consult Barsanufius about how to keep up his prayer life and yet manage to discharge all the duties imposed on him as infirmarian.

The First Disciple: Saint Dosithy

Among the assistants given him was a certain Dosithy. Attached to the manuscript of the Discourses is a brief life of this young man which shows us Dorotheos at work training his disciples. This youngster was the favourite page of a certain general, completely ignorant of the faith and of God. Hearing one day about the Holy Land, he desired to visit it. The general, not wishing to disappoint him, entrusted him to the care of some of his friends who were about to go there on pilgrimage. He was a very delicately bred young man, leading a very soft and probably dissolute life, but while there he was looking with wonder at a picture depicting the torments of the damned in hell, when a lady appeared and began explaining to him all the punishments that the wicked were obliged to endure after they left this mortal life. Knowing nothing of God and the final judgment, he said in all simplicity, 'Madam, what must I do to escape all these terrible punishments?' And she told him, 'You must take up fasting, eat no meat and pray continually.' With that the lady disappeared. Considerably shaken and filled with compunction, he began to do exactly what the lady had told him. The general's friends, who had brought him to the Holy Land, observed what he was doing and were much disquieted, fearing the general would be displeased; but Dosithy persisted.   Some of the soldiers who had accompanied them, however, told him, 'Young man, the way you are living is not suitable for men living in the world; if you want to stick to it you ought to go to a monastery and you will save your soul.'   But he knew nothing of monasteries, and said, 'All right. Take me to some place you know where I can become a monk, because I don't know where to go.' Some of the soldiers, friends of Abbat Seridos, went off to the monastery taking with them their young friend.   When they arrived at the monastery, Abbat Seridos sent Dorotheos to talk to the young man and to find out all he could about him. But the youth could only repeat, 'I want to be saved'. Dorotheos reported that there was nothing bad about the boy and, if he wished, he could receive the boy without fear. The Abbot then said, 'Do me this favour.   Take him under your charge in the infirmary for the sake of his salvation.' This alarmed Dorotheos' modesty, for although he had been in the monastery several years he still regarded himself as a mere novice.   'It is above my state,' he said, 'and beyond my capacity to take charge of anyone.'   But the Abbot did not want Dosithy to be with the brethren for fear that he had committed some crime and would be pursued and brought to justice, and he insisted.   The Grand Old Man was consulted, and he said to Dorotheos, 'You must accept, because it is through you that God will save him.'   So Dorotheos set to work to train him.   When dinner time came he said, 'Eat as much as you want, but let me know how much.'   After dinner Dosithy came back and said, 'I have eaten two whole 2 lb. loaves.'   So Dorotheos asked, 'Do you feel all right?'   To which Dosithy replied, 'Yes Father.'   'You don't feel hungry?'   'No, Father.'   'From now on then, eat one and a half loaves and cut the remaining half in two, eat half of it and leave the rest.'   He did this and the next day Dorotheos asked him, 'Do you feel hungry, Dosithy?'   And he replied, 'Yes, Father, I do a bit.'   After some days Dorotheos again asked him, 'Do you still feel hungry, Dosithy?'   And he replied, 'No, Father, thanks to your prayers, I'm all right now.' 'Then,' said Dorotheos, 'now make do with one loaf and a half and leave the rest.' And so, little by little, the ration was reduced until Dosithy was able to live on as little as half a loaf a day.

In the infirmary Dosithy was a good worker, looking after the sick, making their beds, and making them comfortable. Everything that he did was well done. If it happened that he was put out by a peevish patient or grew angry and rough with his patients, he would weep bitterly and would not be consoled. The others would report it to Dorotheos, who would seek him out and find him seated on the floor weeping his eyes out. 'What's the matter, Dosithy, what are you crying about?' 'Forgive me, Father,' he would say, 'I got angry with my brother and spoke unkindly to him.' 'And so, Dosithy, you were annoyed, and are not ashamed to speak badly to your brother! You don't yet realise that he *is* Christ, and that you have been a cause of suffering to Christ?' Dosithy would lower his eyes, still crying, and say nothing. When he had cried enough, Dorotheos would say, 'God forgive you. Up now! Let us begin again from now, and let us be more attentive and God will help us.' As soon as he heard these words, Dosithy would get up joyfully and run off to his duties, fully convinced that he had been pardoned by God. Similar scenes took place from time to time, and always when Dorotheos said, 'Come on! Up you get! God forgive you. Once more start again from the beginning but correct yourself from now on.' Dosithy would shake off his trouble and go to work again with a will.

Besides being a thoughtful and efficient infirmarian, Dosithy was also simple and sincere in revealing his inward thoughts, and when his master was passing he would sometimes say, 'My thoughts say to me, "I have made that bed very nicely" '. Dorotheos would say, 'O ho, my lad, you are a good nurse, and have become a good workman, but are you a good monk?'

Dosithy would never let himself become attached to any of

the things he had to use.   When he wanted a new cloak, Dorotheos would give him one that was a bit worse for wear, but Dosithy would take it aside and repair it beautifully.   Then he would show it to Dorotheos, who often enough told him to give it to someone else, and gave him another old cloak to repair for himself.   But Dosithy was never put out or complained, or said, 'After I have taken the trouble to make it like new, he takes it away and gives it to someone else'.

One day a fine looking knife was presented to the infirmary.   Dosithy received it and carried it to Dorotheos to ask if it could be kept in the infirmary as it was excellent for cutting bread.   Dorotheos was not keen on having special things in the infirmary, but was content to have things that would do the job, but were of plain quality.   He consented to have a look at it, and saw that it was not only a good sharp serviceable knife, but handsome also.   As he did not want Dosithy to become attached to any material thing, he would not let him keep it.   He said, 'And so, Dosithy, it pleases you very much?   Do you want to become the slave of this knife and not the slave of God?   Is it true that it pleases you so much, and you are bound by your attachment to this knife?   Are you not ashamed to wish to have this knife for your master rather than God?'   Dosithy listened without a murmur and lowered his eyes.   And Dorotheos, after giving him a long talking to about it, finally said to him, 'Put it over there and never touch it again'.   And he never did.   The others used it, but never again did Dosithy touch it, not even to hand it to someone else to use, and he never said, 'Why only me among the lot of them?'   All that he was told to do he did with joy.

Dosithy lived for something less than five years, never seeking to follow his own will or to satisfy the passionate desires that arose in him, but always doing, with complete simplicity, all that Dorotheos asked of him.   When he first became a novice he was often crude and boisterous in his speech.   One day as he was speaking very loudly and not too politely, Dorotheos, to pull his leg and to calm him down a bit, said to him, 'You need a sop of bread and wine, Dosithy! Off you go and get it.' As soon as he heard this he stopped his chatter and went immediately to fetch a jug of wine and some bread. This he brought to Dorotheos for the blessing, but he, not understanding, turned to him in astonishment and asked, 'What do you want now?' Dosithy replied, 'You told me to take a sop of bread soaked in wine, please give me the blessing.' 'Ass!' replied Dorotheos. 'It was because you were speaking like a Goth. Every time their spleen is aroused, they get irritated and begin to raise a clamour. That's why I said to you, "Take a sop of bread soaked in wine"—to stop up your mouth!' Hearing this Dosithy knelt down and asked pardon, then quietly went and put the bread and wine back in its place.

A little later Dosithy began importuning Dorotheos with questions about Holy Scripture, for through his purity of heart he had been given a taste for and understanding of Scripture. One day he came with a rather abstruse question at a time when Dorotheos did not want him to be preoccupied with those things, and chose to train him in the spirit of humility. He replied, 'I don't know.' Soon afterwards, without thinking, back came Dosithy with another question about another text of Holy Scripture. Dorotheos, with some tartness, said, 'I don't know. Go and ask the Abbot [Seridos]!' While Dosithy went off to look for the Abbot, Dorotheos met the Abbot and said to him, 'If Dosithy comes to ask you something about Holy Scripture, take him down a peg!' When Dosithy at last found the Abbot and propounded his question, he was received rather coolly. The Abbot said to him, 'Why don't you learn to keep quiet and not keep on asking all these presumptuous questions? Why don't you think of your own impurity and have contrition for your sins?' And gave him a slap on each of his cheeks. Dosithy returned to Dorotheos and showed him his cheeks, red and still smarting from the blows. 'I have been paid,' he said, 'and well paid for my presumption.' And he did not say, 'Why did you not correct me yourself, and not send me to the Abbot.'

He simply accepted the rebuke. And so it was always; when he consulted any of the Elders about his 'thoughts' he accepted the advice he was given and never returned to the subject again. His training was hard, and by our standards perhaps a little cruel, but well in accord with the spirit of the times. So he lived for five years, profiting from Dorotheos' training and guidance, in all humility, never seeking to gratify his own will or to satisfy the cravings of his heart. As the infirmary was separated from the community dwelling, the others knew little or nothing of what he was doing or how he was acting. After something less than five years he fell sick of tuberculosis and began to spit blood. One day he heard that lightly boiled eggs were good for people in his condition. It so happened that Dorotheos, who loved him and would have done anything to relieve him, was so preoccupied with his infirmary and other duties, that he did not happen to think of this remedy. But the idea and the desire to try it tormented Dosithy. One day he said to his master, 'Father, I have heard speak of a remedy that is supposed to be good for my condition, but I don't want you to give it to me, because my thoughts obsess me about it.' 'Tell me what it is, Dosithy.' 'Promise me that you won't give it to me, because my thoughts obsess me about it.' 'Very well, I will do as you ask.' Then Dosithy told him what he had heard, and added, 'But for the love of Our Lord, if you agree, since it did not occur to you to get me some, don't give me any because of my thoughts.' With some hesitation Dorotheos agreed, but did all he could to procure the best remedies he could except that one. And so even in sickness Dosithy fought against his own will. In prayer he was constant too, for Dorotheos had taught him the Prayer of Jesus, 'Lord Jesus Christ have mercy on me,' or 'Son of God, come to my aid.' When he was already ill, Dorotheos used to say to him, 'Dosithy, pay attention to your prayer, don't let it escape you.' And he would reply, 'Yes, Father, but pray for me too!' When his illness seemed to be getting worse, Dorotheos asked, 'And now, Dosithy, how is the prayer

going? Are you keeping it up?' 'Yes, Father, thanks to your
prayers.' Later, when he was so bad he had to be carried on
a stretcher, he was asked, 'How is the prayer now, Dosithy?'
He said, 'Pardon me, Father, I have no longer the strength
to keep it going.' Dorotheos said to him, 'Never mind, leave
your prayer now, just remember God and think that he is
there at your side.'

As time went on Dosithy became worse and worse. His
sufferings increased, and he was afflicted with a continuous
cough and great loss of blood and vomiting. He sent a
message to the Great Old Man, and asked him for pardon for
his sins. He received the following reply:

'Have no fear, brother, but rather let your soul rejoice and
exult for joy in the Lord. Believe me, for it is the truth! For
God has, according to your request, forgiven all your sins
from your childhood until now. Blessed be God whose will it
is to forgive you everything. Do not be sad, therefore, for no
evil remains in you. You will have more pain but it will have
an end.'

As the illness progressed and Dosithy became even worse,
the other brethren asked the other old man, John, 'Is it a
question of life or of death?' He replied, 'It is a question of
death! But the Grand Old Man could ask God to spare his
life if he received God's inspiration to do so.' On hearing
this the brethren wrote Barsanufius to beg him to ask Him to
obtain Dosithy's cure. They received this reply:

'How merciful is my God! And may He fill you with yet
more joy in the Holy Spirit now and always. Amen. But as to
your brother, it is enough for him to receive what he has
merited, for in an instant he has become rich, and from a
slave he is become a free man. Blessed be God who was
pleased to answer your prayer. Say nothing at present to
Dosithy, so as not to sadden him, but keep it secret. For in
truth, for him it is not death but passage into eternal life,
from affliction into repose. Be joyful, my sons, in the Lord.'

At last Dosithy was at the end of his tether and could
endure no more. He sent to ask the Grand Old Man, 'Allow

me to depart, for I can endure no more.' And he received the reply, 'Patience, my child, for God's mercy is near.' A few days later he again sent word, 'Master, my strength is ebbing fast.' Then the Great Old Man said, 'Go forth in peace! Take your place in the presence of the Holy Trinity, and intercede for us all!'

When they heard this, some of the hardy old ascetics who had spent long years in prayer and severe penance were inclined to grumble. 'What has he done? No special penances and only a short time in the monastery, that he should merit to hear that?' And it was true, he could never fast a whole day, was never able to be up for the whole night office. He had never been seen to practise any special mortification and was always receiving special concessions with regard to food. But they did not know what he *had* done—his obedience in all things and his complete surrender of his own will, his simplicity under reproof and his pure, disarming humility. Not knowing all this, some of the elders went on murmuring until God made known the glory reserved for Dosithy because of his humility and obedience. It happened that a holy old man visited the monastery and conceived a desire to see the saints who had graduated from there to heaven, and he prayed to the Lord about it. He was granted a vision of all the Ancients who had died in that place, ranged as it were in choir with the angels; among them, in a place of honour was one who was little more than a boy. When he came to himself he described him and asked the elders who it was. Immediately they recognised from his description that it was Dosithy; and they glorified God who had brought him so soon to perfection and glory through his simple obedience and humility.

Guest-Master

From this time on, the jealousy and persecution that

Dorotheos had suffered for a long time died down. Several of
the brethren began to seek direction from him and to tell him
their secret thoughts. **Abbot** Seridos and the two Old Men
fully approved. In his Discourses he describes one such
instance.

About this time he seems to have fallen ill himself and to
have had to give up charge of the infirmary. When he had
recovered, but was still not completely restored to strength,
he was given charge of the guest-house, where there was
plenty of work awaiting him. Not only were there visitors to
be interviewed and looked after by day, but sometimes
passing muleteers, with animals loaded with merchandise,
would arrive by night and ask to be put up. They had to be
attended to and fed, and the animals taken care of, so that he
hardly lay down to sleep before it was time to be for Vigils.
He confesses that he would answer the watcher's knock and
immediately fall asleep again, so that he was late for, or
missed, Vigils. To remedy this he got two of his trusty
brothers to see that he was properly awake and up for Vigils,
and he pointed out later how we should look on the watcher
as a benefactor who helps us earn our eternal reward.

Dorotheos was fond of his friends, as he tells us in one of
his Discourses, and he loved to be in their company. As a
young man, however, he was able to abstain from their
company when he had a special object in view. Later, when
he had been several years in the monastery, this liking for
company and conversation seems to have sprung to life again,
especially when his duties brought him into contact with the
many visitors to the Monastery. He was also a very sensitive
man; sensitive, that is, not only to the way he was treated by
others, but to the needs of the spiritual life, for in one of his
letters to Barsanufius, [15] 'What shall I do, for I am afraid of
the shame of being despised? Sometimes I meet certain
people and I am caught up and captivated by this fear, and
forget the needs of the spiritual life, and yet I am afraid to
send them away?' Barsanufius' reply seems particularly
sound and human. 'If your conversation is likely to bring

them spiritual profit and you have no other pressing duties to perform, you can remain in conversation with them. If the conversation is indiscreet or dangerous, say, "Forgive me, I am a weakling" and depart. As for being put to shame, take your stand in common with Our Lord. He was not ashamed to be with sinners; you despise being shamed in this world.' Part of the illness of which he complains from time to time seems to have come from a bad digestion, for on another occasion he asks, [16] 'If, when eating with the brethren, I have quickly had enough, ought I leave the table immediately, or ought I to stay to the end of the meal, or should I take with my ration of bread some of the vegetables or fruit provided?' He is told that it is best to take a tiny portion of everything; next best is to remain seated when he has eaten what he can; but if he were unable to sit with the brethren without con- tinuing to eat, he could rise when he had had enough and leave the table.

Again he asks about the relationship between contempt and humility: [17] 'If someone holds himself in contempt, humiliating himself in his heart, is there need to have external disgrace and ill-treatment from men, or to do dirty and degrading work? Also, should a man in search of humility just be prepared for humiliations, or must he also be humble in speech?' The reply is very revealing. 'There are indeed two forms of contempt, one coming from the heart, the other coming from men. That which comes from men is greater than that from the heart. For that coming from the heart does not cause us so much pain and labour as does that coming from men. Running after things that are easily paid for does not bring much profit, but quickly leads to vainglory. To be ordered to do something degrading and not to resist, but to carry it out, and to do it with unmurmuring obedience, this brings great profit, and by this you possess true contempt of self. True humility is never, in any circumstance, to give oneself a vote of thanks; it is to cut off your own will on all occasions, so that you are subject in all things and bear with equanimity all that comes upon you.

This is true humility in which no place can be found for vain-glory. As for speaking with humility, this brings in its train a certain vainglory and is hurtful rather than helpful. It is enough to say, "Forgive me and pray for me." '

Like all the saints, Dorotheos' spiritual life was no easy one. To begin with there was his property. He had some difficulty in giving up his possessions completely. Even after he had been at the monastery for some time he still retained a small parcel of land for his sustenance, because of the weakness of his body. For this his director chided him, very gently pointing out the spiritual weakness involved. Then there was the difficulty of giving up his own will and not trying by hook or by crook to get his own way, and keeping control of his tongue, for he was rather talkative by nature, ever eager to please and to win approval, tending to boastful-ness and vainglory. All these defects he came to see and to fight against, revealing them all with perfect candour to the Ancients. There was a prolonged period when he was a prey to temptations of the flesh, which were so severe that he was at times on the border of despair. He received long letters from Barsanufius on their causes and the way to combat them. Even from the beginning of his monastic life he aspired to the life of hesychia, i.e. a life of enclosure and solitary contemplation; but he was a very able and practical man. His practical abilities were used to the full, so that at times he complains of the excessive amount of work he has to do. No doubt the Ancients recognised his spiritual capacity, but saw the need for long hard training in the works of practical charity in order to prepare him adequately for a life of deeper prayer and contemplation. Later he reports that his 'thoughts' keep saying to him, 'Go away to some other place and your salvation will be assured.' [18] He receives in reply a very interesting letter which begins with a stinging rebuke, 'Brother, cursed be the one who sowed such thoughts in your heart, to make you break the Rule; it is the Devil. He does this to make mock of you, by inspiring you with a claim to virtue, only to make you an object of scandal to others, and

you will have to take the blame for it. And you suffer this
only because of your negligence and vainglory. This is what
you say to yourself, "I shall go away to some foreign part,
and I shall endure being despised." With your negligence,
the demons put into motion your vainglory to make you lose
your soul.'

Some considerable time later Dorotheos writes to John,
'My "thoughts" say to me that hesychia is the most
necessary thing of all, and that it would be profitable for me.
Is this right?' John replies that hesychia means to recollect
the heart, to stop giving and receiving from men, to stop
trying to please men and to concentrate on activities of a
different kind. He then reminds him of our Lord's saying, 'I
want Mercy and not Sacrifice.' 'If then you are convinced
once for all that mercy is better than sacrifice, turn your heart
to works of mercy. To be frank, hesychia can easily lead to
pride so long as a man is not completely master of himself,
that is to say until he has become irreproachable. For then it
is true hesychia, because a man is then carrying his cross. If
you act with compassion, you will find help [from God], but if
you force yourself in claiming something that is beyond your
strength, you will lose what you even now possess. Walk then
neither towards the "interior" nor towards the "exterior",
but between the two, understanding what our Lord wants of
you, because the days are evil.'[19] Despite its severity, this
letter does not seem to have disturbed Dorotheos, but rather
to have perplexed him, for he asks for a clearer indication as
to how he is to fulfill it. Has he to keep some days for
hesychia, and some days for temporal affairs? He is told,
'not to be presumptuous about hesychia, nor contemptuous
about temporal business,' and he will arrive at the middle
way and not fall away, but preserve humility in hesychia, and
true vigilance in the embarrassment of work-a-day things.
There is no set time for recollection; one must be recollected
at all times. He must endure with thanksgiving whatever
presents itself and have compassion for all those in the
monastery. He must suffer with those who suffer, console

them, comfort them. That is what true compassion is, to be sympathetic with those who are sick and to help them to care for themselves.

At another time he writes, 'What I resolve to do when I am alone, I let slip when I am with the brethren. I am afraid of falling into habits of sin.' And yet he comes to realise that afflictions of his heart are good for him, because they break down the hardness of his heart. As for continuous prayer, the ability comes and goes; one little hour of joy and fervour, then a half hour of strain and labour to keep up the remembrance of God. Then he is captivated by the things of the senses, and asks for the Old Man's prayers that he may make progress in vigilance and understanding. There is a touching admission which, I am sure, must find an echo in the heart of every spiritual man, for he says in effect, 'When I am at peace and in recollection in my cell, I get a message to carry out some special duty. I go and do it, but when it is done I don't go back to my cell, but stay around on one pretext or another, doing this and that, and I get tied up with things that can well go on without any need for my intervention. Then I get back to my cell in the evening, full of dryness and disgust with the things of the spirit, full of darkness and spiritual sloth and discouragement.'

He asks about discernment: how can one know that one is acting according to God's will? When he is told that it is through prayer and taking counsel, he writes back, first, what is he to do if, when he has prayed long about the problem in question, he still cannot be certain whether it is God's will or not? And secondly what is he to do when an immediate answer or action is needed, and he has no chance to pray or take counsel about it? Or if a project seems straight away to be good and pleasing to God, how is he to know whether there is not underlying it something secretly tortuous and tending towards spiritual loss or disaster? And so we see him going through life probing into the deepest corners of his conscience, humbly confessing his weaknesses, asking the advice and prayers of his spiritual Fathers, making the small efforts of which he was capable to eliminate them, and waiting the help from God that they constantly promise him. As time goes on he is more and more occupied with the question of prayer and the acquistion of real humility. He writes, 'Since you tell me that to have a job to do and to put my heart into doing it *is* submission and the remembrance of God, I beg you to teach me also how it is possible in all the turmoil occasioned by this service, according to God and among men, to preserve unceasingly in my consciousness the remembrance of God; and [tell me] if it is possible to ask of God, "Father, what is most advantageous for me. For to you and God everything is possible." '[20] 'Every time that God, through your prayers, gives me a little sorrow for my sins, I lose it little by little in showing myself off. I pray you, Father, to strengthen also even that [sorrow for sin], so that everything comes from God's mercy and yours, and nothing from myself.'[21]

He goes on to say that the initiative needed to conduct the infirmary helps to drive him towards vainglory and excessive freedom of speech; and the provision of foodstuffs for the infirmary impel him towards gluttony. And then, 'If you think that I would make some progress in more humble duties if I were relieved somewhat, I will set myself at once more to be of service [to the brethren]. You know, Father, that it is not that I have taken a dislike to these duties, that I say these things. For what in fact am I doing, miserable fellow that I am? I fear, Father, that in remaining where I am, I shall arouse in myself these passions, either through my own fault or through the onslaught, I think, of the demons, I do not know, but you, dear Father, show me what is God's will, and deliver me from these thoughts that trouble me and by your prayers give me the strength to do what you tell me.' Having obtained the assurance of the Grand Old Man that he will not abandon him even when he leaves this world, Dorotheos asks the same assurance of the other Old Man. 'If on any occasion I am defeated and fall, my thoughts tell me it is because of your pride. God will not allow you to attain mastery over your passions, lest you fall into vainglory because of your victory....' [22]

MYSTICAL EXPERIENCES

Through these letters written to his spiritual Fathers we see Dorotheos struggling on towards that spiritual maturity which consists in establishing in the soul as a permanent endowment the meekness and humility of heart to which Our Lord invites us when He says, 'Learn of me for I am meek and humble of heart' (Matt 11:29).

Many times Dorotheos says in effect to his readers: 'If you are willing to labour a little, be patient, and pray much, God will come to your assistance.' In the Discourses he explains to us what this labour entails in practice. He is telling us incidentally how he himself laboured, and here and there he lets us catch a glimpse of how the Lord came to his assistance by lifting, ever so slightly, the veil in his own mystical experiences.

It may perhaps at first sight come as a surprise to find Dorotheos relating publicly incidents of his life which demonstrate—to say the least—a considerable degree of virtue. In England especially this surprise may be coupled with a certain amount of pain and distaste which may be derived from the legend of the British stiff upper lip, from the attitude it produces in the those who hide their natural emotions and often enough conceal the things most dear to their heart, or keep any discussion of them merely at an academic level, especially with those who do not form part of one's inner circle of special friends. This applies specially to religious convictions, aspirations, and experiences, which, like it or not, enter into our human make-up. It is a habit of mind which has been bred into us for a dozen or more generations and stimulated by religious persecution and bigotry of one kind or another. It is an attitude of mind that may well be spreading to other parts, formed and fostered by the restrictive complexity and the existing conditions of urban life today. The reaction against this inhibited attitude of mind towards personal relationships already set in motion by the younger generations—thanks be to God!—was newly under-lined by the Vatican Council after a radical re-examination of Christ's teachings and an attempt to formulate them in a more understandable way.

The need for communication with our fellow men is now felt as an imperative. In St Paul's terms, 'we are members one of another (Eph 4:25). In the terms of modern philoso-phers, it is an expression of the brotherhood of man and a means to the full development of our true and full human personality. In reading the Discourses our first impression of Dorotheos' self-revelation may be a little displeasure and our first reaction perhaps to dismiss them as 'blowing his own trumpet', but they are worth looking at it again. For there is a difference between 'boastfulness' and genuine fraternal communication, which is a sharing of valuable experience, a channel for human growth and encouragement.

A summary acquaintance with the Apophthegmata of the Desert Fathers, the Lausiac History, and a pile of similar documents from the third to the seventh centuries reveals that this was the method universally used by the Seniors for the building up of the spiritual life of their disciples. It was a genuine communication of the Spirit that had been given to them. Not a little of their charm and that of their sayings lies in their disarming simplicity. As we read them, we become conscious of how relevant any self-revelation was to the matter in hand, and we experience how powerful it could be in making the instruction come to life in us.

Finally, humility is truth. To confess the good that God, directly or through the experience of other men, has done to you, is simply to tell the truth. This is just what the most wonderful and most humble of all purely human creatures 'the hand-maid of the Lord', did when she said, 'My soul magnifies the Lord.... All generations will call me blessed.... For he who is mighty has done great things for me.'[23]

The mystical life experienced at Thawatha was pro-

portionate to the highly supernatural atmosphere in which the
monks lived; it was extensive and intense, in the words of
Dorotheos, 'there were many Great Old Men living there'.
First, doubtless, was St Barsanufius, who sometimes was so
rapt in God for days on end that he had no earthly food at
all.[24] Dorotheos lifts the veil, certainly once, possibly twice,
on his own mystical experiences.

On the first occasion he describes a state which succinctly
evokes the Dark Night described much later in detail by St
John of the Cross. 'There came to me once only a great and
unspeakable trial, and I was in such straits that I was drawn
almost to the point of departing this life.... Although it did
not last very long it was most grievous while it lasted. My
heart was heavy; my mind was dark; nothing could comfort
me and there was no relief anywhere. I was shut in on all
sides; completely stifled. But swiftly comes the grace of God
to the soul, when endurance is no longer possible... and I was
then *in* such a state of temptation and distress.'[25] Then he
describes a visionary visitor, dressed like a bishop, who led
him into the Church. And after standing at prayer with him
and for him in front of the altar, he turned and approached
Dorotheos, and the darkness began to clear. He touched him
on the chest and recited the words of the Psalm:[26]

> I waited, I waited for the Lord
> and he stooped down to me;
> He heard my cry.
> He drew me from the deadly pit.

Immediately I was a different man and there way joy with
sweetness and comfort in my heart. I was a different man.'

That vision had its permanent effect—as St John of the
Cross asserts every true mystical experience should have.
Dorotheos tells us: 'From that moment... I have not known
myself to be troubled by sorrow or fear, but the Lord has
sheltered me till now through the prayers of the Ancients.'

The second experience may have been told about another,

although I would say that relating it in the third person was a bit of camouflage for a personal experience—such as St Paul used when he said: 'I know a man... who was caught up to the third heaven.' [27]

The word Dioracticus [28] in Greek can mean 'gifted with spiritual insight' or it can be proper name.   Some of the manuscripts spell it with a capital.   This may have come from the original stenographer, who wrote it like that because of the way in which it was said.   Personal names in ancient times were given for their meaning.   For example, Dorotheos is 'Gift of God'.   Rachel dying in child-birth called her son Benoni, son of my sorrow. [29]   Hence those who heard it could have taken it as a proper name.

Dorotheos recounts a vision of an angel who put a mysterious seal on those who were present at the Vigils, or on the places of those who had a genuine desire to be present but were absent for pressing and legitimate reasons.   But the places of those who were absent through laziness or faint-heartedness, were not sealed.   The reason why I would say that this recounts his own experiences is its effect on him: he made heroic efforts to be up for the Night office in spite of what to many a man would be a perfectly legitimate excuse for staying in bed.   He relates how, when he was guestmaster and just recovering from a serious illness, 'strangers would arrive and I would spend the evening with them or there would be a caravan, and I would attend to their needs; after that I would go to bed and I was often awakened for some other emergency.   In these circumstances I had usually snatched very little sleep before it was time for the Night office, and the watcher would come to wake me.   What with my labours and weakness and the intermittant fevers that attacked me, I was in a bad way and hardly knew what I was doing.   I would reply like one in a dream: "God love you, Master, you called and I am coming".   He went away, and I was asleep again.'   And what was his reaction?   He persuaded two of his confrères to keep him awake, one after call-up; the other during Vigils.   'Believe me, Brothers,' he commented, 'I was devoted to them as if my very salvation depended on them; I very nearly worshipped them.' A result hardly possible from just hearing a story, but very likely the result of a supernatural visitation.

THE TURNING-POINT

Such then was the life of Dorotheos until the death of Abbot Seridos. This Abbot, before he died, between AD 540 and 543, appointed his successors, as was the custom in many of the palestinian monasteries of the time—or rather, he left a whole list of those who were to succeed him in turn, for there were several worthy men living at Thawatha, of whom Dorotheos was certainly one of the most outstanding. At the end of the list was a certain Elien, a laymen—'should he become a monk'. This provision was unknown to Elien, who had known the two Old Men for a long time and had been attracted to the monastic state. He had put himself under the direction of the two Ancients, and this attraction had gradually turned into a positive and powerful desire, but his hesitations continued because he was a married man and had several children. Even before the death of Abbot Seridos he had begun to consult both John and Barsanufius about the disposal of his property and the provision to be made for his wife and children. To the Old Man he wrote, confessing his faults and his weakness, 'begging you not to turn away from my miseries, but to consent to the request of the sinner that I am. What do you order me to do? Leave [the world] at one fell swoop without making any provision, or wind up my affairs and then retire? I don't want the remembrance of all those things to come and trouble me in my retreat and suggest troublesome thoughts and choke the good fruit of the spirit. Should you order me to put my affairs in order first, please tell me if I should apply myself to the disposal of my small properties, and ask God to help me. I ask you, not because I am confident of being able to do what you tell me, but because I hope in your prayers about these orders and the help that you will give me. For if you ask God for me that the Lord lead me towards what is good and useful and give me the strength to stick to it, he will not despise your request.'[30]

In his reply, Barsanufius says among other things, that the best thing is to break at once and completely. 'What then? We have not abandoned everything? Very well! Since, because of our weakness, we have not been able to do it, let us at least bow our heads, recognising our weakness and stay to put our affairs in order, and not get puffed up as if we were doing something great, when we are only acting the way that people do who are weak.... Make provision for your wife and the disposal of your other property according to the advice that Brother John has already given you.' In another reply Barsanufius says, 'My child, you do well to talk of forgetfulness, for if you had not forgotten the things that were written you on my behalf, you would know from them that our Master and all-providing Lord has persuaded me to treat you as a true spiritual son; and I have confided to you secrets that I have not confided to many. This is a proof of my adopting you as a spiritual son. For whom should a father confide in, if not his son? And that progressively as he grows up, in the measure that he can carry and keep that confidence.... May God send you his Holy Spirit to teach you everything, and may you not be separated from us in this present world nor in the future life. For God sees clearly that the remembrance of you is firmly fixed in my heart, and I am confident that it will never be blotted out. Believe me! God has already granted me your soul for eternal life.... Do what you can, do not bring shame on my old age. For God knows that I am doing all that is in my power for your salvation, asking him to put you for all eternity among the number of the saints.'

In the meanwhile, Abbot Seridos had died, and the abbacy was offered to the first nominee, who, with much modesty and humility, refused the honour. About this time Elien, still in ignorance of the last testament of Abbot Seridos, fell into a great sadness over the tribulations of this life and the punishments to come. He was so overcome by these sombre thoughts that he was at risk of falling into despair. He wrote to enquire of **Abbot** John and to ask for his prayers and a word of consolation. Abbot John, foreseeing that all the nominees for the abbacy would refuse, wrote to Elien especially on the subject of obedience: 'Beloved Brother, faith in God for a man who has delivered himself up to God consists not in having free disposition of himself, but in abandoning himself to him up to his very last breath. All that happens to him he receives as coming from God, and this is what St Paul means by, "in everything give thanks". If, in effect, a man refuses what comes from God, he disobeys God, seeking to fulfill his own will. In truth, faith *is* humility, "Those whom he has called, he justifies and glorifies" (Rom 8:29). From now on throw off your sadness which works death, for only sadness which is according to God works salvation. Pray, therefore, for me and be from now on without fear. Otherwise you will annoy God, by persevering in your own will. May our Lord Jesus Christ give you the grace to do his will and to find mercy before him; to him be glory and power for ever. Amen!'[31]

Having received this surprising letter, Elien was freed from his sadness, but he was at a loss to know what the Old Man was getting at, for the reply did not seem to be a reply to his letter. So the Old Man told him clearly what had happened and that he was to be successor to Abbot Seridos. Elien was astonished that anyone could even dream of such a thing. He judged himself completely incapable of the task but he dared not categorically refuse the Old Man's command. Hence he wrote as follows: 'Father, I no longer know anything. The Spirit of God who dwells in you knows me; as for me, I am full of fear and trembling because of the danger of the situation. If in your opinion I can find mercy in doing as you say, through your protection in Christ, I make no objection; for you have full power over me, and I am in God's hands and yours.' And John replied, 'Lord Brother,

God is my witness that I love you sincerely and my only wish
is that your soul suffer no harm in anything whatsoever.
Confiding completely in your obedience and busying myself
beforehand about your salvation, I have co-operated in a
noble work.   For what is hidden from the eyes of men is
visible to God.'[32]   He goes on to warn him about the cares
and responsibilities of an abbot, reminding him at the same
time that it is God's work.   'It is for you to collaborate and
suffer with Him, so as to find yourself one day in the
company of those who are saved.   Since all this is God's
doing, you cannot refuse.   Be courageous in the Lord and
have confidence in Jesus.   He is the one who keeps us from
evil.   Hesitate no more, and pour out your heart to God, in
Our Lord and the Holy Spirit.'   Elien finally accepts: 'I am
your servant, be it done to me according as you say.'   At the
command of the brethren he was clothed with the monastic
habit, and the bishop was called in to ordain him priest.   He
was then formally installed as abbot.   His first visit was to
Abba John whom he had never yet seen in the flesh, and he
was received by him in all humility as his venerable abbot.
On being asked for his abbatial blessing, he was abashed and
hesitated, but when John insisted he gave it and then they
sat down together.   John told him that a long time ago Abbot
Barsanufius had predicted that he would become a monk and
abbot of the monastery.   'And so it has happened according
to God's good pleasure.'   This was John's *nunc dimittis*, for
he had already foretold that he would die on week after
Seridos.   Elien importuned Barsanufius to obtain the pro-
longation of John's life so that he could give him some
instruction on his duties as abbot and he obtained an extra
fortnight. [33]   John then retired to his cell, lay down, and died
peacefully.   Nothing more was heard or seen of Barsanufius,
and fifty years later he was still believed to be living alone in
his cell with God, without need for earthly sustenance. Finally
the reigning Patriarch, Eustochius (552-563) commanded that
his cell be opened, and legend has it that a sheet of flame
leapt out and scorched some of the witnesses.[34]

A critical point, then, in the history of the monastery at Thawatha and the life of Dorotheos had been reached somewhere between the years 540 and 543 with the disappearance of three of the leading lights of the place. Seridos was dead; John the Prophet was dead; and most important of all, Barsanufius had gone into complete retirement. There was a new abbot, Elien, who, though he had long been a friend of the monks and had been under the direction of the Ancients for several years, had first to be clothed as a monk and then ordained before he could take up his duties as abbot. All this was done with the consent and approval of the Community and of all the elders, including Dorotheos, who had out of humility refused the office. Who was this Elien? The facts stated above are all that we know for sure about him. We know that he was a man of ideas and initiative. From one of the letters he wrote of Abba John during the few days off allowed him for the purpose of instructing the new abbot in his duties, for Elien had asked whether it was permissible to change any of the rulings of the dead Seridos. The extraordinary thing is that there was someone known to us from the letters of the two Old Men to have a relationship to the Community corresponding with that of Elien. That was Dorotheos' brother. There is also a sentence in one of the letters quoted above which would appear to add weight to the hypothesis that Elien was, in fact, Dorotheos' brother. I refer to Letter Forty, in which we learn Dorotheos was being tormented by the idea that he should go away and find salvation in some other place.[35] This was about the time when Dorotheos was building the infirmary with the financial and material help of his brother. After administering a stinging rebuke and pointing out that he would be transgressing the monastic code, and that it was a subtle temptation of the devil, Barsanufius implies that there had been some kind of rumpus between the two brothers, for he says, 'How does it come about that your heart is troubled merely on learning that your brother spoke one word against you, and that you do not want anyone to know that you have committed a fault?

Be assured in the Lord that but for the hand of God and the prayers of the true servants of God who are here, you would not be capable of staying one whole year in the monastery. But you are so blind you do not see what beneficence God has extended and continues to extend to you, through the prayers of the saints and of blessed Abraham who has said both *to you and to your brother*, "If you remain in this place, you will have me for your intercessor"'. Apart from the well-known devotion of the early monks to the Patriarchs of Israel, the area around the wadi Gaza and the region of Gerara was consecrated by the sojourn of Abraham in that neighbourhood. Whereas I am fully aware of the difficulties, both psychological and others, that can and do arise, when blood relations are members of the same religious community —and in the event of my hypothesis being correct, it would help to explain why St Dorotheos should go off and form a monastery at a considerable distance away, it was this letter that sowed a doubt in my mind about the foundation attributed to him in the current legend of his life.

The following reasons transform my doubt almost into a certainty that he did not found another monastery, but lived out the remainder of his life at the monastery where he started his religious life, Thawatha.

First, a careful comparison of the teaching he received from two Ancients there, with the teaching contained in his own Discourses, shows his fidelity to what he had learned from them. It is true that his exposition of the doctrine was more formal and schematic, but the content is almost identical. One of the points on which he is particularly forceful and definite is precisely this; the idea of going off and seeking salvation in another place is a particularly insidious temptation of the devil. I cannot see that it is psychologically possible for a man so obviously sincere and in earnest about his spiritual life to act contrary to his own teaching.

Secondly, the expressions which seem to imply that he left Thawatha have been interpreted in too wide a sense. Where he uses such phrases as, 'when I was in the *monastery*', translators have added in brackets on their own authority, [of Seridos]. What he actually says is 'when I was in the *coenobium*.' In the Palestine of the sixth century there were two kinds of monastic communities, the 'cenobium' and the 'lavra'. The first was a monastery devoted to the common life, very much on the lines of a monastery as we know it today. The second was a colony of hermits living in separate cells, coming together for the celebration of the liturgy and a limited number of communal exercises, but in general following each his own timetable and programme of prayer and ascetical practices. Now at Thawatha as we have seen clearly manifested in the letters of John and Barsanufius the two kinds of life were going on at the same site; those who joined the community started their training in the 'cenobium' where they lived the common life, and as they became proficient in the spiritual combat they moved on progressively into degrees of the eremitical life. So when Dorotheos says, 'when I *was* in the cenobium', he is not implying that he is no longer living at Thawatha, but that he had passed from one section of the monastic complex to another, viz. from the common life to the solitary life. There were at varying distances from the communual buildings, separate cells where the solitary life was practised with varying degrees of severity. Witness the incident about the dumping of rubbish outside Dorotheos' cell; he must have been near enough to the centre of things to make it convenient. The life of hesychia, i.e. solitary contemplation, was very much the monastic ideal of the time, though a couple of centuries of experience had made it clear that a solid training in community life was a necessary preparation for it in most cases. Also, there were men who were capable of striving for and making progress towards perfection only in community life but who were quite unfitted for eremitical life in any degree. St Benedict was quite as clear about the dangers of the solitary life as he was about its being a spiritual ideal and he stipulated that those who were called to it should first have learned to fight the devil and their own evil tendencies in the community of the brethren. In this he is only echoing the experience of the desert. It seems to me that when Dorotheos says, 'When I *was* in the "cenobium"' he is not implying that he had left Thawatha, but that he had left the cenobium proper to settle in the 'lavra' attached to it. That is, he made his home at the monastery in one of the more solitary hermitages outside the enclosure of the cenobium, there to pursue the contemplative life with more concentration and intensity. In this he is not rejecting the instruction given him by his spiritual director, John the Prophet. We must remember that when he wrote to John of his desire for the more contemplative form of life, 'hesychia', he had been only a comparatively short time in the monastery. And as we saw above, John's letter was in answer to a particular problem at a particular moment in Dorotheos' spiritual life. Without decrying the excellence of the hesychastic way of life—which after all he himself was leading—John simply pointed out that a great deal of strength was needed for it. In order to become 'irreproachable' he advised the mixing of his active service of the brethren with a certain amount of solitude and contemplation. Such advice seems to me inevitable to one who was relatively young in monastic life, and it would not exclude the possibility of later graduation to a life of greater calm and solitude. This is what, in my opinion, happened when, with the departure of Seridos and the Two Ancients, the new abbot was appointed. Dorotheos retired to some more secluded hermitage and devoted himself in greater concentration to the contemplative life. We know from his own mouth that Dorotheos ministered to John the Prophet for nine years and that the same John lived at Thawatha for eighteen years until his death. Some of the letters to John imply that Dorotheos was no longer his personal attendant and we can, therefore, conclude that Dorotheos had been engaged in monastic life for something less than eighteen but more than nine years—surely time enough for one of his intensity to acquire the strength and stability to pass on to a more intense form of eremitical life. Even while he was John's personal attendant, he had graduated from complete identification with the cenobitic life, and was occupying a separate cell apart from the common dormitory. A further indication of his growing spiritual maturity was that certain monks began coming to him with their spiritual problems and this with the consent and approval of Abbot Seridos and the Two Ancients. It seems fairly obvious that as one of the older and more experienced monks at the time of Seridos' death he would have been among those nominated to succeed him, and one of those whose refusal of the office had been accepted by John and Barsanufius before they departed. This acceptance of his renunciation of the abbacy was tantamount to agreement that Dorotheos should pass on to a further degree of solitary life. Nor would it be surprising if, in view of their long and intimate association, he moved into John's hermitage and took on some of his functions. For unlike Barsanufius, who enclosed himself in his cell and was never seen again, John retired to his cell where he died peacefully. We have testimony that he was buried by his brethren.

Before going on to my final reasons for thinking that Dorotheos did not found a monastery of his own, I must say a word about the title of archimandrite given him. In the Palestine of the sixth Century the title archimandrite was not applied, as it was later in other parts of the Empire, to an ordinary abbot as the head and father of a community of monks. The ordinary term for an abbot in that sense was 'hegumen' (ἡγούμενος, a leader, ruler, chief). Seridos was the hegumen of the monastery of Thawatha. Also the term *abba*, which we are accustomed loosely to translate as abbot, did not mean abbot in the sense that we use it for the head and father of a community of monks; it was often merely a title of respect given to a holy man who had spent long years living the life of a monk while in pursuit of holiness. Professor Chitty, in his book *The Desert A City*,[36] remarks that Palladius refers to Saint Pachomius as an archimandrite because he was in general charge of some three thousand monks spread over several monasteries, although the application of the term to the Egypt of those days was an anachronism.[37] Further on,[38] he speaks of the special sense the term had acquired in the patriarchate of Jerusalem by the end of the fifth century and the beginning of the sixth, viz. the one who had the oversight of all the monks of a region or diocese. He also cites the fact that in the year 492, when the Archimandrite Marcian died, all the monks of the wilderness went to the Patriarch and asked for and obtained Sabas as the archimandrite of the anchorites and cell-dwellers and for Theodosius as the archimandrite of all the cenobia. Each of these was given a second in command: Sabas the hegumen of the lavra of St Gerasimus and Theodosius the head of the cenobium of Martyrius. Dorotheos' retirement to an anchorite cell at Thawatha would be perfectly consistent with duties of archimandrite for all the region around Gaza. The duties of the archimandrite would be somewhat on the lines of an abbot visitor in our days. Periodically he would make the rounds of all the monasteries under his charge, to see that monks were maintaining a serious religious life, to draw attention to abuses, to straighten out difficulties, and to give conferences and encouragement to all those in need of it. This would explain the genesis of the Discourses, and the words of the anonymous writer that he had *collected* all that he could come by, though it was certainly only a small part of Dorotheos' output. This seems to me to imply that he could not find them all in the same place but had to go in search of them to the different monasteries where Dorotheos had given talks. Such a task would have given Dorotheos the occasion for putting into practice the advice of Abbot John to combine the life of contemplation with that of serving the brethren, in a spiritual sense, which he was extremely well fitted to do. It would also be perfectly consistent with the words of John Moschus in the *Pratum Spirituale* which contains the most ancient reference to Dorotheos after the death of Barsanufius and John, and which, I suspect, gave rise to the current legend that Dorotheos founded a monastery of his own.

John Moschus became a monk in the Cenobium of St Theodosius at Jerusalem and later lived in the desert near the Jordan and in the New Lavra of St Saba, where he was for a time precentor. He died about 620 AD. He could, therefore, have been a youngster at the time when Dorotheos was at the height of his powers. He spent a considerable part of his life on pilgrimage in Egypt and Syria and even in the west, collecting materials for his famous lives of the monks. He relates a story, told him by Abbot Sabbatius, of the robber who came to Abbot Zozimun the Cilician, confessed that he had committed many murders and asked to do penance and to become a monk. Zozimus agreed, and clothed him with the monastic habit but after a time, fearing that he would be taken and killed by his enemies, Zozimun said to him, 'Take my advice and let me take you to the cenobium of Abbot Dorotheos near Gaza and Maiuma', (πλησιον Γα ζαζ και Μαιουμαζ). [39]   The Latin version is *prope Gazam et Majuman.* The *Dictionnaire de Théologie* renders it *entre* - 'between', but this is jumping to a conclusion which is not justified by the original text. Maiuma was the Port of Gaza and was two miles distant. Until the time of Constantine, they were, both from the civic and the ecclesiastical point of view, one place. Constantine in 337, granted both civic rights and a bishopric to Maiuma and named it Constantia. However, Julian the Apostate withdrew its civic rights and reunited it to Gaza, but it kept its bishopric. Hence at the time when Moschus was writing, Gaza and Maiuma were regarded as *one city*, and the phrase, 'near Gaza and Maiuma' could perfectly apply to Thawatha, which was only a couple of miles away. Seridos and the Two Ancients were not long dead, but long enough to be suffering that temporary eclipse that so often comes to famous men soon after their death. Elien seems to have made no mark on history and may not have lived long after his appointment as abbot. Dorotheos was at the height of his fame when Moschus was a young man. What could have been more natural than to

refer to the cenobium united to his place of retirement as the
cenobium of Dorotheos.   This then is a further reason for
doubting the assertion that Dorotheos founded a monastery of
his own.

Finally, I come to a statement which at first sight seems
to knock the bottom out of all my reasoning.   The editors of
the *Oeuvres Spirituelles* state that in the ancient manuscripts
the title of the *Discourses* is *Instructions given by Abbot
Dorotheos to his disciples after he had left the monastery of
Abbot Seridos and founded, with the help of God, his own
monastery, after the death of Abbot John the Prophet and the
last silence of Barsanufius.*   Unfortunately the editors do not
state in which old manuscripts it appears, or whether it
appears in the majority of manuscripts.   The editors of the
Migne edition do not seem to have been aware of it, for they
entitle their edition, *Various teachings of our Holy Father
profitable for the soul*, which seems to echo the commendatory letter of the original collector of the Discourses.
The editors of the *Oeuvres* mention that there are a number
of manuscripts existing of a Georgian translation, one of
which goes back to the end of the tenth century, and an
Arabic translation, the earliest copy of which is perhaps
earlier than the earliest we have in Greek.   One wonders
whether they bear the title refering to Dorotheos founding a
monastery or not. Unfortunately I have not the means to find
out. It has often been demonstrated that the titles appearing
on manuscripts are the inventions of copyists and not of the
originators of the work. This makes one cautious in accepting
statements which appear in the titles of ancient works,
especially if there is a considerable gap, as in this case,
between the date of the work itself and the date of the
manuscript in which it is found.   The editors of the *Oeuvres*
suggest that the original collection was made 'some decades'
after the death of Dorotheos. So be it. The date of his death
is said to fall between 560 and 580. For the sake of argument
let us put the date of compilation at 600 and the date of the
earliest extant manuscript at 1000. We have a gap of 400

years. The place of origin of the said manuscript was probably not the area of Gaza or Jerusalem, but Mount Athos or some other distant place. The copyist's knowledge of geography and civic governance could not have been as precise as that of John Moscus who died about 620, who had travelled extensively throughout Egypt and Syria and the whole of Palestine, and would certainly have known of the moral and civic unity of Gaza and Maiuma.

DEATH AND AFTER

Given Dorotheos' history of continual ill health and the compiler's remark that he was brought to perfection in *a short time*, I would be inclined to put his death nearer 560 than 580; and to suggest that the compilation took place very soon after his death, perhaps not more than a decade. Although the writer of the preface nowhere states specifically that he knew Dorotheos personally, he does give two hints that he did. First he says in his letter, as he is talking of Dorotheos following the example of Peter, who stripped himself of all attachment to visible things: 'So he [Dorotheos] gave himself up according to God to his [spiritual] Fathers so as to say, *I know very well*, with complete frankness to our Saviour, "behold we have given up everything and followed you"'. The second occurs when he is talking about Dorotheos' personal characteristics in dealing with other people. He says: 'He was compassionate and affectionate, truly worthy to instruct and enlighten souls; great by his wisdom, greater still by his personal devotion; sublime in contemplation, even more sublime in humility; pleasing to *listen to* and *even more pleasing to converse with.*' Add to this the fact that he calls Dorotheos 'our holy Father', refers to his correspondent's great love for Dorotheos; and makes no specific mention of having known him personally. Does this not imply that the recipient of his letter had also known him personally and, therefore, it was superfluous to mention it? All together these clues give fairly solid ground for concluding that the Collector had known Dorotheos personally and that the collection was in fact made very soon after Dorotheos' death.

About the life of St Dorotheos after the death of Abbot John, the only definite information I have so far come across comes in John Moschus' *Pratum Spirituale*, already mentioned. It is worth looking at a little more closely since, besides being remarkably interesting in itself, it may contain a precious clue to chronology. John Moschus was visiting the monastery of Abba Firminus. Abba Sabbatius related it of Zosimos the Cilician, who was presumably dead. The same Zosimos was present at the Council of Constantinople in 536, for he, as hegumen, signed the *Acta* of *IV Actio*. Dorotheos was certainly alive in 543. This is, in brief, the story: A certain man came to Abbot Zosimos and said, 'For the love of God, Father, make me a monk, for I have been guilty of committing many murders and I want to stop and do penance.' So Zosimos with suitable exhortations gave him the monastic habit and he started to follow the monastic observance. After a few days, Zosimos said to him, 'My son, you cannot stay here because either the justices will hear of it and come to arrest you or your enemies will come and kill you. You must take my advice; I will take you to the cenobium of Abbot Dorotheos near Gaza and Maiuma.' This he did, and the murderer-turned-monk stayed there nine years, doing penance and fulfilling all the observances of the life. After nine years he went back to the monastery of Firminus, and said to Abbot Zosimos, 'Give me back my own clothes, and take back the monastic habit.' At this the old man was profoundly saddened, and he asked, 'Why is this, my son?' He replied, 'For nine years I have fasted as well as I could and lived soberly. I have lived in quiet subjection in the fear of God, and I know that in his infinite goodness he has forgiven me my many sins, but now I have always before my eyes the face of a small boy who says to me, "Why did you kill me?" And I am haunted by this face day and night; in the church when I go to Communion, in the refectory—

everywhere. He never gives me any peace, but is always asking, "Why did you kill me?" Father, I want to go and give myself up to die for that little boy whom I wantonly killed.' So he put on his secular clothes, went away to Diospolis, was tried and executed the next day. It would seem, therefore, that Dorotheos was certainly alive in 552, continuing to live in one of the hermitages attached to the cenobium of Thawatha, exercising the function of overall spiritual director, much in the same way that John and Barsanufius had done, with this difference, that instead of executing his spiritual ministery exclusively by letters dictated to a secretary, he from time to time made the rounds of the monasteries under his charge. There he gave his conferences or took part in their meetings and discussions until his death, which, in view of his constant ill health, I would put nearer 560 than 580. It is notable that among the hesychasts of his time, moving around in furtherance of the prayer life or to consult spiritual fathers is not regarded as incompatible with their kind of life. Many instances could be brought forward. St Sabas, for instance, would go off by himself into the wilderness for the whole of Lent to prepare for the celebration of Easter. John Moschus relates a story told him by Denis, the priest of Ascalon, about a certain anchorite named John who lived in a cave near Sochus, about twenty miles from Jerusalem. From time to time he would go to a certain place in the 'vast solitude' for a period of intense communion with God, or to Jerusalem to venerate the holy places, or to visit some martyr's shrine or to be present at the Eucharist at the monastery of St Thecla in Seleucia or to Mount Sinai. He might be absent for a few days or a week and sometimes for months at a time. In his cave he had a statue of Our Lady holding the Child Jesus. Before it it was his custom to keep a candle burning day and night, and before leaving he would trim and light a new candle and say to Our Lady, 'Holy Lady, Mother of God, I am going to be away on a journey which will take many days, you take care of your candle. Do not let it go out, but keep it alight as I have resolved always to do. For I am going away with you as the helper and companion of my journey.' And when he returned he always found the candle burning brightly, quite as large as when he set it up. [40]

Of the exact date of Dorotheos' death we have no precise indication; nor do we know what he died of, except that it was not of old age. Nor have we any document which tells us where he died and where he was buried. Having read his Discourses and seen something of the kind of man he was, we must conclude that most probably he died in his hermit's cell in the neighbourhood of Thawatha and was buried there.

In the *Acta Sanctorum* the author of the monograph on Dorotheos, the Archimandrite of Gaza, asserts that he found no trace of Dorotheos' being honoured as a saint. This is not surprising, even if it needs, perhaps, a little qualification. Palestine and Syria for a large part of the sixth century was a theological battle-ground. The inhabitants were excitable; feelings ran high; controversy was vigourous, often acri-monious and sometimes broke out into armed combat. The ascetics were numerous, running into thousands. Mono-physitism and Nestorianism were rampant, and many among the ascetics were unlearned men, incapable of mastering the subtleties of theological thought, and unable to accept the definitions of the Council of Chalcedon. Also, it must be confessed, a fair proportion of them were unable, or unwilling, to stick to their profession of a life of prayer and severe discipline. In consequence they were not slow to accept the diversion of assembling under some theological banner and forming whole armies, ready to vindicate their views by force. On the other hand, some of the intruded bishops, like the notorius Severus and his disciple Peter, used to stir up their followers to attack the monasteries, and reinforced them by any rabble they could find. Even when these two were condemned at the Council of Tyre and removed from the Sees of Antioch and Apamea, they continued to work behind the scenes. Their particular brand of Monophysitism claimed a following even among the monks. Among their adherants were men whose names were the same as our Dorotheos, Barsanufius, and Isaias. At intervals during the sixth century not a few of the episcopal sees of Palestine and Syria, even the patriarchal see of Constantinople, were occupied by men holding varying monophysite views. All of them were ready to call those not of their own party heretics. It is not, therefore, surprising to find a good deal of confusion, not only in the minds of their contemporaries, but especially in the minds of their successors. In consequence, Dorotheos was branded a heretic not only during his life-time, but also afterwards.

However, with the accession of Tarasius to the patriarchate peace was in view. He had been the secretary of Theodora when she became a devout orthodox Christian. Tarasius held orthodox views and was in communion with the See of Rome. According to the testimony of St Theodore of Studios, Tarasius examined the work of Dorotheos of Gaza, and pronounced them in accord with the true faith; they were indeed extremely profitable for the soul. Saint Theodore wrote this in his testament, where he clearly distinguishes our Dorotheos, Barsanufius and Isaias from their heretical namesakes. A statement of this, written by a Studite monk at the beginning of the ninth century, was prefixed to the manuscript and all the subsequent manuscripts derived from it. This forms the first preface of the Greek text in use today.

Another thing that needs to be remembered is that in the sixth century a saint was universally expected to be a wonderworker, or at least to have the gift of prophesy. If he did not work miracles during his life, there was every chance that he would not be recognised unless he worked miracles at his tomb. Dorotheos' tomb was lost to view a short time after his death, so that there was not much time for his *cultus* to grow and spread. Then, too, Barsanufius' fame overshadowed the quieter fame of Dorotheos. His life was externally so much more remarkable both for wonders and prophesies that he was immediately recognised as a saint; his fame and *cultus* spread so rapidly that he was depicted with St Ephrem on the altar frontal of Sancta Sophia.   The life of Dorotheos was a hidden one, he lived in the shadow of a greater name, and made a point of keeping aloof from the polemics of the day and the place where he lived.   He adhered firmly to his monastic life and principles.   The wonder of his life was not manifested by any miracles, and his teaching was to the intimate circle of his own brethren and the monasteries immediately under his care.   Violence was afoot in his days because of theological disputes, yet greater violence was to come, for the Persians were on the march by 610 AD.   By 614 they had taken Jerusalem and the region beyond the Jordan, thence they passed on into Egypt to capture Alexandria in 616.   The monastery of Thawatha stood almost directly in the line of the victorious Persian army's advance and could easily have been pillaged and destroyed with all its inhabitants by 615.   Gaza would have been by-passed, as a fortified city.   If this is so, we can date the end of monastic life about 615; but even if it were spared then it certainly came to an end in 534 during the Arab invasion, when Gaza, after a seige of several months, capitulated.   During that invasion some 90,000 Christians were said to have been slaughtered in the neighbourhood of Jerusalem alone.   Gaza, so slow in accepting the faith, and probably brought to it finally by the monasteries in the area, proved equally slow to relinquish it. When the city capitulated to the Arab general Ama, many of the citizens, including 60 christian soldiers of the garrison, died for the faith.   Ten were taken to Jerusalem and executed on the sixth of November, and the remaining fifty were executed at Elutheropolis on December the 17th, 634. [41]

The ruins of the monastic city in which Dorotheos lived have not yet come to light, but in the area where we should expect to find it many remains of the christian Byzantine era have been discovered.   Taken all in all then, it comes as no surprise that no traces should be forthcoming of an offical *cultus*.   To sum up: his life was by its nature a hidden one; his tomb is lost; soon after his death christian living was eliminated from the place where he lived.   This is not to say that he was not honoured for his holiness and revered for his doctrine. He was venerated as one of the Holy Fathers by the monks of the Studite tradition and of Mount Athos, where his instructions were much used in the training of novices. It is even likely that he did have a share in the public *cultus* of the St Dorotheos, who from monastic life was translated to be bishop of Tyre. It was Dorotheos' lot to be mistaken in dishonour for Dorotheos the heretic in life, but in honour for Dorotheos the bishop and saint after death. While his monastery and his body lie buried under a pile of sand and rubble in an unknown place, his life of sacrifice and his work for the monastic life has borne fruit down the ages. It continues, and—please God—will continue for ages to come. My hope is that one day will be uncovered that hidden sanctuary, the tomb of Dorotheos, Archimandrite of Gaza.

FOOTNOTES

1. London: S.P.C.K., 1943.

2. For a collection of *The Sayings of the Desert Fathers*, see the book of the same name, translated into English by Benedicta Ward SLG (Cistercian Studies Series Number 59, 1975). Hereafter cited as CS 59.

3. Nbr. 39: *Maîtres Spirituelles de Gaza* (Solesmes, 1971) p. 95.

4. PG 88.

5. *Dorothée de Gaza. Oeuvres spirituelles*, Sources chrétiennes, 92. Edd. Dom L. Regnault et Dom J. de Préville. Paris: Editions du Cerf, 1963. [The translation here presented has been thoroughly checked against this edition—ed.]

6. Of the name Δωρωθεος, I suppose the convention anglicization would be Dorothy, hardly suitable in this case because Dorothy in English has been adopted as a name for a girl; nor do I see much point in latinizing it to Dorotheus. The meaning of the Greek is 'a gift offered to God' or a 'gift from God', which would be suitable for any child, male or female. I therefore keep it in its Greek form, simply transliterating it to Dorotheos.

7. AA SS 21:582.

8. See page 83.

9. See Discourse X.

10. Pt 2; PG 87:2792.
11. E.g. 36, 37, 39; MSG, pp. 90-94.
12. Ltrs. 58-9.
13. EAO (1896) p. 12.
14. PO 8:176.
15. PG 88:1822.
16. PG 88:1810.
17. PG 88:1816.
18. MSG 40:96.
19. MSG 56:110.
20. MSG 61:114.
21. MSG 62:115.
22. MSG 64:117.
23. Lk 1:47-9.
24. MSG, p. 18.
25. Pg. 127.
26. Ps 40:1-2.
27. 2 Cor 12:2.
28. See page 176.
29. Gen 35:18.
30. MSG 95:145.
31. MSG 97:149.
32. MSG 98:151.
33. Chitty, p. 138.
34. Ibid.
35. MSG 98:96.
36. Oxford: Blackwells, 1966.
37. Pg. 25.
38. Pg. 86.
39. PG 87/2:3033.
40. PG 87/2:3052.
41. *Echo d'Orient* 8:1905.

THE DISCOURSES

OF

ABBA DOROTHEOS

I

N RENUNCIATION

IN THE BEGINNING when God created man he set him in paradise (as the divine holy scripture says),[1] adorned with every virtue, and gave him a command not to eat of the tree in the middle of paradise.[2]   He was provided for in paradise, in prayer and contemplation in the midst of honor and glory; healthy in his emotions and sense perceptions, and perfect in his nature as he was created.   For, to the likeness of God did God make man,[3] that is, immortal, having the power to act freely, and adorned with all the virtues. When he disobeyed the command and ate of the tree that God commanded him not to eat of, he was thrown out of paradise and fell from a state in accord with his nature to a state contrary to nature, i.e. a prey to sin, to ambition, to a love of the pleasures of this life and the other passions; and he was mastered by them, and became a slave to them through his transgression.   Then little by little evil increased and death reigned.[4]   There was no more piety, and everywhere was ignorance of God.   Only a few, I say, of the Fathers moved by the law of nature acknowledged God; such were Abraham and the rest of the Patriarchs, and Noah and Jacob.   And to speak simply, very few and rare were those who knew about God. For then the Enemy deployed all his wickedness so that sin ruled.   Then idolatry began and the worship of many gods, divining, murders and the rest of the devil's wickedness. Then God in his goodness had mercy on his creatures and gave Moses a written law in which he forbade some things and allowed others, saying 'This you shall do, that you shall not do'. He gave the commandments, and said 'The Lord, your God, is one Lord,'[5] so as thereafter to turn their minds from polytheism, and then: 'You shall love the Lord your God with all your soul and with all your mind,'[6] everywhere proclaiming that God is one, and there is no other. For in saying 'You shall love *the Lord*, your God,' he showed that God is one and one is the Lord.   So also in the decalogue: 'The Lord your God shall you adore, him only shall you worship. You shall adhere to him and swear by his name.'[7] Then he adds, 'You shall have no other gods, nor any likeness to anything in heaven above or on earth beneath'[8]—for they used to bow down before all sorts of creatures.

The good God, then, gave the law as a help, for their conversion, for putting right what was evil, but they did not reform.   He sent the prophets, but they were able to do nothing.   For evil prevailed as said Isaiah, 'no injury, no bruise, no wound was cauterized; no chance of soothing dressings; no oil, no bandaging of wounds,'[9] as much as to say that the evil was not in one member, or in one place, but in the whole body.   It took in the whole soul and all its powers.

Everything was a slave to sin, everything was under the control of sin.   As Jeremiah said, 'We would heal Babylon but she would not be healed.'[10]   That is to say, we have revealed your [God's] name, we have announced your commandments, your benefits and your warnings.   We have put Babylon on her guard against enemy risings.   All the same she is not healed; she has not been converted, she has not feared, she has not turned from her wickedness.   In another place he says, 'they have not submitted to discipline',[11] that is, correction and instruction.   And in the psalm it says, 'Their soul abhors all nourishment and has come near to the gates of death.'[12]

Then at last the good, man-loving God sends his only begotten Son. It was for God alone to heal and prevail against such miseries; and the prophets were not ignorant of this. Wherefore David clearly said, 'O you, who are seated above the cherubim, show yourself; stir up your power and come to save us.' [13] And again, 'Lord, bow down the heavens and come down' [14] and more to the same effect. The other prophets also, each in his own way, proclaim many things about it, now begging him to come down, now revealing that he certainly will come. Therefore our Lord did come, by being made man for our sakes, so that, as the scripture says, like should be healed by like, soul by soul, flesh by flesh, for he became completely man—without sin. He took our very substance and took his origin from our race and he became a New Adam, like the Adam he himself had formed. For he renewed man in his nature, restored the depraved senses and sensibility of human nature to what it had been in the beginning. Having become man, he lifted fallen man up again. He freed him from slavery to sin which had mastered him by force. For with violence and tyranny the Enemy was leading man to sin, reluctantly, without really wanting to sin, as the Apostle speaking in our person says, 'I do not the good which I would but the evil I would not, that I do.' [15] Having become man, then, for our sakes, God freed man from the Enemy's tyranny. He took away his power, broke his strength, took us out of his hand, and freed us from slavery to him—unless we spontaneously choose to obey him by sinning. For the Lord gave us power, as he told us, to trample on serpents and scorpions and all the power of the enemy, [16] since he cleansed us of all sin by baptism. For Holy Baptism purges us of iniquity and washes away all stains. Therefore again, recognizing our weakness and knowing for certain that even after baptism we would fall again—as it is written, 'For the heart of man is prone to evil from his youth' [17]—God from his goodness gave us holy precepts which purify us, so that, if we really want to, through the keeping of these commandments we can be purified not only from our sins but from those innate tendencies which lead us to evil. Sin is one thing but instinctive reaction or passion is another. These are our reactions: pride, anger, sexual indulgence, hate, greed, and so on. The corresponding sins are the gratification of these passions: when a man acts and brings into corporeal reality those works which were suggested to him by his innate desires. It is impossible to exist without natural desires arising, but not to give way to them is by no means impossible.

Therefore, The Man [God] gave us instructions, as I said, which purify our passions and those evil dispositions which come from our inner man.[18] He instilled into man's inner conscience the power to judge good and evil; he woke it from sleep; he showed the causes from which sins rise and he says to us, 'The Law says, "Do not commit adultery", but I say to you, do not entertain desire. The Law says "Do no murder", but I say, do not give way to anger.[19] If you do entertain a fleshly desire and today you do not commit adultery, it does not cease inwardly troubling until it whips you into action. If you are irritated and stir up your anger against your brother, then you strike him, speak evil against him, then plot against him and so go forward little by little and at last you come to murder him.' Again the Law says, 'An eye for an eye and a tooth for a tooth,'[20] etc., but Our Lord admonishes us not only to bear patiently the blows of one who strikes us, but humbly to turn to him the other cheek.[21] And so the object of the Law is to teach us not to do to others what we do not wish to suffer, and therefore it cuts away our wrong-doing through our fear of suffering. Now the object must be, as I am always saying, to cast away our hatred, our love of pleasure, our vainglory and the rest of our unruly desires.

I repeat that the aim of Christ, our Master, is precisely to teach us how we come to commit all our sins; how we fall into all our evils. First he sets us free through Holy Baptism, as I have already said, giving us the forgiveness of our sins, and he has given us the power to do good if we desire to and no longer to be dragged down into sin, so to speak, by force. For one who has consented to sin is weighed down and dragged away by it. As it is written: 'By his sins is everyone put in bondage.'[22] Then he teaches us by his holy precepts how to be cleansed from our own passions so that we do not fall again into those same sins. Finally he shows us how we come to despise and disobey the commandments of God and adds the medicine that all may be able to obey and be saved. What then is the medicine and what the cause of our contempt? Listen to what the Lord himself tells us: 'Learn of me, for I am meek and humble of heart and you shall find rest for your souls.'[23] There you have it in a nutshell: he has taught us the root and cause of all evils and also the remedy for it, leading to all good. He shows us that pretentions to superiority [pride] cast us down and that it is impossible to obtain mercy except by the contrary, that is to say, by humility. Self-elevation begets contempt and disobedience begets perdition, whereas humility begets obedience and the saving of souls. And I call that real humility which is not humble in word and outward appearance but is deeply planted in the very heart;[24] for this is what he meant when he said that 'I am meek and humble of heart'.

Let anyone desiring to find true humility and rest for his soul learn lowliness of mind and see that in it is all joy and all glory and all tranquility, and in pretentions to superiority, just the contrary. From where do all those afflictions of the mind come to us? Is it not through our arrogance, our thinking too much of ourselves? Is it not through extolling ourselves and our evil self-preference? Is it not the bitterness of ourselves that will master us? But how did this come about? Was man not created in all comfort, in all joy, in perfect peace and in all glory? Was he not in paradise? He was sent away. Why? God said you shall not do this, and he did it! Do you not see the pride in that, the obstinacy, the insubordination? And so God said, the man is mad; he does not know how to be happy, unless he experiences evil days he will go away and completely perish. Unless he knows what tribulation is he will never know what rest is. He then gave

him what he deserved and expelled him from paradise. Then
he delivered him to his own self-will and to his own desires,
that he may grind down his own bones and learn that he
cannot go straight on his own, but only by the command of
God; so that learning the poverty of disobedience may teach
him the tranquility that comes from obedience. As the
prophet says, 'Your rebellion shall teach you.'[25] Nevertheless, the goodness of God, as I have said many times, did not
despise what he had formed, but again urged him [to obey],
again exhorted him. 'Come to me,' he said, 'all you who
labor and are heavily burdened and I will refresh you'[26]—as
much as to say, 'See how you have to work! See the misery
you have brought on yourself! See how you are tried by evil
and your own unruliness!   But come change your ways,
acknowledge your own powerlessness so that you can come to
your rest and your own true glory. Live through lowliness of
mind instead of going to your death through pretentious
pride. Learn of me, for I am meek and humble of heart and
you shall find rest for your souls.

See brethren, what arrogance does? See what lowliness is
able to do! What need was there for all these contortions? If
from the beginning man had humbled himself and listened to
God and obeyed his command, there would have been no fall.
Again, after Adam had done wrong, God have him a chance
to repent and be forgiven and yet he kept on being stiff-
necked and unrepentant. For God came to him and said,
'Adam, where are you?'[27] instead of saying, 'From what
glory are you come to this? Are you not ashamed? Why did
you sin? Why did you go astray?'—as if urging him sharply
to say, 'Forgive me!' But there was no sign of humility.
There was no change of heart but rather the contrary. He
replied, 'The wife that *you* gave me'—mark you, not 'my
wife'—'deceived me,'; 'the wife that *you* gave me,'[28] as if to
say, 'this disaster *you* placed upon my head'. So it is, my
brethren, when a man has not the guts to accuse himself, he
does not scruple to accuse God Himself. Then God came to
Eve and said to her, 'Why did you not keep the command I

gave you?' as if saying, 'If you would only say, "Forgive me", to humble your soul and be forgiven.' And again, not a word! No 'forgive me'. She only answered, 'The Serpent deceived me!' [29]—as if to say, if the serpent did wrong, what concern is that to me? What are you doing, you wretches? Kneel in repentance, acknowledge your fault, take pity on your nakedness. But neither the one nor the other stooped to self-accusation, no trace of humility was found in either of them.

And now look and consider how this was only an anticipation of our own state! See how many and great the evils it has brought on us—this self-justification, this holding fast to our own will, this obstinacy in being our own guide. All this was the product of that hateful arrogance towards God. Whereas the products of humility are self-accusation, distrust of our own sentiments, hatred of our own will. By these one is made worthy of being redeemed, of having his human nature restored to its proper state, through the cleansing operation of Christ's holy precepts. Without humility it is impossible to obey the Commandments or at any time to go towards anything good. As Abba Mark says: without a contrite heart it is impossible to be free from wickedness or to acquire virtue. [30] Therefore, by compunction of heart you get a grip on the Commandments, are free from evil, gain virtue and, what is more, peace of mind returns to you. The holy men of old thoroughly understood this and through all their training and guidance in humility were zealous in uniting themselves to God. Thereby becoming friends of God, they were able, after Holy Baptism, not only to cut out sins arising from evil passions, but to conquer the passions themselves and to acquire complete control of their passions. Such were Saint Anthony [of the Desert], Saint Pachomius and the rest of the God-bearing Fathers.

Their aim was to purify themselves, as the Apostle says, 'from every blemish of the flesh and the spirit'. [31] They knew that by the keeping of the Commandments the soul is purified and the mind too is enlightened, and they perceived that it starts functioning as nature intended it to. 'The command of the Lord gives light and enlightens the eyes.'[32] Being in this world they knew very well that it was not possible, without trouble, to make progress in virtue, and they worked out for themselves an unusual kind of life, a strange way of passing their time, I mean the solitary life. They began to flee the world and to live in the desert, in watching and fasting and sleeping on the bare earth[33] and other forms of mortification. Having left their homeland and their relations, riches, and possessions, they simply crucified themselves to this world. And not only did they keep the commandments, but made a gift to God.

The commandments were given to all Christians and it is understood that every Christian observes them; this is, as it were, the tribute appointed to be paid to the King. Anyone who says, 'I will not pay tribute,' will he escape punishment? There are, however, in the world great and illustrious men who not only pay the appointed tribute, but also offer gifts and they are thought worthy of great honor, great benefits and esteem. So also the Holy Fathers not only kept the commandments but also offered gifts to God. These gifts are virginity and poverty. These are not commanded but freely given. Nowhere is it written, you shall *not* take a wife or beget children. Neither did Christ give the *commandment*, 'Sell your property!' He did not choose to do so when the lawyer approached him saying, 'Good Master, what shall I do to inherit eternal life?' He replied, 'You know the Commandments. Do not kill, do not steal, do not commit adultery, do not bear false witness against your neighbour' etc. When the answer came, 'All these things I have kept from my youth', he added, 'If you want to be perfect, sell your property and give the money to the poor,' etc. See, he did not say 'sell your property' as a commandment, but as a counsel. This is clear from the condition imposed, '*if* you wish to be perfect.'[34]

As we said, therefore, the Fathers offered to God besides

all the other virtues, their virginity and poverty as a gift. They crucified the world to themselves, and struggled to crucify themselves to the world. As the Apostle says, 'The world is crucified to me and I to the world.'[35] What is the difference? The world is crucified to a man when a man renounces the world to become a solitary, and leaves parents, wealth, possessions, business dealings, and the giving of present. Then he is crucifying the world to himself, for he has left himself, and this is what the Apostle means by, 'the world is crucified to me.' But then he adds, 'and I to the world'. How can a man be crucified to the world? When, after being freed from external things he begins the combat against pleasure itself, against the desire of having things, against his own will, and he puts to death his evil passions. Then he himself is crucified to the world and is worthy to say with the Apostle, 'the world is crucified to me, and I to the world'.

Our Fathers, as I said, having crucified the world to themselves, were earnest in the fight to crucify themselves to the world. We thought to crucify the world to ourselves when we left it and entered the monastery, but now we have no desire to crucify ourselves to the world. We have still the taste for it; we are passionately attached to its glories, to delicate food and clothing. Suppose there is a good tool to which we become attached. We allow that miserable tool to have the same effect on us as Abba Zosimos says, as if it were a hundred gold sovereigns.[36] 'We reckon to come out of the world and leave the affairs of the world'—and yet we come to the monastery and through trivial things we reveal, and give way to, our desire for the things of this world; and we suffer this way through our own folly because, having given up great and honourable things, we satisfy our inordinate passions with things of very little value. Each one of us has given up something—perhaps great possessions, or perhaps very small—at any rate, each one has given up what he had to give. We come to the monastery and, as I said, we satisfy our own desires through trivial things which are worth nothing. We ought not to do this, for as we are set apart from the world and its affairs, so we ought to be set apart from the desire for material things, and to know what renunciation is and why we came to the monastery, [to know] what is the objective we have set ourselves, and so adjust our conduct to correspond with it, and throw ourselves into the contest as our Fathers did.

traditio

Our habit consists of a tunic with short sleeves, a leather belt, a scapular, and a cowl. Each one of these is a symbol, and we ought to know what they symbolize. [37]

Why do we wear a tunic with short sleeves when others wear them long? Long sleeves signify hands. Hands are given to do things with. When the thought occurs to do anything suited to the 'old' man—for example, to steal, or to strike someone—it is in fact to do something sinful with our hands. We ought to pay attention to our habit and take note that we have no long sleeves, that is, we have no hands for doing what unredeemed man did.

There is another sign in the tunic: it is the purple mark and what does this mark signify? Anyone fighting for a king has purple in his mantle. For because a king wears purple, all those who fight for him put purple on their clothes; this is the royal uniform which shows they are the king's men and that they fight for him. So we put the purple mark on our habit to show that we fight for Christ, our King, and that we desire to endure for him all the sufferings he endured for us. For when Our Master was suffering for us he wore a purple robe; [38] first as king, for he is King of Kings and Lord of Lords, [39] and then because he was mocked by impious soldiers. Therefore, also having purple for a sign, we promise, as I said, to suffer all that he suffered. A soldier does not leave his service [regiment] and withdraw secretly to become a farmer or a merchant, for that would bring him into disgrace. As the apostle says, 'No one fighting for God mixes himself up with secular business so that he is able to please Him to whom he has engaged himself.' [40] So also we ought to contend, neglecting worldly affairs, and to be occupied with God alone and, as it says, to be like "A maiden who is both devoted and without distraction".'[41]

We also have a belt, and why do we wear it? The belt which we wear is a symbol first of all that we are ready for work. Everyone who wants to work first girds himself so that he is not hindered by his robes. As the Apostle says, 'They stood with their loins girt.'[42] Again, as the belt is made of deer skins, it is a sign of bodily mortification, and so we should mortify our fleshly desires.[43] The belt is worn around the loins, from which area voluptuous pleasures [are said to] proceed. This is what the Apostle says, 'Mortify your members on the earth against fornication and uncleanness'[44] etc.

We wear also a scapular and the scapular is placed across our shoulders: this signifies a cross on our shoulders as He said, 'Take up your cross and follow me.'[45] What is the cross, but the perfect mortification set up through our faith in Christ. For faith, as the teaching of the Fathers again has it, 'always gets round obstacles and frees us for the work which brings us to this perfect mortification'[46]—that is, that a man puts to death in himself the affection for the things of this world. He has given up parents, possessions, riches, all that a man can give up to take up the contest; let him also renounce self-will and the desire for these things. This is what we mean by perfect renunciation.

We wear also a cowl or hood: this is a symbol of abasement. Little ones, not full-grown men, wear the cowl without malice. We wear the cowl for this reason: that we may be little ones in malice. As the Apostle says, 'Do not be little ones in understanding, be little ones in malice.'[47] What is being a little one in malice? A baby has no malice. If he is not treated with honor he is not angry; if he is honored, he is not subject to vainglory. If what he has is taken away he is not troubled. To be a little one in malice means having no desire for revenge and laying no claim to glory.

And again the hood is a symbol of God's grace. Because as the cowl covers and warms the head of the child, so the grace of God covers the mind, as the Book of the Fathers says, 'that the cowl symbolizes the grace of God our Saviour, our direction-finding apparatus, our childhood in Christ, on account of the devil's continuous attempts at striking and wounding us.'[48]

And so we have about our waist the belt which is mortification of unreasoning passions; on our shoulders the scapular which is the cross; the cowl [hood] which is the sign of innocence and childhood in Christ.

Let us lead a life in agreement with our appearance, as the Fathers say, lest we take on a character alien to it.[49] But as we have given up the great things let us give up the little things; as we have renounced the world, so let us give up passionate attachment to it. For through certain small and worthless things our inordinate desires bind us again to the world without our realizing it. If, therefore, we desire to be set free and to enjoy perfect freedom, let us learn to cut off our desires and so, with God's help, in a little while, we shall make progress and arrive at a state of tranquility. For nothing helps men so much as to cut off self-will, for thereby a man prepares the way for nearly all the virtues.

If a traveller is on his way and finds a staff and uses it, he does away with much of his journey's labor. So it is in pursuing this way of cutting off instinctive desires. From this cutting off of self-will a man procures for himself tranquility and from tranquility he comes, with the help of God, to serene indifference.[50]

In a short time a man can cut off ten such desires. He takes a little walk and sees somthing. His thoughts say to him, 'Go over there and investigate,' and he says to his thoughts, 'No! I won't,' and he cuts off his desire. Again he finds someone gossiping, and his thoughts say to him, 'You go and have a word with them,' and he cuts off his desire, and does not speak. Or again his thoughts say to him, 'Go up and ask the cook what's cooking?' and he does not go, but cuts off his desire. Then he sees something else, and his thoughts say to him, 'Go down and ask, who brought it?' and he does not ask. A man denying himself in this way comes little by little to form a habit of it, so that from denying himself in little things, he begins to deny himself in great without the least trouble. Finally he comes not to have any of these extraneous desires, but whatever happens to him he is satisfied with it, as if it were the very thing he wanted. And so, not desiring to satisfy his own desires, he finds himself always doing what he wants to. For not having his own special fancies, he fancies every single thing that happens to him. Thus he is found, as we said, to be without special attachments, and from this state of tranquility he comes to the state of holy indifference.

You see how much profit it brings us to cut off, little by little, our own will. This is what happened to Blessed Dosithy, a man who left a life of pleasure and idleness, who had never heard a word about God. You have heard to what heights it brought him in a short time. How he mastered himself by obedience, and cut off his own will.

How God glorified him and did not allow such virtue to fade from man's memory, but revealed it to one of the Holy Elders who saw him in the throng of all the Saints rejoicing in their happiness.

I will tell you another thing which likewise happened in my time, that you may learn how obedience, and not following one's own will, snatched a man from death. At the time when I was one of Abba Seridos' disciples there came a disciple of a great old monk from the region of Ascalon about some business for his abbot. He had the command from his senior to return after vespers to his own cell. When the time came to leave, a violent thunderstorm arose, with rain heavy enough to cause flooding, and yet he wanted to leave as the senior had told him. We begged him to stay, seeing that it was impossible to get safely across the river. He would not be persuaded to stay with us. At last we said, 'Let us go with him as far as the river. When he sees it, he will return of his own accord.' So we went off with him, and when we reached the river he took off his cloak and bound it round his

head, tied up his scapular and jumped into the raging waters
of the river. We just stood there astonished and fearful that
he would be drowned, but he kept afloat, and very soon he
was seen on the other bank. He put on his cloak, threw us a
profound bow from there, received ours in return, and went
off at a run. But we stood in wonder, astonished at the
power of virtue. We came near with fear, but he went
through without danger because of his obedience.

Another Brother was sent by his abba on some necessary
business to a correspondent in the country. When he saw
himself solicited by the [man's] daughter to a shameful act
and himself in danger of falling, simply cried out, 'O God of
my Father, deliver me', and straightway he was found on the
road to Skete, fleeing towards his spiritual father.[51]

Notice the power of virtue, notice the efficacy of prayer.
How much help has he who cried out for the prayers of his
spiritual father—as if he would say, 'O God, through the
prayers of my father, deliver me'—and straightway he was on
the road [for home]. Mark well the humility and discretion of
both. They were in a tight spot, the Ancient wished to send
the brother to their man of business and he did not say to
him, 'Go' but, 'Would you like to go?' And the brother did
not say, 'Right, I'll go,' but 'I'll do what you want me to do.'
He was afraid that he might fall into sin and he was afraid of
not being obedient. Then, as they were in a very tight spot,
the Ancient said to him, 'Get up and go!' He did not say to
him, 'I trust in my God that he will protect you,' but said, 'I
trust in the prayers of my spiritual father that they will
protect you.' Likewise the brother did not say, when he was
tempted, 'O my God, deliver me' but, 'O God, through the
prayers of my father, deliver me.' Each of them was
counting on the prayers of his father. See how they yoked
obedience to humility! Just as horses are yoked together in a
chariot so that one does not outstep the other, so obedience
needs to have humility yoked together with it. How can a
man be worthy of this grace, unless, as I said, he treats
himself harshly to cut off the desires of his own and to give

himself, after God, to his [spiritual] father, without hesitation, doing everything with full confidence as though obeying God. Such a man is worthy to find mercy, such a man is worthy to find salvation.

The story is told of Blessed Basil[52] that, making a visitation of his monasteries, he said to one of the Heads, 'Have you any saints here?' The Abba said, 'Through your prayers, my Lord, we all desire to be saints.' And again Blessed Basil said to him, 'No! I mean have you *got* any saints here?' And the Abba tumbled to it (for he, too, had spiritual insight). 'Yes,' he says, and he sent for a certain brother. When he arrived, the Saint said to him, 'Wash my feet' and he went and fetched what was necessary. And after his feet were washed, Basil said to the brother, 'Wait till I wash your feet.' And without a murmur he allowed himself to be washed by the holy man. After testing the brother in this way, he said, 'When I enter the sanctuary, you come, too! And remind me to ordain you.' Again without a murmur, the brother obeyed, and when he saw the holy Basil in the inner sanctuary he went up and reminded him, and Basil ordained him and took him with him, for who else but this blessed brother was suitable to be with this holy god-bearing father? You do not have experience of this unmurmuring obedience; neither do you know what real internal peace is.

At one time, before I knew the power of this virtue (that is, humility), hearing that through much tribulation we must enter the Kingdom of Heaven,[53] I became afraid because I had no troubles. And when such thoughts came upon me I used to take up a pen and write to one of the Ancients. On this occasion I wrote and asked Abba John, the disciple of Abba Barsanufius, and while I was writing, even before I had finished, I was sensible of help and relief, and this itself increased my freedom from care and my sense of peace. And this is what I said: 'Master, since the scriptures say that through much tribulation we must enter into the Kingdom of Heaven and I do not seem to have single affliction, what shall

I do? Shall I not lose my soul if I haven't a single affliction or anxiety?' When I had explained my thought to him in this way, he wrote back declaring, 'Do not be afraid, you have no cause to be, for everyone who throws himself completely into obedience to the Fathers shall surely possess this state of freedom from care and peacefulness of soul.'

FOOTNOTES

1. Gen 2:25. [Scriptural citations follow the enumeration of The Jerusalem Bible—ed.]

2. Gen 2:16-17.

3. Gen 1:27.

4. Rom 5:14

5. Deut 6:4.

6. Deut 6:5.

7. Deut 6:13.

8. Deut 5:7-8.

9. Is 1:6.

10. Jer 28:9.

11. Jer 2:30.

12. Ps 107:18.

13. Ps 80:2.

14. Ps 144:5.

15. Rm 7:19.

16. Lk 10:19.

17. Gen 8:21.

18. Cf. Rm 7:22, Eph 3:16, Plato, *Republic* IX. 589.

19. Mt 5:27,21; Ex 20:14,13.

20. Ex 21:24.

21. Cf. Mt 5:38-9.

22. Prov 5:22.

23. Mt 11:29.

24. Cf. Cassian, *Conf.* 18:11.

25. Jer 2:19.

26. Mt 11:28.

27. Gen 3:9.

28. Gen 3:12.

29. Gen 3:13.

30. Mark the Hermit, *De his qui putant*...197; PG 65:961A.

31. 2 Cor 7:1.

32. Ps 19:8.

33. See DS 2:451-4: *Chameunie.*

34. Cf. Mt 19:16-22.

35. Gal 6:14.

36. *Alloq.* 1:5; PG 78:1689.

37. Cf. Evagrius, *Praktikos* (PG 40:1220f; CS 4:13-14), Cassian. *Inst.* 1 (CSEL 17:8-16).

38. Cf. Jn 19:2.

39. Rev 19:16.

40. 2 Tim 2:4.

41. Cf. 1 Cor 7:34-5.

42. Lk 12:35.

43. Cf. Cassian, *Inst.* 1:11.

44. Col 3:5.

45. Cf. Mt 16:24.

46. Evagrius, *Praktikos*; PG 40:221; CS 4:14.

47. 1 Cor 14:20.

48. *Praktikos*; PG 40:1220; CS 4:13.

49. Apo Nau 55; ROC (1907) p. 180.

50. ἀπάθειαν.   Cf. Evagrius, *Prak.*; CS 4:19, 32-4.

51. Apo Amoun 3; PG 65:128; CS 59:27.

52. Apo Basil 1; PG 65:137; CS 59:33.

53. Ac 14:22.

II

N HUMILITY

ONE OF THE FATHERS used to say, 'Before anything else we need humility: a being ready to listen whenever a word is spoken to us, and to say, "I submit", because through humility every device of the enemy, every kind of obstacle, is destroyed,' What is the force of this saying? Why did he say, 'before anything else we need humility', and not, 'we have need of self-control'? Because, the Apostle says, 'Everyone who strives for mastery abstains from all things.'[1] Or why did he not say, 'Before anything else we have need of the fear of God'? For it is written, 'The beginning of wisdom is the fear of the Lord'[2] and again, 'With the fear of the Lord a man turns away from evil.'[3] Or why did he not say, 'Before all else we need almsgiving, or faith'? For it is said that by faith and almsgiving we are cleansed from sin, and the Apostle says, 'Without faith it is impossible to please God.'[4] If, therefore, it is impossible to please God without faith, and faith and almsgiving cleanse from sin, and by fear a man turns aside from evil, and the beginning of wisdom is the fear of the Lord, and a man who strives for the mastery abstain from all things, why does he say, 'Before all else we need humility' and leaves aside all these very necessary things? The holy man wishes to show us that neither the fear of God, nor faith, nor self-control, nor any one of the other virtues can set us right without humility, and therefore he says, 'Before anything else we need humility, being ready to listen whenever a word is said to us, and to say, "I submit", because through humility every device of the enemy and every kind of obstacle is destroyed.'

Consider well, brothers, how great is the power of humility. Consider how great is the spiritual energy behind saying, 'Pardon me'. Why is the devil called not only 'enemy', but also 'adversary'? He is called 'enemy' because he is a hater of men, one who hates what is good, a traitor; an 'adversary', because he always puts obstacles in the way of good. If someone wants to pray he puts obstacles in the way through evil suspicions, shameful thoughts, and spiritual torpor. If a man wants to give alms he obstructs it through avarice or procrastination. If a man wants to keep vigil he obstructs it with hesitations or laziness. In every single thing he is against us when we desire to do good. This is why he is called the enemy and the adversary and why, by lowliness, all his attacks and devices are brought to nothing. Lowliness is really a great thing, for every kind of good is advanced by lowliness, and by working at it we cut short our journey, as it says, 'See my humility and my toil, and take away all my sins,'[5] and 'I was humiliated, and the Lord saved me'![6] For humility *alone* can bring us into the spiritual life (as Abbot John used to say)[6] even if slowly. Therefore, let us also be humble for a short time and we shall be saved. Even if we cannot endure much labor because we are weak, let us be set on humbling ourselves. I firmly believe that, in the mercy of God, the little thing done with humility will enable us to be found there, in the same place as the saints who have labored much and been true servants of God. Yes! We are very weak, and cannot labor very much, but can we not at least be humble? Happy indeed, brothers, is the one who has true humility. A great thing is humility; rightly was it pointed out by that holy man who had true humility and who said, 'Humility does not grow angry, and does not anger anyone.'[7]

This seems a strange thing, for humility alone is opposite to vainglory, and it is from this, I suppose, that it guards a man. But a man grows angry over riches and what he has to eat; why then does he say that humility does not get angry, or provoke to anger? Humility is a great thing (as we keep on saying) and it is powerful to bring down grace to the soul. For the rest, the grace of God itself, coming into the soul, protects it from these other two grievous passions, for what is more grievous to a man than to grow angry and to anger his neighbor? As one of the Seniors says, 'It is completely foreign to a monk to grow angry, and if one should grow angry, unless he is swiftly protected by humiliating himself, in a short time, troubled as he is, and troubling others, he comes under the power of the devil.'[8]

For this reason he says that humility does not get angry or provoke to anger; but why am I saying that it protects from these two passions? In point of fact humility protects the soul from all the passions and also from every temptation. When Blessed Anthony saw all the snares of the devil spread out everywhere, he sighed, and asked God how anyone could ever avoid them. God answered him, 'Humility. It is humility that enables you to escape them all!' And what is more astonishing, he added, 'They cannot even touch you'.[9]

Now do you perceive the power of lowliness? Do you see the grace attached to this virtue? In point of fact there is nothing more powerful than lowliness. If a painful experience comes to a humble man, straightway he goes against himself, straightway he accuses himself as the one worthy of punishment, and he does not set about accusing anyone or putting the blame on anyone else. For the rest, he goes on his way untroubled, undepressed, in complete peace of mind, and so he has no cause to get angry or to anger anyone else. And so you see, the holy man quite rightly said, 'Before anything else we need humility'.

Now there are two kinds of humility, just as there are two kinds of pride. The first kind of pride is when a man despises his brother, considers him worth little or nothing, while he puts a much greater value on himself. Such a man, unless he speedily repents and takes great care, will come in a short time to that second kind of pride by which he lifts himself up against God, and ascribes what he does right not to God, but to himself. Really, brothers, I knew a man who came to this miserable state. From the beginning, if one of his brethren said anything to him, he used to say, 'Who the devil is he? He is not Zosimos or one of his lot.' Then he began to cheapen them and to say, 'There is no one of any importance but Macarios' and after a little while, to say, 'Who is Macarios, anyway? There is no one any good, except perhaps Basil or Gregory.' And then in a short while he began to debunk them, saying, 'Who is Basil? Who is Gregory? There is no one who counts but Peter and Paul.' And I say to him, 'Really, brother, you are going to despise these soon.' And believe me, after a short time he began saying, 'Who is Paul? Who is Peter? There is no one but the Holy Trinity'! And so at last he lifted himself up against God—and there he gave up! Therefore, we ought, my brothers, to take up the fight against the first kind of pride, lest little by little we fall into this absolute pride.

There is also the pride of this world, and the pride of monastic life. The pride of this world is when you are lifted up above a brother because you are richer or more handsome or have more beautiful possessions. When therefore we see ourselves getting vainglorious about these things, or because we have a better monastery, or one that is more convenient, or when we have more brethren, we ought to see that we have reached a high point of this worldly pride. This is when a man is vainglorious about material things. And what shall I say when a man is puffed up about a good voice or his beautiful psalmody, or his reasonableness, or because he does his work neatly? All these are similar to the first, and more like the pride of this world. But the pride of monastic life is when a man grows vain about keeping vigils, or fasting, or his piety, or his rule of life, or his zeal. There is even the case where a man humbles himself to win glory. All this, I say, is the pride of monastic life. Admittedly we are not without pride, but if we are proud of our monastic observance, at least let us not be proud about material things. This concludes what I have to say about the first kind of pride, and also the second: the pride of this world, and the pride of monastic life. It remains [for us] to learn something of the two kinds of humility.

The first kind of humility is to hold my brother to be wiser than myself, and in all things to rate him higher than myself, and simply, as that holy man said, to put oneself below everyone. [10] The second kind is to attribute to God all virtuous actions. This is the perfect humility of the saints. It is generated naturally in the soul by the performance of the commandments. [It is] just like a tree bearing much fruit: it is the fruit that bends the branches and lowers them down, but when there is no fruit, the branches point upwards and grow straight.

There are certain kinds of trees which never bear any fruit as long as their branches stay up straight, but if stones are hung on the branches to bend them down they begin to bear fruit. So it is with the soul. When it is humbled it begins to bear fruit, and the more fruit it bears the lowlier it becomes. So also the saints; the nearer they get to God, the more they see themselves as sinners. I remember once we were speaking about humiliation and one of the great lights of Gaza, hearing us say, 'The nearer a man is to God the more he sees himself to be a sinner', was astonished, and said, 'How is this possible?' He did not know, and wanted to know the answer. I said to him, 'Master of the First Rank, tell me, how do you regard yourself in respect to the other citizens here?' And he said, 'I regard myself as great, and first among the citizens.' I said then, 'If you went away to Caesarea, how would you regard yourself then?' 'I would value myself somewhat less than the great folk there.' So I said, 'If you went away to Antioch, what then?' And he replied, 'I would regard myself as one of the common people.' I said, 'And if you went from the city of Caesarea into the presence of the Emperor, what would you think of yourself then?' He replied, 'I should think of myself as just one of the poor.' Then I said to him, 'There you are! In the same way, the saints, the nearer they approach to God, the more they see themselves as sinners!' Abraham, when he saw God, called himself 'dust and ashes'.[11] And Isaiah said, 'Unhappy am I, for my lips are unclean.'[12] Similarly Daniel was in the lion's den and Habakkuk came to him with a meal and said to him, 'Accept the food, which the Lord has sent you.' And Daniel replied, 'For the Lord has remembered me!'[13] He had great humility in his heart when he was in the lion's den because they did not devour him once and for all, not even afterwards, and so with astonishment he cried, 'the Lord has remembered me'.

Do you see the humility of the saints and how their hearts were set on it? Even when messengers straight from God were sent to them to help them they were not turned away from humility but fled from self-glorification. As men clad all in silk flee if a filthy rag is thrown at them, so that their noble robes will not be stained, so the saints, clad in virtue, take flight from human glory lest they be stained by it. Those who desire that sort of glory are like the naked man who always wishes to find a few rags, anything at all, to cover his shame. So too one who is naked of virtue desires to be praised by men. Therefore the holy men who are sent from God to help men, do not let go of humility. Hence on one occasion Moses said, 'I beseech thee, Lord, send another more eloquent than me for I am hard-voiced and a stammerer.'[14] Jeremiah said on another occasion, 'I am a child!'[15] So every single one of the saints, as I have said, acquired this humility from the fulfilment of the Commandments. No one can explain how this comes about, how humility is generated in the soul. Unless a man learns this by experience, he cannot learn it by verbal teaching.

One day Zosimos was talking about humility. There was a certain sophist present who, hearing what he said, wanted to enquire more deeply into it and he said, 'Tell me how you can reckon yourself a sinner. Do you not see that you are a holy man? Do you not see that you have already acquired virtue? Do you not see that you are fulfilling the Commandments? How can it be that doing all these things you still reckon yourself a sinner?' The old gentlemen did not quite know how to answer, and he said, 'I do not know how to explain it to you, but it is quite true.' The sophist then brushed this aside and repeated his request to know *how* this could be true. But the old gentlement still could not find a way of explaining it and began to say with his usual holy simplicity, 'Do not try and confuse me. I tell you this is exactly how I feel.' Since I saw the old gentlemen hesitating over how to reply, I said to him, 'Is this not rather like sophistics or medicine? When a man is studying it carefully and is practising it little by little, by doing the work he acquires the state of mind proper to a sophist or a doctor, and he is unable to say and does not know how to explain how little by little he was led into that state of mind, for the soul absorbed it imperceptibly. The same sort of thing is found as regards humility; the work of fulfilling the Commandments generates a state of humility and the process cannot be explained in words.' When he heard this Abbot Zosimos was glad and embraced me and said, 'You have found the answer; it is as you say.' The sophist, hearing this, had his difficulty laid to rest and accepted the explanation. For the elders used to say that by doing certain things we intend [to cultivate] humility; when the state of true humility is generated [in the soul], no one can find an adequate description of it.

When Abba Agathon was on his death bed the brethren said to him, 'Father, are you afraid?' He said, 'As far as it was in my power I have kept the Commandments, but I am only a man. How do I know if my work satisfies God? The judgment of man is one thing; the judgment of God is another thing altogether.'[16] See how he brought humility to our notice, guided us toward attaining it. How it is generated in the soul, as I keep on saying, no one finds words to describe, nor is it possible to take possession [of it] by thought, if the soul by its works be not worthy to learn it. But the Fathers used to say repeatedly what produces it. Among the seniors it used to be told how a brother asked one of the elders, 'What is humility?' And the elder replied, 'Humility is a great and divine work and the road to humility is labor, bodily labor, while seeking to know oneself and to put oneself below everyone else and praying to God about everything: this is the road to humility, but humility itself is something divine and incomprehensible.'

Why is it said that bodily labors bear the soul on towards humility and how can it be said that bodily labors have an effect on the soul?

About being below everyone, we have spoken above because it is contrary to the first kind of pride. For how can a man think himself greater than his brother, be puffed up about anything, or blame or despise anyone, if he thinks himself lower than everyone? In like manner to pray all the time is clearly the antidote to the second kind of pride. It is more than clear that the humble man, the god-fearing man, knows perfectly well that nothing good, nothing straight and sure, happens in the soul without the help and the supervision of God, and therefore he does not stop praying unceasingly that God may act mercifully towards him. A man standing in need of everything from God is ready to make progress; he knows how he will make progress, and cannot be puffed up. He does not rely on his own abilities but attributes to God everything he does right and always gives thanks to him. He is always calling on God for fear that God may stop helping him, and so let his native weakness and powerlessness appear. So through his act of humility he prays, and through his prayer he is made humble. In as much as he is always making progress in virtue, he is always growing in humility. The more humble he is, the more help he gets [from God], and so he advances [in the spiritual life] through this virtue of humility.

Now to return to the question why physical labor induces the state of humility, and what influence bodily labors have on the state of the soul. As I said before, it is because the soul, having fallen away from the Commandments into disobedience, was delivered, as St Gregory says,[17] to love of pleasure and to the independence which fosters error, so that it comes to love the satisfactions of the body, and in a certain sense it is found to have taken on the same characteristics as the body, and to have become completely fleshly.' As it says, 'My spirit shall not persist in men, for they are made of flesh.'[18]   Inasmuch as the wretched soul at the same time suffers and co-operates with the things done by the body, the elder says that bodily labor leads to humility.

The dispositions of soul of a healthy person are one thing: those of a sickly person, another; of a hungry person, another; of a well-fed person, another.   Similarly the dispositions of a man riding a horse differ from those of a man riding a donkey; those of the man seated on a throne from those of a man sitting on the floor.   The dispositions of one beautifully clothed differ from one clad in rags.

Let work humble the body, and when the body is humbled the soul will be humble with it, so that it is truly said that bodily labors lead to humility. This is why Evagrius, when he was at war with a temptation to blasphemy, as a person with true insight, knowing that blasphemy comes from conceit and that when the body is humbled, the soul is humbled with it, spent forty days naked in the wilderness, without shelter, so that his body like a wild beast was covered with insects—and so his labor did not result in blasphemy, but humility. So the elder was right in saying that bodily labor leads to humility. May God, who is so good, grant us the grace of humility which delivers man from so many evils and delivers him from the greatest temptations.

FOOTNOTES

1. 1 Cor 9:25.
2. Ps 111:10.
3. Prov 15:27.
4. Heb 11:6.
5. Ps 25:18.
6. *Biblos* 277. Cf. PG 88:1816A.
7. Apo Nau 115; ROC (1907) 402; PL 73:1037.
8. Apo Macarius, cited by Zosimos; PE II:35, p. 112.
9. Apo Antony 7; PG 65:77; CS 59:2. Cf. PL 73:785.
10. Apo Nau 323; ROC (1912) 209; PL 73:967.
11. Gen 18:27.
12. Is 6:5.
13. Dan 14:36-7.
14. Ex 4:10.
15. Jer 1:6.
16. Apo Agathon 29; PG 65:117; CS 59:21. Cf. PE III, 9, p. 23.
17. Gregory Nazianzen, *Orat*. 39.7; PG 36:341C.
18. Gen 6:3.

III

N CONSCIENCE

WHEN GOD CREATED man, he breathed into him something divine, as it were a hot and bright spark added to reason, which lit up the mind and showed him the difference between right and wrong. This is called the conscience, which is the law of his nature. This is compared to the well which Jacob dug, as the Fathers say, and which the Philistines filled up.[1] That is, to this law of conscience adhered the patriarchs and all the holy men of old before the written law, and they were pleasing to God. But when this law was buried and trodden underfoot by men through the onset of sin, we needed a written law, we needed the holy prophets, we needed the instruction of our Master, Jesus Christ, to reveal it and raise it up and bring to life through the observance of the Commandments that buried spark. It is in our power either to bury it again or, if we obey it, to allow it to shine and illuminate us. When our conscience says to us, 'do this!' and we despise it and it speaks again and we do not do it but continue to despise it, at last we bury it and it is no longer able to speak clearly to us from the depths where we have laid it. But like a lamp shining on a damaged mirror, it reflects things dimly and darkly, just as you cannot see the reflection of your face in muddy water. We are found unable to perceive what our conscience says to us so that we think we have hardly any conscience. No one is without a conscience, since it is something divinely implanted in us, as we have already said, and it can never be destroyed. It always patiently reminds us of our duties, but sometimes we do not perceive that we are despising it and treading it underfoot. This is why the prophet bewails Ephraim and says, 'Ephraim prevails against his adversary and treads down judgment.'[2] The adversary here is 'conscience.' Here the Gospel says, 'Come to an agreement with your adversary while you are on the way with him, lest he deliver you to the judge and the judge to the warders and they put you in chains. Amen, I say to you, you shall not leave the place until you have paid the last farthing.'[3] Why does he call conscience the adversary? It is called the adversary because it always opposes our evil desires and tells what we ought to do and we do not, or what we ought not to do and we do; and it accuses us, and so conscience is called our adversary, and Our Lord admonishes, 'Come to an agreement with your adversary while you are on the way;' for the 'way' as St Basil says, is this world.[4]

Let us be zealous, brothers, to guard our conscience for as long as we are in this world and not to neglect its promptings in anything. And let us not tread it under foot even in the least thing, for you can see that from the smallest things, which of their nature are worth little, we come to despise the great things. When we begin to say, 'What is it if I say just these few words? What does it matter if I eat this morsel? What difference if I poke my nose in here or there? From this way of saying, 'What does this or that matter?' a man takes evil and bitter nourishment and begins presently to despise greater and more serious things and even to tread down his own conscience and so, at last destroying it, bit by bit, he falls into danger and finally becomes completely impervious to the light of conscience.

Therefore, brothers, see to it that we do not neglect little things; see to it that we do not despise them as of no account. There are no 'little things'—for when it is a question of bad habits, it is a question of a malignant ulcer. Let us live circumspectly, let us give heed to trivial matters when they are trivial, lest they become grave. Doing what is right and what is wrong: both begin from small things and advance to what is great, either good or evil. Therefore Our Lord warns us to take account of our conscience as one giving evidence of his own experience and saying 'Be careful, simpleton, see what you are doing, come to an agreement with your adversary while yet on the road' and he shows the danger to be feared: 'Lest he deliver you to the judge, and the judge to the executioner and he throw you into prison.' And what else? 'Amen, I tell you, he shall not go from there until he has paid the last farthing.'[5] Conscience then warns us, as I said, about what is good or what is bad and shows us what to do and what not to do, and in the world to come it will accuse us. Therefore it says, 'Lest he deliver you to the judge...' etc.

In attending to our conscience, we need to consider many different factors. A man needs to satisfy his conscience towards God, towards his neighbor, and towards material things. As regards God: he must not despise God's precepts, even those concerning things which are not seen by men or those things for which one is not accountable to men. A man should obey his conscience in relation to God; for example, did he neglect his prayer? If an evil thought came into his heart, was he vigilant and did he keep control of himself or did he entertain it? He sees his neighbor saying something or doing something; does he suspect it's evil and condemn him? To put it simply, all the hidden things that happen inside us, things which no one sees except God and our conscience, we need to take account of. This is what I mean by our conscience towards God.

To respect our conscience towards our neighbor means not to do anything that we think may trouble or harm our neighbor in deed, or word, or gesture, or look. For there are gestures, as I very often tell you, which hurt our neighbors and there are looks capable of wounding him and, to speak plainly, whatever a man does readily, knowing it gives his neighbor a bad thought stains his own conscience because it means that he is ready to harm or trouble his neighbor—and this is the sort of thing I mean by keeping a good conscience towards our neighbor.

As regards keeping a good conscience in respect of material things: not to use things badly, not to render things useless, not to leave things about, and when we find things left about not to leave them even if they are of small value, but to pick them up and put them in their proper place. Not to be slovenly about our clothes or wear them out too quickly: for example, when one can wear a shirt a week or two, to want to wash it every day and so by constant washing wear it out too quickly and always be asking for new. These things are against the conscience. Similarly about the bed, often when one can make do with a small mattress, one asks for a large one; and when one has a blanket, one wants to exchange it for a new one or a better one for the sake of prestige or from mere thoughtlessness. Or where a rush mat is adequate one asks for a carpet and is quick to protest unless one gets it; or one approaches one of the brethren and says, 'Why has so-and-so got such a thing and I haven't?' Such a man is not on the right road. Or a man hangs his tunic or blanket in the sun and through negligence leaves it there to spoil—this is all against the conscience. It is the same about food: a man is perfectly able to satisfy the needs of his body with bread, vegetables, and few olives, but he gives up doing so and seeks something more tasty and more expensive—all this is against the conscience.

The Fathers tell us that a monk ought not to give his conscience occasion to reproach him about anything at all.[6] It is necessary, therefore, brothers, to keep watch over ourselves always and to keep ourselves away from all these things lest we fall into danger. For Our Lord also will bring an indictment against us, as we have said above. May God grant we listen and be attentive to these things, lest the sayings of our Fathers turn out to be for us words of condemnation.

FOOTNOTES

1. Cf. Gen 26:15.
2. Hos 10:11.
3. Mt 5:25-6.
4. *Hom in Ps. i;* PG 29:200-21.
5. Mt 5:26.
6. Apo Agathon 2; PG 65:109; CS 59:17.

IV

N THE FEAR OF GOD

SAINT JOHN in one of his epistles says, 'Perfect love drives out fear'.[1] What does the holy man signify to us by this? What sort of love and what sort of fear is he talking about? The psalmist says, 'Fear the Lord all you who love him',[2] and we find thousands of similar sayings in Holy Scripture. If, therefore, the saints who so loved him feared him, how can he say, 'Love casteth out fear'? St John wishes to show us that there are two kinds of fear: one preliminary, the other perfect; the one found in beginners—as someone called it 'of the devout'; the other in those perfected in holiness, of those having arrived at true love. One forms a desire of God through fear of condemnation; this is, as we have said, the starting point. His starting point is not 'what is good' but the fear of torments. Another forms a desire for God because he loves God himself, loves him and knows what is acceptable to God. Such a man is goodness itself, knowing what it is to be with God. See! This is the man who has true love, which St John calls perfect love, and that love leads a man on to perfect fear. Such a man fears and keeps to God's will, not for fear of punishment, not to avoid condemnation, but, as we have said, because he has tasted the sweetness of being with God; he fears he may fall away from it; he fears to be turned away from it. This is the perfect fear which is generated from perfect love and throws out that preliminary fear. And this is why he says that perfect love casts out fear. But it is impossible to come to perfect fear except through that preliminary fear.

There are, as St Basil says, three states through which we can be pleasing to God.[3] The first, that of fearing punishment; this makes us acceptable and we are in the state of slaves. The second, the state of servants working for wages, fulfilling orders for our own advantage and, by doing so, earning our wages. The third is the state of sons, where we strive for the highest good. For a son, when he comes to maturity, does his father's will not for fear of being beaten, nor to receive a reward from him, but because he knows he is loved. He loves and honors his father, and is convinced that all his father possesses is his own. Such a man is worthy to hear, 'You are no longer a slave, but a son, an heir of God through Christ'.[4] As we said, he no longer fears God with that preliminary fear, but really loves him, and so blessed Anthony can say, 'I no longer fear God',[5] and when the Lord said to Abraham after the immolation of his son, 'Now I know that you fear God',[6] this signifies that perfect fear that is generated out of love. What does he refer to in saying, 'Now I know'? Abraham was charitable, he did so many things (at God's bidding), he obeyed God and did not spare his only son, he wandered from place to place in a foreign land among idolatrous peoples, where there was not an atom of the fear of God, and on top of all this he endured the fearful test of sacrificing his only son. And after all this, God said to him, 'Now I know that you fear God'; clearly he meant that perfect fear that belongs to the saints. So no longer through fear of punishment nor to receive reward do they do the will of God, but loving, they fear to do anything apart from the will of the Beloved, and so he says, 'Love casts out fear'. No longer do they act from fear, but they fear out of love.

This, then, is the perfect fear, but perfect fear cannot come about if a man has not that preliminary fear. For Scripture says, 'The beginning of wisdom is the fear of the

Lord,'[7] and again, 'The beginning and the end is the fear of God'.[8] He calls the beginning that preliminary fear which is the final perfect fear, that of the saints. The preliminary fear belongs to our own state; this preserves the soul, like an enamel. It is written, 'By the fear of the Lord every man turns away from evil'.[9] If every man turns from evil for fear of punishment, like a slave who is afraid of his master, he comes in some measure to do good, and begins to hope for a certain recompense for his good works as would the hired servant. When therefore, he persists in fleeing evil, as we say, out of fear like a slave, and again doing good out of hope like a hired servant, spending time with God, and proportionately being united to God, at last he tastes and comes to a certain experience of Good as it is in itself and he wishes to be separated from it no longer. For who, says the Apostle, is able to separate him from the love of Christ?[10] Then he attains the measure of a son and loves good for its own sake and fears, because he loves. And this is the great and perfect fear. For this reason the Prophet teaches us the difference in this fear and says, 'Come, my children, listen to me and I will teach you the fear of the Lord.'[11] Fix your minds on this saying of the Prophet, see how every word has its force. First he says, 'Come to me', calling us on towards virtue. And he adds, 'children'. The saints call 'children' those who are converted by their words from evil ways to virtue, as the Apostle says, 'Children of whom I am in labor again until Christ be formed in you.'[12] Then after calling us to him and urging us on to this conversion he says, 'I will teach you the fear of the Lord'. Consider well the saint's confidence. When we wish to say something about the spiritual life, we always say, 'Do you wish to discuss and lay bare something about the fear of God or some other virtue?' But he acts differently and confidently says, 'Come, children, listen to me, and I will teach you the fear of the Lord; who is the man who desires life and loves to see good days?' Then as though someone replied, 'I do, teach me how to live and see good days,' he sets out to teach him saying, 'Refrain your

tongue from evil and your lips that they speak no guile'. [13]
See, meanwhile, he cuts off a source of evil through the fear
of God. *To refrain your tongue from evil:* that is, do not
offend the conscience of your neighbor by anything, do not
speak evil, do not be irritable. *And your lips that they speak
no guile:* that is, do not speak to deceive your neighbor.
Then he adds, 'Turn aside from evil'. First he speaks of
particular sins, backbiting and deceit, and he goes on to
speak globally of all evils. 'Turn aside from evil': as much as
to say, simply flee from all evil and turn aside from
everything that leads to evil. Nor again does he only say that
and keep silence, but he adds, 'and do good'. For it can
happen that although a man does no evil, he nevertheless
does no good. When a man does not harm anyone, he does
not, however, show pity; when he does not hate, he does not
love. Therefore, quite rightly, the Prophet says, 'Turn away
from evil and do good'. See how he shows the consequence
of the three states of which we spoke: how through the fear
of God we are lead by the hand to reject evil and so we come
to be united with the good. For if a man is worthy to leave
evil and to flee from it naturally, he can work at good, led
along the way by the example of the saints. Having said this,
quite rightly, he leads on to its consequences adding, 'Seek
peace and pursue it'. Not content to say only 'seek it', he
must add, 'run after it quickly, so that you may take hold of
it'.

Fasten your mind firmly on this saying and consider the
zeal of the holy man. When a man is worthy to turn away
from evil and is keen to rest with God and to do good, battles
with the enemy come swiftly upon him. Henceforth he has to
compete, to labor, to be ground down; not only does he fear
to turn back towards evil, as we said about the slave, but
hopes, as we said before, for the reward of good like a hired
laborer.

As he is being attacked, fighting with weapons and with
his fists, he does good, but with much trouble and
exhaustion. But when assistance from God is generated in

him and afterwards he begins to take on a certain stability in his pursuit of what is good, then he is in sight of rest, then he steps forward towards peace, then he knows from experience the struggle of war and the joy and happiness of peace; and for the rest he ardently desires it and is keen to run in pursuit of it. And finally he obtains it, so that he possesses it and builds it into himself. And what is more fortunate than the soul of one who is worthy to attain to this measure? Such a man, as we have often said, attains the measure of a son. For so blessed are the peacemakers that they are called the very sons of God. [14] What, more than anything else, makes a soul do good if not the joy that good itself brings it? Who knows that joy except the man who has experienced it? Such a man discovers what that perfect fear is, as we often say.

Now we have heard what the perfect fear of the saints is and what is the preliminary fear which belongs to our lowly state, how we escape from it, and where we come to through the fear of God. Lastly, we desire to learn how the fear of God comes about, and to do this we must say what it is that banishes us from the fear of God.

The Fathers tell us [15] that a man gains possession of the fear of God by keeping the thought of death before his mind and remembering eternal punishment, by examining himself each evening about how he has passed the day and each morning about how he has passed the night; by never giving rein to his tongue and by keeping in close and continual touch with a man possessed of the fear of God, as his spiritual director. A brother once said to one of the elders, 'What shall I do, Father, that I may learn to fear the Lord?' And he said, 'Go and become a disciple of a man possessed of the fear of the Lord and from his fearing the Lord you, yourself, will learn to fear the Lord.' [16] We chase away from us the fear of the Lord by the fact that we do just the opposite; we do not keep before us the thought of death, or punishment, nor do we attend to our own condition, or examine how we spend our time, but we live differently and are occupied with

different things, pandering to our liberty, giving way to ourselves, self-indulgence—this is the worst of all, this is perfect
ruin. What chases away the fear of the Lord as effectively as
indulging our fancies? Hence when Abba Agathon was asked
about self-indulgence he said that it is like a great conflagra-
tion from which, when it burns up, men flee and the fruit of
the trees around it is utterly destroyed. [17]   Good Lord! You
understand the strength of this passion and its destructive-
ness.   And when he was asked again, 'Is it so very
dangerous?' he said, 'Yes, there is nothing more dangerous
than self-indulgence. It prepares the ground for all the vices
because it chases out from the soul the fear of God.' For if
every man turns aside from evil by the fear of the Lord, there
is good reason why, where there is no fear of the Lord, every
vice is to be found.   May God deliver us from the deadly
disease of self-indulgence. [18]

Self-indulgence takes many forms.   A man may be self-
indulgent in speech, in touch, in sight. From self-indulgence
a man comes to idle speech and worldly talk, to buffoonery
and cracking indecent jokes.   There is self-indulgence in
touching without necessity, making mocking signs with the
hands, pushing for a place, snatching up something for oneself, approaching someone else shamelessly.   All these things
come from not having the fear of God in the soul and from
these a man comes little by little to perfect contempt. For this
reason when God delivered the Commandments of the Law,
he said, 'Treat with respect the sons of Israel.' [19] For without
mutual respect, God himself is not honored, nor is it possible
to fulfil a single commandment.   Therefore, there is nothing
worse than this abuse of freedom and it is the seed-bed of all
the vices. For it does away with the respect of others, drives
away the fear of God, generates contempt.   Exercising this
dangerous liberty towards one another leads to effrontery,
speaking ill of one another, and coming to blows.

If one of you sees, sometime, something unedifying and
so much as goes on to pass it on and put it into the heart of
another brother, in doing so you not only harm yourself but

you harm your brother by putting one more little bit of knavery into his heart. Even if that brother has his mind set on prayer or some other noble activity, and the first arrives and furnishes him with something to prate about, he not only impedes what he ought to be doing, but brings a temptation on him. There is nothing graver or more deadly than this doing harm, not only to himself but also to his neighbor.

Therefore, it is a great thing to cultivate this respect for our brethren so that we fear to harm ourselves and one another, that we honor one another and that we keep a careful check on our gestures and on our countenance towards one another. For these latter, as one of the elders points out, can come under the heading of 'taking liberties'. Should it happen that you see a brother doing wrong, don't despise him and wipe your hands of him and keep silence and let him be destroyed, nor again curse him or speak ill of him. But with sympathy and the fear of God speak to someone who is able to set him up again, or you yourself speak to him with love and humility saying, 'Pardon me, brother, but I consider—being careless myself—we probably do not act rightly in doing so-and-so.' If he does not listen to you, speak to another in whom you see he has full confidence, or to his dean, or to the abbot, according to the gravity of the fault; but above all, as we have said, speak with a view to setting him straight again, not to gossip idly or to defame him or despise him, not, so to speak, to hold him up as a bad example, nor to condemn him or to pretend to be righteous by doing so. If a man having any of the dispositions I mentioned above speaks to the abbot himself, he is not speaking for the correction of his brother, nor is he if he speaks only on account of injury done to himself; that is a transgression, it is speaking ill of his brother. But let him grope about in his own heart and if he experiences there a movement of anger or resentment let him not speak. Should he perceive accurately that he desires to speak out of concern for his brother and a need to help him and if this thought brings a certain emotion which troubles him, let him humbly make the

facts known to his abbot, both his own and his brother's
saying, 'My conscience bears witness that I wish to speak for
the correction of my brother but I perceive that some thought
of self is mixed up with it. Maybe I was at some time
holding something against my brother, I don't know. Or
maybe slander is prompting me to speak and bring about a
correction, I don't know.' The abbot will tell him if he ought
to speak out or not. There is a time when a man speaks not
to come to the aid of his brother, not because of his own
feelings, not because he bears a grudge but because he is led
on, as it were, by frivolity. And what need is there for idle
talk? Often a brother learns that he is being discussed and is
very distressed about it. Trouble arises from this and further
harm is done. But when a man speaks up purely out of a
desire to help his brother and that alone, God does not permit
any commotion to arise and he does not allow any trouble or
harm to follow on its heels.

Take great care, as we have said, to keep guard over your
tongue, so that no one speaks ill of his neighbor or plagues
anyone by word or deed or gesture or any means whatever;
and do not let yourself become so touchy that when a man
hears a sharp word from a brother he is put out or makes a
contentious answer or remains vexed with him. That is not
the way of those who desire to be saved, that is not the way
of the spiritual athlete. Go in search of the fear of God, but
with discretion, so that you go to meet one another as
friends, each one bowing his head before his brother, as we
say, each one humbling himself before God and before his
brother, and cutting off his own will for the sake of his
brother. Actually if a man does this rightly, and gives way to
his brother and gives him the place of honor, this very
deference will be of greater help to himself than to the other
man.

I do not know if I have done good at any time, but if I
have been protected from this vice of 'taking liberties' I know
that I was protected because I never judged myself better
than my brother, but I always reckoned my brother ahead of

me [in virtue].

Some time ago while I was a disciple of Abba Seridos, the minister of old Abba John, a disciple of Abba Barsanufius, fell sick and my abba ordered me to serve the old man. I used to reverence the door of his cell with as much devotion as one would pay the Cross of Christ. How much more reverently would I serve him? Who would not desire to be worthy to serve such a holy man? He had a wonderful way of speaking and each time I had completed my service, I bowed to him and asked for a word of advice before going away, and he always spoke to me. The old man had four words of advice, and, as I said, each time I was about to leave he used to say one or other of these four words. He used to speak like this, 'Once for all,'—for it was his custom so to begin every oracle he spoke—'Once for all, brother, may God preserve you in love. The Fathers used to say: "That guarding of your neighbor's conscience brings forth humility".'[20] Again another evening he said to me, 'Once for all, brother, may God preserve you in love. The Fathers used to say: "I used never to grasp my own desires in preference to my brothers." ' On another occasion, he said, 'Once for all, brother, may God preserve you in love. The Fathers used to say, "Flee the ways of man and you will be saved."' Again he said, 'Once for all, brother, may God preserve you in love. The Fathers used to say, "Bear one another's burdens and so you will fulfil the Law of Christ." '[21]

The old man always had an exhortation from one of these four to give me as I went away each evening, as though giving me provisions for a journey, and so I hold them as a safeguard all my life. Nevertheless though I had such great confidence in the holy man and was so well disposed to do him service and obey him, when I perceived that one of the other brothers was disturbed by his desire to serve the old man, I went to the abbot to persuade him that this brother could perform this service better than I. But the abbot did not allow him to do so, nor did the old man. Yet I had done my best to give place to the brother, and although I did this service for nine years, I know that I did not speak one disparaging word to anyone, and I kept up this service although I had other duties to discharge. I say this lest anyone should say I had nothing else to do.

Believe me, I know one brother walked behind me from the infirmary to the church, abusing me all the way. But I went on ahead without uttering a single word. When the abbot learned about it—I don't know who told him—he wanted to rebuke him. I fell at his feet saying, 'Do not do so, for the Lord's sake. It was I who failed. He has done nothing wrong.' And another brother, whether to provoke me or out of simplicity, the Lord knows which, during the night silence, made water all over my head and soaked my bed. Similarly some of the other brethren began, during the day, to shake their rush-mats in front of my cell, and I saw such a horde of flies and stinging insects coming into my cell that I could not kill them all. They were in such great numbers because of the heat. When I came back to lie down they all settled on me. Sleep came upon me, I was so tired from my labor, but when I woke up I found my body bitten all over. But I never said anything to any of them, not 'You are not to do this', or 'Why do you do this?' I am not conscious, as I said, of having said a bitter or complaining word. Learn then to bear one another's burdens, learn to reverence one another. And if any one of you hears a disobliging word, or if one of you suffers at any time from a deliberate provocation, do not straight-way become timorous, do not immediately get worked up, do not be found faint-hearted in the time of contest, unprepared in time of need, untuned, not able to meet such attacks as are bound to come. Don't be like a pumpkin that immediately goes rotten if a gnat comes up to it and punctures it, but rather have a stout heart, have patience that our love for one another may conquer everything that comes up against us. If anyone should have a charge [in the monastery], or if anyone should be given a commission for the cook, or the gardener, or the cellarer, in short for anyone of those who have a job to do for us, let him take care to seek the answer himself or to render the service himself, and before all things let him stick to his position and not for any reason allow himself to cause a disturbance or to give way to his likes or dislikes, or any other kind of self-will, and so depart from the commandment of God. And whether the business is thought to be of little importance or great, let him never despise it or neglect it. For neglect is a bad thing. Again, let him not be puffed up on account of the position he holds, because if this happens he will do himself harm by the job entrusted to him. If you are concerned with any business whatever, even if it is very urgent and important, I do not want you ever to do it with contentiousness or disorder, but to be fully convinced that all the work you do, whether it is important or trivial, as we have said, is only one-eighth part of the thing we are seeking. But keeping one's proper state [of submission to God and respect for the brethren], even if it means losing our job, is four out of eight parts, i.e. half of the thing we are seeking. See then how great the difference is. When you do anything, therefore, if you wish to do it perfectly and completely, you must take care to do it while considering it, as it is, the eighth part [of what we aim to do], and to keep unharmed our own interior disposition as four-eighths. If from the pressure of the work we have to do, we have to dispense ourselves from some rule, and we are hurt, or hurt someone else, in carrying out our administration, it is certainly not good to destroy the half in order to preserve the eighth. And if you know that someone is doing this, he does not have a proper understanding of the job he is doing. If either through ambition or through seeking to please men, he remains contentious, he punishes both himself and his neighbor, so that later he can hear it said of him that nobody got the better of him. God bless my soul. What great manliness! That is not a victory gained, brothers, it is sheer loss; it is mere destruction. Look! I tell you that, should I send one of you on any necessary business whatever and should he see any commotion arising or anything else harmful, let him cut it off and not harm himself or anyone else. Let the business go rather than let a commotion arise; only see to it that you do not provoke one another. Otherwise you will destroy the four parts, and this is manifestly irrational. I don't tell you this that you should immediately become timid and run away from what you have to do, or become neglectful, throw up the matter and stifle your conscience because you do not want to take the trouble to do your duty; nor again, when you are given an order, that one of you should say, 'I cannot do that. I shall be harmed by it; don't pick on me.' By this sort of reasoning no one would render any kind of service or be able to fulfil God's commandment. But hold all your strength in readiness to do every service with love, with humility, deferring to one another, honoring one another, consoling one another. Nothing is more powerful than humility. If, however, someone knows that his brother is temporarily troubled, or he himself is troubled, break off and retire from one another, and do not remain until real harm follows from it. For it is a thousand times better that the business not go as you wish, but go according to the needs of the situation; not go on at one fell swoop or by judicial decree even if it is a reasonable, if you thereby disturb yourself and trouble one another and so lose four out of eight parts. There is a great difference in the loss incurred. It does happen that a man loses the whole eight and yet accomplishes nothing at all. This is the whole story about contentiousness. Our basic principle is that all the work we do, we do through the help we get from others. How useful it is for us to be humble towards one another. By doing the contrary we only trouble and give pain to each other. Do you know what someone says in the Book of the Elders? 'From the neighbor is life and from the neighbor is death.'[22] At all times each one of you must take this saying of the Seniors to heart, in order to put it into practice so that you may be zealous in seeking—with great love and the fear of God—to benefit each other as well as yourselves. And so you will be able to profit from everything that happens to you and to make progress by the help of God. God himself, the lover of men, will grant us this fear of him, for it is written, 'Fear God and keep his precepts, because this is required of all men.'[23]

FOOTNOTES

1. 1 Jn 4:18.
2. Ps 34:9.
3. *Reg. fus. tract., proemium;* PG 31:896. Cf. Cassian, *Conf.* 11:6-7 & DS 2:535-6: *Charité.*
4. Gal 4:7.
5. Apo Antony 32: PG 65:85C; CS 59:6.
6. Gen 22:12.
7. Ps 111:10.
8. Cf. Prov 1:9, 9:10, 22:4.
9. Prov 15:27.
10. Rm 8:35.
11. Ps 34:11.
12. Gal 4:19.
13. Ps 34:13.
14. Mt 5:19.
15. Cf. Apo Nau 182; ROC (1908) 267 & 264; ROC (1900) 369. Apo Nisteros 5; PG 65:308; CS 59:130.
16. Apo Poemen 65; PG 65: 337B; CS 59:147-8.
17. Apo Agathon 1; PG 65: 109; CS 59:17.
18. παρρησία
19. Lev 15:31.
20. Apo Isaac; PE I, 45, p. 168.
21. Gal 6:2.
22. Apo Antony 1; PG 65:77; CS 59:2.
23. Qo 12:13.

V

N THE NEED FOR CONSULTATION

That a man ought not to rely exclusively on his own judgment

IN THE BOOK of Proverbs it says, 'Those who have no guidance fall like leaves but there is safety in much counsel.'[1] Take a good look at this saying, brothers. Look at what Scripture is teaching us. It assures us that we should not set ourselves up as guide posts, that we should not consider ourselves sagacious, that we should not believe we can direct ourselves. We need assistance, we need guidance in addition to God's grace. No one is more wretched, no one is more easily caught unawares, than a man who has no one to guide him along the road to God. It says, 'Those who have no guidance fall like leaves'. Leaves are always green in the beginning, they grow vigorously and are pleasing to look at. Then after a short time they dry up and fall off, and in the end they are blown about by the wind and trodden under foot. So is the man who is not guided by someone. At first he has great fervor about fasting, keeping vigil, keeping silence, and obedience and other good customs. Then after a short time the fire is extinguished and, not having anyone to guide him and strengthen him and kindle his fire again, he shrivels up and so, becoming disobedient, he falls and finally becomes a tool in the hand of his enemies, who do what they like with him.

Concerning those who make a report about what concerns their interior life and do everything with counsel, it says, 'There is safety in much counsel'. When it says 'much counsel' it does not mean taking counsel from all and sundry, but clearly from someone in whom he has full confidence. And he should not be silent about some things and speak about others, but he should report everything and take counsel about everything. To a man doing this consistently, there is indeed safety in much counsel. But if a man does not bring to light everything about himself, especially if he has turned away from evil habits and a bad upbringing, and if the devil finds in him one bit of self-will or self-righteousness, he will cast him down through that. For when the devil looks at a man who sincerely desires not to sin, he is not so unintelligent as to suggest to him (as he would to a hardened sinner) that he go and commit fornication or go and steal. He knows we do not want that and he does not set out to tell us something we do not want to hear; but he finds out that little bit of self-will or self-righteousness and through that, with the appearance of well doing, he will do us harm. Hence again, it is said, 'A bad man does evil when he mixes it with righteousness'.[2] The 'bad man' is the devil and he does evil when he mixes it with righteousness, i.e. our self-righteousness, for then he is stronger, then he can do more harm, then he can operate more freely. For when we are masters of our own affairs and we stand in our own righteousness, as if we were doing great things, we are giving ourselves counsel— and we do not know how it is we are destroyed. For how can we know the will of God or seek it completely if we believe only in ourselves and hold on to our own will?

For this reason Abba Poemen used to say that 'The will is a brass wall standing between God and Man'.[3] Take a look at the force of this saying. And he adds another thing about self-will. 'It is a rock jutting out as if going out to meet and push back the will of God.' Therefore, if a man relinquishes it he can truly say, "In my God, I have leapt

over the wall. My God, blameless in his way'.[4] How marvellously he speaks! When a man gives up his own will he
sees at once that the way of the Lord has no blemish or
obstruction; when a man has a fondness for his own will, he
does not see that the way of God is without blemish or
obstruction. And if he happens to be cautioned about his
condition, he is angry and contemptuous, and he turns away
and rejects it. For how can a man have experience of this or
be persuaded by the counsel of anyone, if he is mastered by
self-will. Then the elder says about self-righteousness: 'If
self-righteousness combines with self-will, a man will turn in
the wrong direction.' My God! How terrible are the consequences suggested by the seniors' words!

Death is properly the judgment to be expected after self-
will! A great danger! A thing to be greatly feared! Then
sometimes the wretched man falls completely. Who can
persuade such a man that another man can see better than
himself what is fitting for him, and then that he should give
up entirely following his own will and his own way of
thinking? But no! The enemy gets his way, he makes him a
corpse. Wherefore it says: 'The evil one does evil when he
mixes it with justice. He hates a whisper of caution.'[5] It is
said that because the evil one hates caution not only can he
not hear the sound of it, he hates even the very echo of it,
that is, the mere mention of caution; for example, if a man
proposes to do something, he enquires whether it is profitable
before he forms an opinion on whether or not it is the enemy
who suggests it, on whether he keeps to what he hears or not
(that is what the devil utterly hates); he asks someone else
and listens to what those who have to share his life have to
say about it. The very sound, the mere echo of such discourse the devil hates and flees away from. And why do I
say this? Because the devil knows that his malice is brought
to light through this enquiry and discussion about the
advantage of doing a thing, and there is nothing he hates and
fears so much as to be known, because then he finds himself
unable to lay snares as he wishes. If a man would safeguard

his soul, he will do so by laying bare all his secret thoughts and hearing from an experienced director, 'Do this, avoid that. This is right, the other is not. This is virtue, that is self-will.' Or again he hears, 'It is not the right *time* for doing this', or at another time, 'Now is the time for this', and the devil finds no opportunity to do him harm or to strike him down, since in everything he is controlled and he takes precautions about everything and is made secure. 'There is safety in much counsel.' The devil does not want this, and hates it. What he wants is to do evil and he rejoices the more over those who do not accept direction.[6] Why? 'Because they fall like leaves.'

Take a look at the brother whom the evil one loved, about whom he used to say to Abba Macarius: 'I have one brother' he said, 'who when he sees me changes like the wind.'[7] Such people the devil loves and he always rejoices over them, the ungoverned, those who are not subject to one who has power, under God, to help them and to give them a hand. Did not that cunning demon, whom the holy man saw carrying his savory drinks in little flasks, go after all the brothers? Did he not offer [drinks] to all alike? But all of them ran and made known his thoughts to his spiritual father and so found help in time of temptation, with the result that the evil one was powerless against them? But the devil found this miserable brother depending on his own strength and having nobody to support him, and he made a plaything of him. And he went off congratulating himself and raging against the others, but he was careless when he told Abba Macarius about it, and gave away to him the brother's name. The holy man ran to him quickly and he found that this very thing was the cause of his undoing: he found him unwilling to talk about his troubles; he found he had not formed the habit of revealing his inner thoughts and for this reason the enemy was twisting him round his little finger. Being asked by the holy father, 'How are things with you?' he would say, 'Thanks to your prayers I am quite all right!' And again Macarius asked, 'Your thoughts and imaginations are not troubling you?' And he replied, 'So far I'm all right.' He did not want to admit anything until the saint, by using all his skill, persuaded him to speak out about himself. He spoke the word of God to him and guided him back to the right way. Then the enemy came again, according to his habit desiring to strike him down and make him act shamefully. He found him stiffened up and no longer bidable. He departed at last without success; he departed put to shame, and by this very brother. And so when he was again asked by the saint, 'How is your friend?', he no longer called him friend but enemy, and cursed him saying, 'Even he has turned away from me and I can no longer influence him; he has become more savage to me than all the rest.' Now you understand why the enemy hates anyone who takes the precaution of revealing his secret thoughts: because he wants to destroy us. Now you understand why he loves those who stake out their own paths: because they work together with the devil, they themselves lay snares for themselves.

I know of no fall that happens to a monk that does not come from trusting his own judgment. Some say, 'A man falls because of this, or because of that,' but I say, and I repeat, I do not know of any fall happening to anyone except from this cause. Do you know someone who has fallen? Be sure that he directed himself. Nothing is more grievous than to be one's own director, nothing is more pernicious. God has protected me from this, and I am always afraid of this danger. When I was in the cenobium I used to reveal everything to old Abba John, for I never set out to do anything contrary to his judgment. And there were times when my thoughts said to me, 'Will he not say the same as I am telling you? Why do you want to disturb him?' And I used to say to my thoughts, 'Damn you and your judgment and your sagacity, your discernment and your knowledge, because what you know, you know from the devil.' Therefore, I went and asked the old man, and often it happened that his reply coincided with the judgment I had already formed, and then my thoughts said to me, 'What about that? Don't you see it is as I told you, and you have disturbed the old man unreasonably?' And I used to say to my thoughts, 'Yes! But now it is right to do this. Now it comes from the Holy Spirit. What is purely your own is bad, it is from the devil, from the state of your emotions.' And so I never allowed my thoughts to persuade me without consulting someone else, and believe me, brothers, I was in a complete state of rest and freedom from care. So much so that I was even a little troubled, as I think I told you, when I heard the text, 'We must enter into the kingdom of heaven through many tribulations,'[8] and I saw myself without a single tribulation. I was afraid and puzzled, not knowing the cause of such peace of soul until Abba John made it clear to me by saying, 'Don't be troubled. Everyone who puts himself under obedience to the fathers has this peace and freedom from anxiety.'

Be careful to make enquiries, brothers, and do not set yourselves up as your own judges. Learn by experience how much freedom from anxiety, how much joy, how much peace this brings. But although I was saying that I am never troubled now, listen what happened to me some time ago. When I was still in the cenobium, there came to me only once a great and unspeakable trial. I was in such dire straights that I was almost at the point of departing this life. But this affliction was contrived by the devil; a trial of this kind could only be brought upon us by the devil's jealousy. Although it did not last long it was very grievous while it lasted. My heart was heavy; my mind dark; nothing could comfort me and there was no relief anywhere. I was shut in on all sides, completely stifled. The grace of God comes swiftly to the soul, when endurance is no longer possible. I was then, as I said, in a state of temptation and distress. On one of the days I was in this condition I was standing inside looking abstractedly out into the court of the monastery in the early hours and beseeching God about it. Suddenly I turned towards the church and perceived someone having the appearance of a bishop come into the sanctuary, as though carried by wings. Ordinarily I never used to approach a

stranger unless I had to do or had been ordered to do so, but
at that moment something drew me powerfully after him, so I
went in behind him. He remained standing for some time
with his hands stretched up towards heaven, and I stood
there behind him in great fear, praying, for I was very
alarmed at the sight of him. When his prayer was finished,
he turned and came towards me, and as he drew nearer to
me I felt my pain and dread passing away. Then he stood in
front of me and, stretching out his hand, touched me on the
breast and tapped me on the chest with his fingers, saying:

> I waited, I waited for the Lord
> And he stooped down to me;
> He heard my cry.
> He drew me from the deadly pit,
>   from the mirery clay.
> He set my feet upon a rock
>   and made my footsteps firm.
> He put a new song into my mouth, [a song of]
>   praise of our God. [9]

He repeated all these verses three times, tapping me on the
chest, as I said. Then he departed. And immediately light
flooded my mind and there was joy in my heart with comfort
and sweetness. I was a different man. I ran out after him
hoping to find him, but I could not. He had disappeared.
From that moment on, by God's providence, I have not
known myself to be troubled by sorrow or fear, but the Lord
has sheltered me till now through the prayers of the seniors
[of the abbas].

I have told you all this so that you may know how much
rest and tranquility a man may have—and that with all
security—by not settling anything by himself, but by casting
everything that concerns himself upon God and on those who,
after God, have the power to guide him.

Learn then, brothers, to enquire; be convinced that not to
set one's own path is a great thing. This is humility, this is

peace of soul, this is joy! What is the use of running headlong into folly? Do not form the opinion that there is any other safe way to travel. Similarly do not ponder what you should do if you have no one to ask. If anyone really in truth desires the will of God with all his heart, God never leaves him [to himself] but always guides him according to his [divine] will. If a man really sets his heart upon the will of God, God will enlighten a little child to tell that man what is his will. But if a man does not truly desire the will of God, even if he goes in search of a prophet, God will put into the heart of the prophet a reply like the deception in his own heart. Scripture says, 'If a prophet should speak and be deceived, it is I, the Lord, who deceived that prophet.'[10] That is why we ought to use all our ability to take a straight course towards the will of God, and not to trust the promptings of our own heart. If there is something good to be done, and we hear from some holy man that it *is* good, then we should on the one hand hold that it is good to do it, but not automatically put our trust in our own judgment that it is a good thing to do and that it is good for us to do it. On the other hand, we ought to do our best again to examine it and *how* we ought to do it and to learn whether we have done it in the right way, and even after that not to be self-satisfied about it, but to wait for God's judgment about it. As St Agathon said when he was asked if he was afraid, 'I have done my best, but I do not know if my work is pleasing to God. God's judgment is one thing and man's is another.'[11] May God shelter us from this danger of being our own guides that we may be worthy to take the road our fathers took and pleased God.

FOOTNOTES

1. Prov 11:14. Cf. *Lausiac History* 27.
2. Prov 11:15 (LXX).
3. Apo Poemen 54; PG 65:333-6; CS 59:146.
4. Ps 18:30-31.
5. Prov 11:15. Cf. Cassian, *Conf.* 1:21.
6. Apo Poemen 101; CS 59:152.
7. Apo Macarius 3; PG 65: 261-4; CS 59:107.
8. Acts 14:22.
9. Ps 40:1-2.
10. Ezek 14:9. Cf. Dt 13: 1, 5.
11. Apo Agathon 29: PG 65: 117; CS 59:21.

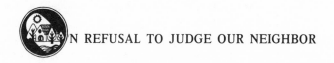

VI

N REFUSAL TO JUDGE OUR NEIGHBOR

IF WE REMEMBER the saying of the holy fathers, brothers, and put them into practice all the time, it will be difficult for us to neglect ourselves. For if, as they used to say, we do not despise little things and think they are of no consequence to us, we shall not fall into great and grievous things. I am always telling you that bad habits are formed in the soul by these very small things—when we say, 'What does this or that matter,'—and it is the first step to despising great things. You know how great a wrong it is to judge your neighbor. What is graver than this? What does God hate and turn away from so much as from this? As the fathers say, what is worse than judging rashly?[1] Nevertheless, from things that appear negligible a man comes to such great evil. For by accepting a suspicion against the neighbor, by saying, 'What does it matter if I put in a word [about my suspicion]? What does it matter if I find out what this brother is saying or what that guest is doing?' the mind begins to forget about its own sins and to talk idly about his neighbor, speaking evil against him, despising him, and from this he falls into the very thing that he condemns. Because we become careless about our own faults and do not lament our own death (as the Fathers put it),[2] we lose the power to correct ourselves and we are always at work on our neighbor. Nothing angers God so much or strips a man so bare or carries him so effectively to his ruin as calumniating, condemning, or despising his neighbor.

There are three distinct things here: running a man down; condemning him unjustly; and despising him. Running a man down is saying that so-and-so has told a lie, or got into a rage, or gone whoring, or the like. A man has already committed calumny if he speaks about his brother's sins as if with sympathy. Condemning a man is saying, 'he is a wicked liar, or he is an angry man, or he is a fornicator. For in this way one judges the condition of his soul and draws a conclusion about his whole life, saying it is of such a kind and condemns him as such. This is a very serious thing. For it is one thing to say, 'He got mad', and another thing to say, 'He is bad-tempered', and to reveal, as we said, the whole disposition of his life. It is serious to judge a man for each one of his sins. As Christ himself says, 'Hypocrite, first take the board from your own eye, then you can see to take the splinter out of your brother's eye.'[3]

You see, he compares your brother's sin to a splinter and your rash judgment to a board. Very nearly the most difficult of all sins to deal with is judging our neighbor! That Pharisee who was praying and giving thanks to God for his [own] good works was not lying but speaking the truth, and he was not condemned for that. For we *must* give thanks to God when we are worthy to do something good, as he is then working with us and helping us. Because of this he was not condemned, as I said, not even because he said, 'I am not like other men', but [he was condemned] because he said, 'I am not like this tax-collector'.[4] It was then that he made a judgment. He condemned a person and the dispositions of his soul—to put it shortly, his whole life. Therefore, the tax-collector rather than the Pharisee went away justified.

Nothing is more serious, nothing more difficult to deal with, as I say repeatedly, than judging and despising our neighbor. Why do we not rather judge ourselves and our own wickedness which we know so accurately and about

which we have to render an account to God?   Why do we
usurp God's right to judge?   Why should *we* demand a
reckoning from *his* creature, *his* servant?   Ought we not to be
afraid when we hear about a brother falling into fornication
said, 'He has acted wickedly!'   If you know what it says about
this in the Book of the Ancients, it would make you shudder.
For an angel brought [Isaac the Theban] the soul of someone
who had fallen into sin, and said to him, 'Here is the person
you have judged. He has just died. Where do you order him
to be put, into the Kingdom or into eternal punishment?'[5]
Can you imagine a more terrible situation to be in?   What
else could the angel mean by these words than, 'Since you
want to be the judge of the just and the unjust, what do you
command for this poor soul?   Is he to be spared or to be
punished?'   The holy old man, frightened beyond measure,
spent the rest of his life praying with sighs and tears and
continuous hard work to be forgiven this sin, and this in spite
of having fallen on his knees before the angel and been
forgiven, for the angel said to him, 'You see, God has shown
you how serious a thing it is to judge; you must never do it
again.'[6]   This was the way he granted forgiveness but the
soul of the old man would not allow him to be completely
comforted from his pain and repentance until he died.

Why are we so ready to judge our neighbor?   Why are we
so concerned about the burden of others?   We have plenty to
be concerned about, each one has his own debt and his own
sins.   It is for God alone to judge, to justify or to condemn.
He knows the state of each one of us and our capacities, our
deviations, and our gifts, our constitution and our preparedness, and it is for him to judge each of these things according
to the knowledge that he alone has.   For God judges the
affairs of a bishop in one way and those of a prince in
another.   His judgment is for an abbot or for a disciple, he
judges differently the senior and the neophyte, the sick man
and the healthy man.   Who could understand all these
judgments except the one who has done everything, formed
everything, knows everything?   I remember once hearing the

following story: a slave ship put in at a certain port where there lived a holy virgin who was in earnest about her spiritual life. When she learned about the arrival of the ship she was glad, for she wanted to buy a small serving maid for herself. She thought to herself, 'I will take her into my home and bring her up in my way of life so that she knows nothing of the evils of the world.' So she sent and enquired of the master of the ship and found that he had two small girls who he thought would suit her. Whereupon she gladly paid the price and took one of the children into her house. The ship's master went away. He had not gone very far when there met him the leader of a dancing troupe who saw the other small girl with him and wanted to buy her; the price was agreed and paid, and he took her away with him. Now take a look at God's mystery; see what his judgment was. Which of us could give any judgment about this case? The holy virgin took one of these little ones to bring her up in the fear of God, to instruct her in every good work, to teach her all that belongs to the monastic state and all the sweetness of holy commandments of God. The other unfortunate child was taken for the dancing troupe, to be trained in the works of the devil. What effect would teaching her this orgiastic dancing have, but the ruin of her soul? What can we have to say about this frightful judgment? Here were two little girls taken away from their parents by violence. Neither knew where they came from; one is found in the hands of God and the other falls into the hands of the devil. Is it possible to say that what God asks from the one he asks also from the other? Surely not! Suppose they both fell into fornication or some other deadly sin; is it possible that they both face the same judgment or that their fall is the same? How does it appear to the mind of God when one learns about the Judgment and about the Kingdom of God day and night, while the other unfortunate knows nothing of it, never hears anything good but only the contrary, everything shameful, everything diabolical? How can he allow them to be examined by the same standard?

Wherefore a man can know nothing about the judgments of God. He alone is the one who takes account of all and is able to judge the hearts of each one of us, as he alone is our Master. Truly it happens that a man may do a certain thing (which seems to be wrong) out of simplicity, and there may be something about it which makes more amends to God than your whole life; how are you going to sit in judgment and constrict your own soul? And should it happen that he has fallen away, how do you know how much and how well he fought, how much blood he sweated before he did it? Perhaps so little fault can be found in him that God can look on his action as if it were just, for God looks on his labor and all the struggle he had before he did it, and has pity on him. And you know this, and what God has spared him for, are you going to condemn him for, and ruin your own soul? And how do you know what tears he has shed about it before God? You may well know about the sin, but you do not know about the repentance.

But there are times when we not only condemn but also despise a man; for it is one thing to condemn and quite another to despise, as I have said. Contempt adds to condemnation the desire to set someone at nought—as if the neighbor were a bad smell which has to be got rid of as something disgusting, and this is worse than rash judgment and exceedingly destructive.

Those who want to be saved scrutinize not the shortcomings of their neighbor but always their own and they set about eliminating them. Such was the man who saw his brother doing wrong and groaned, 'Woe is me; him today—me tomorrow!' You see his caution? You see the preparedness of his mind? How he swiftly foresaw how to avoid judging his brother? When he said 'me tomorrow' he aroused his fear of sinning, and by this he increased his caution about avoiding those sins which he was likely to commit, and so he escaped judging his neighbor; and he did not stop at this, but put himself below his brother, saying, 'He has repented for his sin but I do not always repent. I am never first to ask for forgiveness and I am never completely converted.' Do you see the divine light in his soul? Not only was he able to escape making judgment but he humiliated himself as well. And we miserable fellows judge rashly, we hate indiscriminately and set people at nought whether we see something, or hear something, or even only suspect something! And what is worse, we do not let it stop at harming ourselves, but we go and look for another brother and say, 'Here is what happened!' We harm him and put sin into his heart also and we do not fear the saying, 'Woe to the man who gives his neighbor something dark and dangerous to drink!' But we do the devil's work and are not one bit concerned about it. What else has the devil to do but knock us down and harm us? We are found to work with him for our own destruction and that of our neighbor, for a man who harms his own soul is working with, and helping, the devil. The man who seeks to profit his soul is co-operating with the angels.

How can we put up with these things unless it is because we have no true love? If we have true love with sympathy and patient labor, we shall not go about scrutinizing our neighbor's shortcomings. As it is said, 'Love covers up a multitude of sins',[7] and again, 'Love thinks no evil...hides everything,' etc.[8] As I said, if we have true love, that very love should screen anything of this kind, as did the saints when they saw the shortcomings of men. Were they blind? Not at all! But they simply would not let their eyes dwell on sins. Who hated sin more than the saints? But they did not hate the sinners all the same time, nor condemn them, nor turn away from them, but they suffered with them, admonished them, comforted them, gave them remedies as sickly members, and did all they could to heal them. Take a fisherman: when he casts his hook into the sea and a large fish takes the bait, he perceives first that the fish struggles violently and is full of fight, so he does not try to pull it in immediately by main force for the line would break and the catch would be lost in the end. No! He plays out the line and, as he says, allows the fish to run freely, but when he feels the line slacken and the first struggles have calmed down, he takes up the slack line and begins, little by little, to draw him in. So the holy fathers, by patience and love, draw the brother and do not spurn him nor show themselves unfriendly towards him, but as a mother who has an unruly son does not hate him or turn away from him but rules him with sweetness and sometimes does things to please him, so they always protect him and keep him in order and they gain a hold on him so that with time they correct the erring brother and do not allow him to harm anyone else, and in doing so they greatly advance towards the love of Christ. What did the blessed Ammon do when those brothers, greatly disturbed, came to him and said, 'Come and see, Father. There is a young woman in brother X's cell!'[9] What tenderness he showed to the erring brother. What great love there was in that great soul. Knowing that the brother had hidden the woman in a large barrel, he went in, sat down on it, and told the others to search the whole place. And when they found nothing he said to them, 'May God forgive you!' And so dismissing them in disgrace, he called out to them that they should not readily believe anything against their neighbor. By his consideration for his brother he not only protected him after God but corrected him when the right moment came. For when they were alone he laid on him the hand with which he had thrown the others out, and said, 'Have a care for yourself, brother'. Immediately the other's conscience pricked him and he was stricken with remorse, so swiftly did the mercy and sympathy of the old man work upon his soul.

Let us, therefore, strive to gain this love for ourselves, let us acquire this tenderness towards our neighbor so that we may guard ourselves from wickedly speaking evil of our neighbor, and from judging and despising him. Let us help one another, as we are members one of another. Which of us, having a wound on his hand or foot, or any other member, would despise it and cut it off, even if it turned

septic?   Would he not rather bathe it and take away the
poison and put a plaster on it, sign it with the cross, apply a
relic, and pray and beg the saints to pray for its cure, as
Abbot Zosimos used to say[10]—to put it simply, not to
turn aside or run away from our own members even those of
bad reputation but to do all we can to cure their disease. In
this way we ought to bear one another's burdens, to help one
another and be helped by others who are stronger than ourselves, to think of everything and do everything that can help
ourselves and others, for we are members one of another,' as
the Apostle says.[11]   If we are one body each is a member of
the other.   If one member suffers, all the others suffer with
it.[12]   What does our 'cenobia', our community life mean to
you?   Do you not reckon that we are one body, and all
members of one another?   Those in charge are the head;
those who supervise and correct are the eyes; those entrusted
with instruction are the mouth; those who listen and obey are
the ears; those who do the work are the hands; those who run
messages, who have outside ministries, are the feet.   Are you
the head?   Fulfil your charge.   Are you the eyes?   Be in touch
and consider.   Are you the mouth?   Speak and give help.   Are
you the ear?   Listen.   The hand?   Work.   The foot?   Do your
errands!   Let each one give assistance to the body according
to his ability and take care to help one another, whether it is
a matter of teaching and putting the word of God into the
heart of a brother, or of consoling him in time of trouble or of
giving a hand with work and helping him.   In a word, as I
was saying, each one according to his means should take care
to be at one with everyone else, for the more one is united to
his neighbor the more he is united to God.

And now I give you an example from the Fathers.
Suppose we were to take a compass and insert the point and

draw the outline of a circle.   The centre point is the same
distance from any point on the circumference.   Now concentrate your minds on what is to be said!   Let us suppose that
this circle is the world and that God himself is the centre; the
straight lines drawn from the circumference to the centre are

the lives of men. To the degree that the saints enter into the things of the spirit, they desire to come near to God; and in proportion to their progress in the things of the spirit, they do in fact come close to God and to their neighbor. The closer they are to God, the closer they become to one another; and the closer they are to one another, the closer they become to God. Now consider in the same context the question of separation; for when they stand away from God and turn to external things, it is clear that the more they recede and become distant from God, the more they become distant from one another. See! This is the very nature of love. The more we are turned away from and do not love God, the greater the distance that separates us from our neighbor. If we were to love God more, we should be closer to God, and through love of him we should be more united in love to our neighbor; and the more we are united to our neighbor the more we are united to God. May God make us worthy to listen to what is fitting for us and do it. For in the measure that we pay attention and take care to carry out what we hear, God will always enlighten us and make us understand his will.

FOOTNOTES

1. Apo Nau 97: ROC (1907) 402.

2. Apo Moses 18; PG 65: 289; CS 59: (2) 119, Apo Poemen 6; PG 65:320D; CS 59: 139.

3. Lk 6:42.

4. Lk 18:11.

5. Apo Isaac; PG 65:240; CS 59: 93.

6. Ibid.

7. 1 P 4:8.

8. 1 Cor 13:5-6.

9. Apo Ammonas 10; PG 65:121; PO 11:408; CS 59:24.

10. Zosimos, PE 2, 37: 119. Cf. PG 78:1693A.

11. Rom 12:5.

12. 1 Cor 12:26.

VII

N SELF-ACCUSATION

L
ET US examine, brothers, how it is that at one time a man hears a disparaging remark and passes it by without being disturbed, as if he had hardly heard it, and at another time he hears it and is immediately disturbed. What is the reason for such a difference? Is there only one reason for this difference or are there many? I see many proximate causes for this state of affairs, but there is one thing, one might say, which is the basic generating cause of them all. First, it happens when a man is at prayer or spiritually at rest and being, as one might say, in a good disposition he bears with his brother and is not disturbed. Again it may happen that he has a special affection for the someone who attacks him and for this reason he will suffer without difficulty anything that person does to him. Then there is the person who disdains the one who wants to cause him pain and despises what he does, and does not treat him as a man or attribute any meaning to what is said or done by him. I will tell you about an incident of this kind which will astonish you. There was a certain brother living at the monastery before I arrived there and I never saw him put out or troubled, although at various times I saw many of the brethren insulting him and treating him outrageously. That youngster suffered everything that was done to him by everyone as if no

one were troublesome to him. I, therefore, used to wonder at his excessive forbearance and desired to learn how he had acquired such virtue. Once I took him aside and gave him a profound bow and beseeched him to tell me what thoughts were habitually in his heart, either when he was insulted or when he was treated badly by someone, that he should manifest such patience. He answered naturally and without embarrassment, 'Oh, I just have to regard them as trivialities or put up with it as a man puts up with the barking of a dog.' Having heard this I cast my eyes down and said to myself, 'Has this brother found the way?' And signing myself, I went away praying that God would protect both him and me.

It happens, as I said, that a man may not be troubled through disdain. This is manifestly a loss. Being incensed against a brother who is troublesome to us happens because we are not always in a good mood or because we have an instinctive dislike for him. There are many causes of this which can be explained in different ways. The root cause of all these disturbances, if we are to investigate it accurately, is that we do not accuse ourselves; hence we have all these commotions and we never find rest. It is not to be wondered at that we hear from the holy Fathers that there is no other way but this and we see that no one at any time went by another way and found rest.[1] We reckon to achieve peace of soul and to take a straight road to it, yet we never come to the point of accusing ourselves. This is true, isn't it? If a man were to discipline himself in a thousand ways and not take this road, he would never stop troubling others or being troubled by them, and he would waste all his labors. How much joy, how much peace of soul would a man not have wherever he went, as Abba Poemen says, if he was one who habitually accused himself?[2] For if anything happened to him, some punishment, a dishonor, or any kind of trouble, he would accept it as if he deserved it and would never be put to confusion. That man would have complete freedom from care.

But someone will say, 'Suppose a brother troubles me and

I examine myself and find that I have not given him any cause, how can I accuse myself?' If a man really examines himself, in the fear of God, he will usually find that he *has* given cause for offence, either by deed or word or by his bearing. But if, in scrutinizing himself, as I said, he sees that he has given no cause in any of these ways at that moment, it is likely that at another time he has offended him either in the same circumstances or in others, or perhaps he has offended another brother and he would want to suffer on that account or for some other wrong doing. If, as I was saying, he examines himself in the fear of God and gropes about diligently in his own conscience, he will always find cause [for accusing himself]. Again there is the case of a man minding his own business, sitting at peace and quiet; and when a brother comes up and says an annoying word to him, he is put out by it. And from the circumstances he thinks that he is justifiably angered, and he speaks against the one who troubled him, saying, 'If he had not come and spoken to me and annoyed me I should not have been at fault.' This is a delusion; this is false reasoning! For it was not the one who spoke that put him in a bad mood. He only showed that it already existed in him; so that he could, if he chose, make reparation for his fault. But the man referred to above is like clean-looking winter wheat, externally good and ready for use; but when someone crushes it, its corruption is revealed. He was sitting at peace, as we were saying, but he had this anger inside him and he did not know it.[3] One word to him from the other and the corruption hidden inside him leapt out. If, therefore, he were ready to ask forgiveness and humbled himself before that brother, he would be cleansed and would advance in wisdom and see that he ought rather to thank the brother who had been an occasion of spiritual help to him. Temptations would no longer weigh him down in the same way, but in proportion to his advance in this custom he would find that they became easier to bear. For to the degree that a soul advances it becomes stronger and has the power to bear anything that comes upon it. In the same way, if your beast of burden is strong you put a heavy load on it and he carries it; if he does happen to stumble, he gets up quickly and doesn't seem to notice his fall. But if he is a sickly animal the same load weighs him down. If he falls down it takes a lot of help to get him up. So it is with the soul: if it goes on sinning it becomes sickly. If sin makes a man sickly and he has become weak and unsound because of it, the slightest thing that happens to him will weigh him down; but if a man is advancing all the time what happens to him becomes less and less difficult to bear in proportion to the ground he has gained. And so this habit of accusing ourselves will work out well for us and bring us peace and much profit, and nothing else that we can do will bring this about. Above all let us be convinced that nothing can happen to us apart from the providence of God.

But suppose someone says, 'How can I not be troubled if I need something and don't get it? You see, I am asking for it to satisfy a pressing need.' Yet even here he has no reason to blame anybody or to be incensed against anyone. For even supposing there is a real need as he claims and yet he does not receive it, he ought to say, 'Christ, Our Lord, knows better than I do if I ought to be satisfied. He is the one who is to take the place of this object or this food for me.'[4] The Sons of Israel ate manna in the desert for forty years and the manna appeared exactly the same for all. For each one it became what he needed. If a man was in need of something bitter, it was bitter; if he was in need of something sweet, it was sweet. In short, for each it became what was most suited to his actual condition.[5] So when a man wants an egg but he gets only vegetables, he says to his thoughts, 'If it was good for me to have it, God would certainly have sent it. Besides, these vegetables have the power to do me as much good as an egg.'[6] And he may rely on God, because he becomes a witness *to* God.

If a man is truly worthy of rest God will convince the hearts of the Saracens that they must deal mercifully with him according to his needs; if he is not worthy or if it is not for his good, he may make a new heaven and a new earth, but he will not find rest. [7] Never mind that a man sometimes finds more rest than he needs and sometimes not even what he needs. It is God, who is merciful and grants everyone what he needs, who is building him up when he gives him more than he needs; in doing so he shows the abundance of his love for men and teaches him to give thanks. When he does not grant him what he needs, he makes him compensate for the thing he needs through the working of his mind and teaches him patience. Because it is our duty to attend to the supernatural aspect of all things, whether we suffer good or evil from anyone, we ought to look at [all things] super-naturally and give thanks for everything that happens to us, always taking the blame ourselves and saying, as the Fathers used to say, 'If anything good happens to us it is God's providence; if anything bad, it is because of our sins.' [8] And truly everything we suffer is caused by our sins. For the holy men of old, whatever they suffered, they suffered for God's name, either to demonstrate their virtue and so to help everyone else, or to win greater reward from God. But we miserable fellows, how can we say this? Every one of us goes on sinning and suffering what we deserve. We have left the straight road of blaming ourselves and taken the crooked road of blaming our neighbor. [9] Every one of us is very careful, on every occasion, to throw the blame on his brother and to strike him down with its weight. Every one of us is negligent and keeps none of the Commandments, and we demand in return that our neighbor keep them all.

There came to me once two brothers who were always rowing, and the elder was saying about the younger, 'I arrange for him to do something and he gets distressed, and so I get distressed, thinking that if he had faith and love towards me he would accept what I tell him with complete confidence.' And the younger was saying, 'Excuse me, reverend father, but he does not speak to me with the fear of God, but rather as someone who wants to give orders. I reckon that this is why my heart has not full confidence, as

the Fathers say.'[10] Impress on your minds that each blames
the other and neither blames himself, but both of them are
getting upset with one another, and although they are
begging each other's pardon, they both remain unconvinced
'because he does not [from his heart] show me deference
and, therefore, I am not convinced, for the Fathers say that
he should.' And the other says, 'Since he will not have
complete confidence in my love until I show him deference I,
for my part, do not have complete confidence in him.' My
God, do you see how ridiculous it is? Do you see their
perverse way of thinking? God knows how sorry I am about
this; that we take the sayings of the Fathers to excuse our
own will and the destruction of our souls. Each of these had
to throw the blame on the other. One says: I cannot
sincerely be asking pardon all the time where my brother is
concerned, therefore God does not give him full confidence in
me. The other says: I cannot be reconciled in love towards
my brother before he asks pardon, and for that reason God
does not give him full confidence in me! What they really
ought to do is just the opposite. The first ought to say: I
speak with presumption and therefore God does not give my
brother confidence in me. And the other ought to be
thinking: My brother gives me commands with humility and
love but I am unruly and have not the fear of God. Neither of
them found that way and blamed himself, but each of them
vexed the other.

Don't you see that this is why we make no progress, why
we find we have not been helped towards it? We remain all
the time against one another, grinding one another down.
Because each considers himself right and excuses himself, as
I was saying, all the while keeping none of the Commandments yet expecting his neighbor to keep the lot! This is why
we do not acquire habits of virtue, because if we light on any
little thing we tax our neighbor with it and blame him saying
he ought not to do such a thing and why did he do
it—whereas ought we not rather to examine ourselves about
the Commandments and blame ourselves for not keeping

them? How did that Senior reply when asked, 'What do you find most important in this way of life, Father?' He replied, 'In everything to blame oneself'. And when his questioner agreed with him about this, he underlined it by saying, 'There is no other way but this.'[11] Similarly, Abba Poemen used to say with groaning that all the virtues come into this house except one, without which a man stays in labor. They asked him which one it was, and he said, 'That a man go on blaming himself.'[12] But the blessed Anthony used to say that the proper daily labor for a man is to cast his wretchedness before God, and reckon on temptation until his last breath.[13]

Everywhere we find that the Fathers kept to this [rule] relating everything to God, even the slightest things, and they found peace. Such was the holy old man who was ill and his brother, instead of honey, poured linseed oil over his food—pernicious stuff that it is.[14] Nevertheless the old man said nothing but ate it in silence and even took a second helping to satisfy his need without blaming his brother or saying that he had done it maliciously. Not only did he say nothing, he was not annoyed with him even in thought. And then the brother learned what he had done and began to lament over it saying, 'O Father, I have murdered you! And you have put this sin upon me because you said nothing!' How meekly he replied, 'Don't be troubled, my son. If the Lord wished me to eat honey he would have made you put honey on it', and he immediately confided the matter to God. What has it to do with God, venerable old man? The brother made a mistake and you say, 'If God wished'. What has it to do with God? And he insists, 'Yes! If God had wanted me to eat honey, the brother would have put honey on.' The fact that the old man was so sick that day that he could take no food did not make him angry with his brother, but he referred the whole thing to God; and the old man was quite right to say, 'If God had wanted me to eat honey he would even have changed the oil into honey.' But we, for each little thing, go and accuse our neighbor and blame him as if he were maliciously going against his conscience. And if we hear a word we straight away distort its meaning and say, 'If he did not intend to annoy me he would not have said it.' What about the example of the holy man who said about Shimei, 'Let him curse, for the Lord told him to curse David'. [15] God told a man who was a murderer to curse a prophet? But how did God speak to him? A Prophet is someone who has knowledge and knows that nothing brings God's mercy to the soul like temptation, especially temptation endured in time of trouble, and aggravated by treachery, and he said, 'Let him alone to curse David as the Lord told him.' But why? 'So that the Lord may see my humiliation and turn that malediction to my benefit'. [16] Do you see how the prophet acted with knowledge? He restrained those who wanted to be avenged for that cursing by saying, 'What have I to do with you, sons of Zeruiah. Let him curse as the Lord commanded him.'

We, however, do not come to the point of saying about our brother that the Lord told him to say it. If we hear a word we immediately react like dogs. If someone throws a stone, they leave the one who throws it, run after the stone and bite it. This is how we act. We leave God who grants us occasions of this kind to purify us from our sins and we run after our neighbor crying, 'Why did you say this to me? Why did you do this to me?' And whereas we would be able to reap great profit from things of this kind, we bring just the opposite on ourselves, being unaware that everything happens by the foreknowledge of God for the benefit of each of us. May God make us really understand this through the prayers of his saints. Amen.

FOOTNOTES

1. Apo Theophilus 1; PG 65:198; CS 59:69.

2. Apo Poemen cited by Zosimos: PE 1, 46: 170. Cf. Apo Poemen 95; PG 65: 345; CS 59:151.

3. Cf. Cassian, *Conf.* 18:13.

4. Cf. Mark the Hermit, *De lege spirit.* 2; PG 65:905.

5. Cf. Wis 16:21, St Basil (PG 32:700C), Gregory of Nyssa (PG 44:368C).

6. See Introduction, p. 42.

7. Cf. Apo Poemen 48: PG 65:333; CS 59:146.

8. Apo Sisoes 43; PG 65: 404B; CS 59:184.

9. Cf. Zosimos; PG 78:1688-9.

10. Apo Poemen 80; PG 65: 341C.

11. Apo Theophilus 1; PG 65: 197CD; CS 59:69.

12. Apo Poemen 134; PG 65:356B; CS 59:156.

13. Apo Antony 4; PG 65:77A; CS 59:2.

14. Apo Nau 151; ROC 1908, p. 51.

15. 2 Sam 16:10.

16. 2 Sam 16:12.

VIII

N RANCOR OR ANIMOSITY

THE FATHERS used to say it is foreign to a monk to be angry, or to annoy other people.[1] And again: The man who masters anger masters the devil, but the man who is worsted by this passion is a complete stranger to the monastic life.[2] What ought we then to say about ourselves who give way to violent anger and even bear malice to the point of animosity toward one another? What else can we do but bewail our pitiable and inhuman condition? Let us control ourselves, brothers, and with God's help come to one another's assistance so that we may be delivered from the bitterness of this pernicious passion. There are times when,with apparent sincerity, a man asks forgiveness of his brother after some discord between them or for some quarrel which has arisen, and yet after the reconciliation he still remains troubled and has hard thoughts against his brother. He ought not to dwell on such thoughts but to cut them off immediately, for this is remembering evil. It needs much self control not to prolong such thoughts and fall into danger. Asking pardon in the way the commandment lays down should heal past anger and so combat thoughts of revenge, and yet because of this disagreement there remains a certain irritation with the brother. Now remembrance of evil or rancor is one thing, loss of temper or rage another, annoyance another, and disturbance of mind yet another.

I will give you an example so that you understand this clearly. Someone who is lighting a fire first sets a spark to the tinder; this is some brother's provoking remark, this is the point where the fire starts. Of what consequence is that brother's remark? If you put up with it, the spark goes out; but if you go on thinking, 'Why did he say that to me and what do I have to say to him?' And, 'If he did not want to annoy me he would not have said that, and he must think that I also want to annoy him.' So you add a small bit of wood to the flame, or some bit of fuel, and you produce some smoke, that is a disturbance of mind. This disturbance floods the mind with thoughts and emotions which stimulate the heart and embolden it to attack. And this boldness incites us to vengeance on the person who annoyed us and this becomes that recklessness which the blessed [abba] Mark talks about: The heart is stirred up to rashness when the thoughts are set on malice, but malice taken upon itself by prayer and hope leaves the heart at peace.[3] If, therefore, you put up with a sharp retort from your brother, the little firebrand is extinguished, as I said, before it causes you any trouble. Even if you are a little troubled and you desire promptly to get rid of it, since it is still small, you can do so by remaining silent with a prayer on your lips and by one good heartfelt act of humility. But if you dwell on it and inflame your heart and torment yourself with thoughts about why he said this to me, and what do I have to say to him, you are blowing on the embers and adding fuel and causing smoke! From this influx of thoughts and conflicting emotions the heart catches fire and there you are in a passion. St Basil calls this passion a boiling up of the blood around your heart:[4] this makes you what is called irascible. But even this commotion can, if you wish, be put out before it becomes rage.[5] If you allow yourself to remain disturbed, however, you will begin to let fly at others—you will be like someone piling logs on a blazing hearth and fanning the fire and so making more firebrands. This is how you get into a rage.

This is exactly what Abbot Zosimos said when he was asked to explain the saying, 'Where there is no bad temper fighting dies out.' 'If at the beginning of a dissention,' he said, 'when there is first smoke and sparks begin to fly, if a man forestalls it by blaming himself and humbling himself before he gets drawn into the quarrel and gets into a temper, until, not remaining tranquil but wrangling and becoming reckless, he acts like a man who is piling wood on a fire which gets hotter and hotter until he has made a great blaze. For just as burning logs are reduced to cinders and get covered with ash but do not go out for ages, even if water is thrown on them, so also anger that endures for a long time becomes rancor (malice bearing). And for the rest, unless a man sweats blood he will never be free from it.'[6] You see? He shows us the difference. Keep it in mind. Here you have heard what the first annoyance is, what temper is, what losing your temper is, and what rancor is. Do you see how from one remark a grievous evil is reached? If, from the beginning, you take the blame when you are reproached, without trying to justify yourself or making counter-charges and so repaying evil for evil, you will be delivered from all these ills. This is why I always say to you: when a passion arises, when it is young and feeble, cut it off, lest it stiffen and cause you a great deal of trouble. It is one thing to pluck out a small weed and quite another thing to uproot a great tree. I find it very strange that we do not pay attention to what we sing in the psalms every day: we curse ourselves and we do not realize it. Ought we not to know what we are saying when we sing, 'If I have paid back evil for evil, let me fall down defenseless before my enemies.'[7] What does 'Let me fall down' mean? As long as a man is on his feet he has power to stand up to his enemies, he strikes and is struck, he wins a victory or he is defeated, but he is still on his feet. If, however, he loses his foothold and falls down, if he is lying on the ground, how can he go on struggling with his enemy? We pray earnestly not only to fall before our enemies but to fall down defenseless.

Let us discuss what it means for someone to fall down defenseless before his enemies. The 'falling' means no longer to have the power to get up. The 'defenseless' means not to have anything good left in us by which we may at length get up again. For a man who gets up may again take care of himself and when indeed he does so he comes back into the contest. Then we (in the words of the psalm) say, 'May the enemy pursue my soul and capture me.'[8] Not only 'pursue' but 'capture' as well, so that we become subject to him in everything and we are bested in everything we undertake. And we ask that he may throw us down in this way if we render evil for evil. Not only do we pray for this, but we add, 'let our life be trodden down into the earth.'[9] What do we mean by our life? Our capacity for acting virtuously, our power of right action—we ask for this life to be trodden into the earth, so that we become completely earthly, and for all our thoughts and actions to be bowed down to earthly things. 'Let him plant my glory in the dust.'[10] What is this glory of ours if not the knowledge generated in the soul by the keeping of the commandments. Therefore, we say all this that he [the enemy] may make our glory, as the Apostle says, into our shame;[11] that we may fix it in the dust and make our life and our glory all earthly, that we have no thought of God but only of bodily comfort or the pleasures of the flesh like those of whom God said, 'My spirit will not endure in those men because they are flesh.'[12] Look, when we recite all this in the psalms, this is how we curse ourselves if we pay back evil for evil—to the extent that we do in fact do this—and we pay no attention and show no discernment.

There is a way of rendering evil for evil not only in actions but also in words and in attitude. A man may not seem to render evil for evil by what he does, but he is found, as I say, to do so in word or in his attitude [general behavior]. For there are times when a person, either by his attitude, his movements, or his looks, disturbs his brother—and does so on purpose—and this is to render evil for evil. Another man may not render evil for evil, by deeds or words or attitude or movement, but he is wounded at heart and harbors resentment against his brother. Another man may have no complaint against his brother, but if he hears that someone has annoyed him or if at some time someone murmurs against him or reviles him, he is glad when he hears it; then it is clear that he too is rendering evil for evil in his heart. Another man may not cling to evil and not be glad when someone who has annoyed him is reviled and may rather himself be annoyed if he has caused annoyance, and yet he is not glad when something good happens to his brother and if he sees him praised or at rest he is displeased—even this is a kind of rancor, though it is less serious. Finally there is the man who wants to rejoice that his brother is at rest, does all he can to be of service to him, and arranges everything to promote his progress and tranquility.

At the beginning of this conference we were talking about the man who apologizes to another but retains a slight irritation against his brother, and we were saying that through his apology the 'anger' was healed but he had not yet conquered resentment. Another man, if someone should happen to annoy him and apologize and be reconciled, is at peace with the other person and he no longer retains in his heart any remembrance of it; but if it happens that the same brother, some days later, says something to trouble him, he begins to remember the first offence and begins to be troubled not only about the second but about the first. This man is like a person who has a wound and puts a plaster on it; after a while, through the plaster, the wound heals and forms a scar, but it still remains a weak spot and if someone throws a stone at him, this place is more easily damaged than the rest of the body and begins to bleed. This is what happened to him: he had a wound and he put on the plaster, this is the apology and the reconciliation; soon the wound is healed as in the example, i.e. the anger is cured; he began to take care about the resentment through being zealous not to cling to the remembrance of evil in his heart, and this is the scar of the healed-up wound. But he was not perfectly healed, he still had a slight resentment left behind, this is the scar from which the skin can easily be removed and the whole wound opened up again by a slight blow. He has to make a great effort that the scar is completely blotted out and hair grows again and no disfigurement is left behind, so that the place where the wound was cannot be discerned. How then can this be put right? By prayer right from the heart for the one who had annoyed him, such as, 'O God, help my brother, and me through his prayers.' In this he is interceding for his brother, which is a sure sign of sympathy and love, and he is humiliating himself by asking help through his brother's prayers. Where there is sympathy and love and humility, how can wrath and other passions develop? As Abbot Zosimos says, 'Even if the devil and all his evil spirits were to set in motion all their cunning tricks to promote evil, all his efforts would be in vain and be brought to nothing by that humility which Christ enjoined on us.' [13]   Another of the Seniors used to say, 'The man who prays for his enemies is a man without rancor.' [14] Work at this and understand clearly what you hear, for unless you work you will not absorb it by word alone. For what man wishing to learn a trade can master it by verbal instructions alone? No! Always he has to start by doing—and doing it wrong—making and unmaking, until, little by little, working patiently and persevering, he learns the trade while God looks on at his labor and his humility, and works with him. And do we wish to master the trade of all trades by word alone, without practical experience of the work? How is this possible? Let us fortify ourselves and work with enthusiasm while we have time. May God give us to remember and keep what we have heard, lest it bring us a heavy sentence on the day of judgment.

FOOTNOTES

1. Apo Macarius, cited Zosimos PE 2, 35, p. 112.
2. Ps Nilus (Evagrius), *De malignis cogitationibus* 14; PG 79:1216BC.
3. Mark the Hermit, *De lege spirit.* 14; PG 65:908A.
4. *In Isaiam;* PG 30:424A. Cf. PG 31:356C.
5. δξυχολία
6. PE 2, 35, p. 111.
7. Ps 7:5.
8. Ps 7:6.
9. Ps 7:6.
10. Ps 7:6.
11. Phil 3:19.
12. Gen 6:3.
13. Cf. PG 78:1688A & PE 1, 46, p. 171. Cf. Ps. Nilus (Evagrius), PG 79: 1128C and PL 73:957A.
14. Evagrius, *Sent. aux moines* 14, ed. Gressmann, TUGL 39, p. 154.

IX

N FALSEHOOD

BROTHERS, I want to remind you of a few things about falsehood. For I see that you are not very careful about controlling your tongues, and from this we easily are carried off into many other faults. You see, brothers, in all human affairs, as I am always telling you, there are habits formed which tend either to good or to evil. There is much need for watchfulness lest we be robbed by falsehood. For no one who lies is linked to God; otherwise God would be a liar. It is written, 'Falsehood is of the evil one' and again, 'The devil is a liar and the father of lies.'[1] You see, he calls the devil the father of falsehood. God is the truth. He says, 'I am the Way, the Truth and the Life.'[2] See how we sort ourselves out and what position we take up through lying—clearly on the side of the evil one. If, therefore, we want to be saved, we must with all our hearts love the Truth and guard ourselves from every kind of falsehood so that we may not be separated from truth and from life.

There are three different kinds of falsehood: There is the man who lies in his mind [imagination]; the man who lies in word; there is the man whose very life is a lie. The man who lies in the mind is the one who is given to conjectures. If he sees someone talking with his brother, he is suspicious and says, 'They are talking about me.' And if they stop their conversation he conjectures that they stopped because of him. If anyone should say one word, he suspects that it is to annoy him and in simply everything he says about his neighbor, 'He did this on my account; he said this about me or he did that for this reason.' This man is being a liar in his mind. Nothing he says is true, but only his suspicion. Out of this come useless investigations, slander, deceptions, quarrelling, rash judgments and the like.

Then there comes an occasion when what he suspects is found to be true, and at that point he says he wants to correct himself, and he spends a lot of time thinking, 'I see someone speaking against me, what is the fault of which he is accusing me. I shall correct myself of it.' But this sort of thing is from the devil right from the beginning because it began in a falsehood for, not knowing, he suspected what he did not know. How can a rotten tree bring forth good fruit? If he really wanted to correct himself whenever a brother said to him, 'Don't do that, or, why did you do that?' Let him not be troubled but bow down and acknowledge his fault and thank his brother for correcting him. Then he will really be cured of his faults! For if God sees that such is his meekness he will never let him go astray, but will always send what he needs to put him on the right road. To say, 'To correct myself I shall trust my conjectures' and to be always suspicious and to spend a lot of time in self-examination is the justice of the devil when he is trying to betray you.

At the time when I was in the coenobium I was tempted to deduce from the behavior of a man the state of his soul. Once a woman carrying a pitcher of water passed by where I was standing at prayer, and my mind was carried away, I do not know how, and I was struck by the look in her eyes. My thoughts suggested to me that she was a harlot. When this suggestion came to me, I was troubled and revealed it to old Abba John. 'Master', I said, 'if, without wishing to, I see someone's behavior and my thoughts suggest to me the state of his soul, what ought I to do?' And the old man cleared up the point for me in this way: 'Surely, supposing a man had an innate urge to do certain things and by fighting against it overcame it, you would not think you could learn the state of his soul from this. Never put any trust in suspicions, for a wrong premise leads right reasoning to a wrong conclusion. Suspicions are falsehood and blind your mind. Even if my thoughts suggested to me about the sun: this is the sun; or about darkness: this is the darkness, I would not believe them. Nothing is more serious than suspicion, nothing brings the mind so much blindness, because if we entertain them for a while they begin to persuade us, until we are convinced that we have seen things which do not exist and never could exist.

And I will tell you a wonderful thing which I witnessed from beginning to end when I was still in the coenobium. We had a brother there whose mind was crammed with this kind of trouble and he was repeatedly misled by his own suspicions; he was indeed completely convinced that each of his conjectures was a fact and that everything was always exactly as he thought and could not possibly be otherwise. As time went on, the devil, in order to deceive him, persuaded him to go into the garden to keep watch. Because he was surreptitiously watching and listening intently, he thought he saw a certain brother stealing and eating a fig. Now it was Good Friday, and hardly the second hour. The devil had so misled him that he was convinced that what he saw had really happened, and unobserved he came away without saying anything. He was on the watch again towards the time of the liturgy to see what the brother who had taken and eaten the fig would do about Holy Communion. And when he saw the brother washing his hands to go and receive Communion he ran to the Abba and said, 'Look, brother so-and-so there is going in to partake of the Holy Communion with the brethren. Order it not to be given to him, for I saw him early this morning take a fig and eat it. At that moment the brother came in with great recollection to partake of the sacrifice, for he was a god-fearing man. When the Abba saw him, before he got near the priest who was distributing Holy

Communion, he took him aside and asked privately, 'Tell me brother, what was it that you did this morning?' He was taken by surprise and said, 'Where, Father?' And the Abba said, 'In the garden when you went in very early this morning, what did you do there?' And the brother, even more astonished, said, 'I did not see the garden this morning, Father, nor was I in the coenobium at dawn. I have only just got back from a journey. Immediately after the rising bell the cellarer sent me out on an errand.' The business of which he spoke was several miles away and he had only just returned in time for the liturgy. The Abba then sent for the cellarer and asked him, 'Where did you send this brother today?' And the cellarer confirmed what the brother said, namely, that he had sent him to a certain man at such and such a village; and he knelt down and said, 'Forgive me, Father, because he was absent from vigils and for this reason could not receive the blessing.' The Abba was convinced and he dismissed the two and sent them to Communion. And he called the brother who had been suspicious, rebuked him severely, and forbade him to receive Holy Communion. Not only this; after the liturgy he called all the monks together, and in tears he told them what had happened and made an example of the brother. He had a triple purpose in doing this: to confound the devil and show him up as the sower of suspicions; to allow the brother to make amends for his fault and be forgiven, and receive help from God thereafter; to put the brethren more on their guard against letting themselves be persuaded by their own suspicions. And having admonished both us and the brother at great length about all this, he said, 'Nothing is more harmful than suspicions, as we see by what has happened.'

And the fathers tell us many such things in different ways to secure us against the harm suspicions do us. Let us strive with all our power never to put our trust in our own conjectures. For nothing separates us so completely from God or prevents us from noticing our own wrong doing or makes us busy about what does not concern us, as this. No good comes from it but only troubles without number and they leave us no time to acquire the fear of God. Should worthless suspicions germinate in our minds, let us turn them into charitable thoughts and they will not harm us.   For entertaining suspicions is wrong and it never allows the mind to be at peace. This is all I have to say about falsehood in the mind.

As regards falsehood in word, this is what I mean: Suppose a man shirks getting up for vigils and instead of saying honestly, 'Forgive me, Father, I hadn't the guts to get up,' he says, 'I was feverish and felt giddy and so was unable to get up, I was too weak'—a whole string of lies to avoid kneeling and humbling himself and seeking forgiveness. Or if someone blames him for something, he persists in explaining away his fault so as not to take the blame for it. Similarly it may suit him to bring charges against his brother and to continue to justify himself by saying, 'But what did *you* say,' or, 'what did *you* do?' 'I did not say that; someone else said it'—but this, but that—so as not to be humbled. Again, if he wants to get something he does not come to the point and say, 'I want the thing', he persists in saying it in a round-about way. 'I suffer from this and therefore I need that', or 'I have an order from so-and-so', and he goes on telling lies until he gets what he wants.   Forasmuch as all sins arise through a love of pleasure or avarice or vainglory, we can say that lying has its roots in these three vices: a man has to avoid blame and humiliation to fulfil his own desires or to gain something, and he never stops turning this way and that, using every trick of speech until he accomplishes his purpose.   And in the end no one believes him when he speaks the truth; no one *can* believe him for the truth he speaks is ambiguous.

There are times when urgent necessity arises and unless a man conceals the bitter fact, the affair gives rise to greater trouble and affliction. When, therefore, such circumstances arise a man should know that in such cases of need he may adapt his speech so as to avoid a greater disaster or danger. As Abba Alonios said to Abbot Agathon: 'Suppose two men committed a murder in your presence and one of them fled to your cell. Then the police, coming in search of him, asks you, "Is the murderer with you?" Unless you dissimulate, you hand him over to death.'[3] But if a man did such a thing, in extreme necessity, let him not be without anxiety but let him repent and sorrow before God and consider it, as I said, a time of trial and not let it become a habit but done once and for all.

Just as an antidote for snake poison or a powerful purge is beneficial when taken in time and in case of need, it does harm if taken habitually, without necessity. It may be appropriate to dissimulate once in a while in a case of dire necessity but not to make a practice of it;[4] and if ever the need and the occasion arise, and one acts with fear and trembling in the sight of God, he will be sheltered from transgression, since he is under constraint; otherwise he would be doing himself harm.

We have seen what it is to be a liar in thought and a liar in word, and now we must speak about what it is to be a liar in one's very life. A man whose very life is a lie is one who is licentious and pretends to be temperate, or a miser and speaks of almsgiving and compassion, or ostentatious and goes in raptures over poverty, not wanting to acquire the virtue he praises. For if he spoke about his own intention he would first humbly confess his own weakness. 'These virtues are a reproach to me: I am empty of all goodness.' After confessing his own weakness he would have to admire and set about praising these virtues. Furthermore, when he sings the praises of virtue his aim is not to avoid scandalizing others, for then he would have to reason as follows: 'Yes, I am wretched and suffer for it because I go on giving scandal, because I harm other souls and bring upon myself their burden as well as my own', and he would hold that he had sinned and, therefore, turned others from good. For it is part of humility to scrutinize severely one's own wrong-doing and to be sympathetic and forbearing towards one's neighbor. But a man of this kind does not praise the said virtues in this way; rather he takes to himself the reputation of virtue in order to cover up his own disorders. And he speaks about the virtues either as if he himself possessed them or (often enough) to harm and catch others. No wickedness, no heresy, not even the devil himself can deceive anyone unless he counterfeits virtue, as the Apostle says, 'The devil changes himself into an angel of light.'[5] It is, therefore, no wonder if the devil's ministers take on the appearance of ministers of justice. So, therefore, the falsifier, either fearing to be shamed for his lack of humility or, as I said, desiring to attract and trick someone, speaks about the virtues with praise and admiration as if he had long acquired and practised them. This is the man whose very life is a lie: he is not a simple but a two-faced man; he is one thing on the inside and another on the outside. We have now spoken about falsehood, which comes from the devil, and we have spoken about truth, and God is Truth. Let us flee from falsehood, brothers, that we may be delivered from the hands of the enemy and let us struggle to take hold of the Truth, so that we may be united to the One who said, 'I am the Truth.'[6] May God make us worthy of his Truth.

FOOTNOTES

1. Jn 8:44.
2. Jn 14:6.
3. Apo Alonios 4; PG 65:133B; CS 59:30.
4. Cf. Cassian, *Conf.* 17:17.
5. 2 Cor 11:14.
6. Jn 14:6.

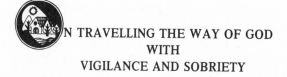N TRAVELLING THE WAY OF GOD
WITH
VIGILANCE AND SOBRIETY

LET US LOOK to ourselves and be sober, brothers. Who will give us back this present time if we waste it? If we actually had to seek these days we would not have found them. Abba Arsenius was always saying to himself, 'Arsenius, what have you come for?'[1] We are in such a negligent and ruinous condition that we don't know why we have come; we don't know even what we want and, therefore, we make no progress, but we are always distressed. This comes about because we have no set purpose in our hearts and actually if we were to resolve to fight a little, in a short time we should not find life distressing or laborious. For if from the beginning a man does violence to himself and struggles with himself a little, in a short time he makes progress and afterwards he goes on peacefully, when God, seeing that he does violence to himself, brings him help. We must, then, do ourselves violence. Let us lay down a good foundation, let us meanwhile desire what is good. Evidently we are not yet perfect, but at least we desire to be so, and this is the beginning of our salvation. For from this desire we shall come in God's company both into the combat and through the combat. So will a man be helped in acquiring the virtues. And this is why one of the Fathers says, 'Give blood, and receive spirit,'[2] i.e. fight and generate a state of virtue.

When towards the end of my childhood I was learning to read, at the beginning I used to wear myself out by working at it too hard and when I went to take up a book I was like someone going up to stroke a wild animal. As I persevered in forcing myself to go on, however, God came to my assistance and I became so engrossed in reading that I did not know what I was eating or drinking, or how I slept, I was so enthused about my reading. I was never drawn away to a meal with one of my friends or to a meeting with him at reading time in spite of the fact that I had many friends and delighted in their company.

When the master[3] dismissed us I used to take a bath—which I needed daily to counteract the exhaustion from excessive study[4]—then I hurried to where I was staying without thinking about eating, for I could not take it easy or order food for myself, but I had a faithful companion and he prepared for me whatever he wished. I took whatever I found prepared for me, propped up a book beside me, and in a short time I was lost in it. For the siesta I had the same book as a companion by my chair, and if sleep overpowered me for a short time I was quickly on my feet again and at my reading. It was the same in the evening when I got back after lamplighting.[5] I used to grasp my lamp and go on with my reading until midnight. So it was that I took no notice of, or pleasure in, anything except what I was reading. When, therefore, I came to the monastery I used to say to myself, 'If for the sake of public speaking so much endurance and fervor is needed fully to acquire the art of reading, how much more is needed for the acquisition of virtue.' From this consideration I received much strength and encouragement. If anyone wants to acquire virtue he ought not to let himself be distracted or be puffed up with vain hopes. If someone wants to become a master carpenter he does not dabble in other trades, so it is with someone wanting to acquire the spiritual craft. He must not interest himself in anything else but, day and night, attend to it, so that he may be able to master it.

Those who do not come to this business [of acquiring the spiritual craft] in this spirit, not only do not make progress, but they wear themselves out like men wandering aimlessly about. For unless a man drives himself and fights against his evil inclinations he readily falls away and diverges from the path of virtue.

Virtue stands in the middle [between excess and defect]. This is the King's highway of which one of the elders used to say, 'Walk by the King's highway and count up the miles.' [6] The virtues, therefore, as we say, are in the middle between too much and too little. Therefore, it is written, 'Do not deviate to the right or to the left but walk the King's highway.' [7] And as St Basil says, 'A man is upright at heart when his estimation of things is not biased towards excess or defect, but goes straight to the middle path of virtue.' [8] For an example I could put it this way: 'Evil in itself is nothing, for it has no being or substance.' God forbid that we should think it has! But the soul deviating from virtue is in a state of violence and this is what makes evil; therefore it suffers injury at its own hands and is deprived of that state of rest which by nature it should have. So it is in the case of wood. Healthy wood has no worms in it, but let it become even a little rotten and out of that rottenness worms develop. Similarly, also, iron makes a little rust, and then the iron itself is destroyed by the rust. Then, too, cloth generates the moth, and the moth spoils the cloth. So then does the soul generate evil in itself; before this the evil had no being, no power, no substance, as I said; and the soul itself suffers injury from the evil it generates. As blessed Gregory rightly says, 'Fire is produced from wood and wood is consumed by fire; so wickedness consumes the wicked.' [9] This is true too in sickly bodies: when someone leads a disorderly life and takes no account of his health, too many or too few of the vital fluids are generated in the body and an unbalance of some kind ensues. Before this the weakness was nowhere nor was it anything positive, and again, when the bodily fluids return to normal, the body is sound again and the weakness then does not exist. So also wickedness is a sickness of the soul depriving it of its own natural health, which is a state of virtue.

Therefore, we say that virtue stands in the middle: and so courage stands in the middle between cowardice and fool-hardiness; [10] humility in the middle between arrogance and obsequiousness. Modesty is a mean between bashfulness and boldness—and so on with the other virtues. If then a man is found to possess these virtues, such a man is esteemed by God, and even if he was always seen to eat, drink and sleep like other men, he would still be esteemed for the virtues he has. But unless a man is watchful and keeps a guard on himself he easily deviates from the road either to the left or to the right, that is by excess or neglect, and so he brings upon himself that sickness which is wickedness. This then is the royal road by which all the saints travelled; the different states of the soul are the milestones a man has to pass—always looking to see where he is, how many miles he has covered and what a state he is in. So suppose we are all on the road, each one has a special objective there in the Holy City. And having left our own city some of us have covered five miles and turned back; some have gone ten, some have got half way there. Others perhaps have not even started on the journey, but have left the city and remain outside the gates on the evil-smelling rubbish dump. There are other travellers who, when they have gone a couple of miles, lose their way and retrace their steps; others travel two miles forward, then five miles backward. Some go back as far as the city itself and hang around outside it without going in. This is how it is with us, for there are some among us who have left the world and come to the monastery with the intention of acquiring the virtues. Some keep straight on for a little, but do not persevere. Others make some progress, others have got half way and then stand still. Others made no progress at all, and although they reckoned they had left the world, they remained attached to it and its evil odors. Others started right and did a little good but soon undid the gooα tney had done. And if some lost more ground than they had gained, others made great progress in virtue, but became proud and despised their neighbors. So they remained outside the Holy City and did not enter in and so they did not attain their end. And so even if they were at the very gates, but remained outside, they too fell away from their own ideals.

Let each one of us then take the trouble to find out where we are: whether we have left our own city but remain outside its gates by the rubbish heap, or whether we have gone forward a little or much, or whether we are half way on our journey, or whether we have advanced two miles, then come back two miles, or perhaps even five miles, or whether we have journeyed as far as the Holy City and entered into Jerusalem, or whether we remain outside and are unable to enter it.

Let each one find out about his own condition, the state of his soul. A man is in one of three conditions: That of giving free rein to his passions or that of checking them or that of uprooting them. In the first he indulges his passions and gives in to vice; in the second he neither indulges his passions nor cuts them off completely but disputes with them and turns them back but allows them to remain inside him; in the third he is working to root them out and he struggles with them and acts contrary to them. There, broadly speaking, you have the three states. You say, 'give us an example. Which of the passions would you like me to expound? Shall we speak about arrogance or sexual desire, or shall we speak rather of vainglory? Suppose a man cannot bear to listen to a word from his brother. For there are those who, when they hear one word against themselves, are put out, snap back five words—or even ten—to every one, and they argue and get excited. And when they have stopped arguing they keep on reasoning against the person who uttered that one word and bearing malice against him, and are sorry they did not say more than they did. And they think up speeches even more disobliging against him, and they always say, 'Why didn't I say this?' Or, 'I ought to have said that!' And they are always raving on. This then is the first state—here you have someone habitually giving way to malice. May God deliver us from such a state. Such a state is subject to punishment, for every sin committed is a step towards hell. And even if such a man should desire to change his ways he has not strength to moderate his passions unless he has the assistance of the saints, as the fathers say. This is why I am always telling you to be careful to cut off your natural inclinations before they become habitual sins.

Another man, when he hears a word [against himself] and is put out, also snaps back five or ten words, and is annoyed that he did not say others three times worse. He is downcast and bears malice and goes on like this for a few days, and then gets over it. Another is like this for a week, or a day, and then throws it off. Another gets abusive and argues and is put out, and puts others out, and quickly gets over it. You see how many degrees there are within the state, and these persons are all tending to hell in as far as their state disposes them to act sinfully.

Let us speak about those who check their passions. A man hears one word and he is troubled, but inwardly; he is sad not because he was abused but because he did not endure it with equanimity. This one is in the state of those who bear up under their passions and check them. Another one struggles and labors and at last is conquered by his passion because it wears him down. Another desires not to answer badly, but is betrayed into it through habit. Another fights never to reply maliciously but he is sad because he was abused, but he condemns himself for his sadness and does penance for it. Another is not sad because he was abused but neither is he glad. All these are standing up to their passions. But two of them are different: one falls into sin because he is defeated in the fight with his passions; the other because he is seized by his passions through force of habit. The other two accuse themselves, not because they fell into sin, but because they could not endure reproof with thankfulness, and are in fear because of the danger of giving free rein to their passions. But I say that the first two are standing up against their passions [in spite of the fact that they fell], because in disposition they were opposing their passions and they did not wish to yield to them, but they were grieved at their fall and went on fighting. For the fathers used to say that everything that the soul does not deliberately intend is of short duration.[11] They ought to grope about in themselves not so much for the *how* and *wherefore* of their passion itself as to come to grips with the cause of their passionate reactions and so to come to see *why* they were defeated or seized by their passions. For there are some, they say, who while fighting to control one passion do so by indulging another passion. For example, a man may keep silent under insults through vainglory; another through the desire to be thought well of or some other passion. These try to right what is wrong by wrong, but Abbot Poemen used to say evil never took away evil.[12] Such as these are classed among those who give free rein to their passions, even if they scoff at the idea.

Finally we must speak of those who are uprooting their passions. If a man rejoices when he is upbraided because it will bring a reward, he is someone who is uprooting a passion but not with knowledge. Another rejoices when he is upbraided and holds that he needs to be upbraided because he has given cause for it; and he would be uprooting a passion with knowledge. For someone to be rebuked and to admit that an accusation against himself is due to himself, whatever comes upon him, this is knowledge. For everyone who prays to God, 'Lord, give me humility' ought to know what he is asking for, viz. that God send him someone to mistreat him. And when he is insulted by someone, he ought to disparage himself and despise his own opinion so that when the other man humiliates him outwardly, he too humiliates himself inwardly.

There is another case where a man not only rejoices to be treated harshly and attributes the cause to himself, but he is also grieved at the commotion in the one who mistreats him. May God bring us all to such a state as this.

Consider then how wide is the subject of these three states, and let each one of us find out, as I said, which condition he is in. [Let him ask himself:] Am I one who desires to develop and gratify his passions to the utmost, or am I one who desires not to do so, but is overcome by his passions, or who is swept into gratifying his passions by force of habit, and after gratifying them, is troubled and repents of it? Or am I one who struggles against his passions with knowledge or checks one bad mood by means of another equally bad—that is, when a man is silent through vainglory or to curry favor, in short for some merely human end? Or am I one who has really begun to root out his unruly inclinations, and then with knowledge and forethought, so that I act contrary to my evil dispositions?

Let everyone find out then where he is; how many milestones he has passed on the road. We ought not only to examine ourselves every day but also over a period of time, every month, and every week. 'The first week I was a prey to such and such a fault—how do I stand now?' Similarly over a period of time: 'Last year I was overcome so many times by such and such a fault, how about now?' And likewise we ought to examine for ourselves each of our faults—whether we have made a little progress or are in the same condition, or have become worse. For so long as we have not uprooted our evil tendencies, may God give us the strength not to give them free rein but to hold them in check. For it is a very grave thing to let loose our passions and not to check them. And I will tell you a parable to illustrate this: A man who gives way to his passions and suffers for it is like a man who is shot at by an enemy, catches the arrow in his hands, and then plunges it into his own heart. A man who is resisting his passions is like a man who is shot at by an enemy, and although the arrow hits him, it does not seriously wound him because he is wearing a breastplate. But the man who is uprooting his passions is like a man who is shot at by an enemy, but who strikes the arrow and shatters it or turns it back into his enemy's heart. As the psalmist says, 'Their own sword shall enter their own heart and their bow shall be broken to pieces.' [13] Let us then take every care, brothers, if we cannot turn their swords back into their hearts, not to take hold of their arrows and plunge them into our own hearts, but to put on our breastplates so that their arrows cannot wound us. May God, who is so good, shelter us from these enemies, and give us self-control, and lead us forward on his road.

FOOTNOTES

1. Apo Arsenius 40; PG 65:105C; CS 59:15.
2. Apo Longinus 5; PG 65:257B; CS 59:104.
3. σοφιστής teacher of rhetoric. See *Antioche*, 447, n. 1, and 449, n. 4.
4. *Antioche*, p. 448, n. 5; 477, n. 6.
5. An old equivalent of Vespers.
6. Apo Benjamin 5; PG 65:145A; CS 59:37.
7. Prov 4:27. Cf. Num 20:17 & Cassian, *Conf.* 2:2, 4:12, 24:24.
8. *In Ps.* 7:7; PG 29: 244D.
9. Gregory Nazianzen, *Orat.* 23:1; PG 35:1152C.
10. Cf. Aristotle, *Nic. Ethics* II.7.2.
11. Apo Poemen 93; PG 65: 345A; CS 59:151.
12. Apo Poemen 177; PG 65:365A; CS 59:161.
13. Ps 37:15.

XI

N CUTTING OFF PASSIONATE DESIRES IMMEDIATELY BEFORE THEY BECOME ROOTED HABITS OF MIND

SET YOUR MINDS, brothers, on looking into your affairs and do not neglect yourselves, since a small neglect may lead us into great danger. I have just paid a call on a brother and found him in a very weak state. At the time he received us I learned that he had had a fever for just seven days. It was then forty days after the fever had left him and he still found he had not regained his former strength. You see, brothers, how laborious and painful it is for someone to fall into an abnormal condition. A man usually despises a small disorder and he does not realize that if a small thing happens to injure his body, especially if it is rather weak, there is very great need both of labor and time before it is put right again. In this case the poor man had a temperature for only seven days; and see how many days he suffered without rest and without regaining his strength. So it is with the soul; a man commits a little sin and what a long time he goes on dripping blood before it is put right! For bodily weakness [which follows a disease] we find there are different causes: either the medicines are old and don't work, or the doctor is inexperienced and tries one drug after another, or the patient is undisciplined and does not keep to what the doctor ordered. We cannot say the same about the soul, that the Doctor lacks experience or does not give the appropriate medicine. For Christ is the Doctor of souls, and he knows everything and applies the right remedy for every sickness.[1] For example: for vainglory, the commandment about humility; for love of pleasure, temperance; for avarice, almsgiving. In short, each disease of the soul has a commandment which is its appropriate remedy, so that the Doctor is not inexperienced, nor again are the remedies old and impotent, for Christ's commands never go stale. Therefore, there is no impediment to the soul's healing except its own unruliness.

Let us attend to ourselves, brothers, let us learn self-control while we have time. Why do we neglect ourselves? Let us be doing something good all the time so that we may find help in the time of trial. Why do we fritter away our lives? We are always hearing a great deal about the spiritual life and we don't care about it, we even despise it. We see our brothers snatched away from our midst and we don't abstain [from passion and excess] even when we know that in a little while we too shall be near death.   Look! Since the time we sat down at this conference we have used up two or three hours of our time and got that much nearer to death. Yet we take care to exclude time from our thoughts and we have no fear. Why do we not remember that saying of the Senior that, 'If a man lose gold and silver, he can always find more to replace it. Time once lost cannot be found again by living in idleness and negligence. No matter how hard we try to regain one hour of this time we shall never find it.'[2] How many desire to hear the word of God and find no one to expound it, while we hear and despise it and are not stirred up by it. God knows, I am frightened by our imperviousness. We who can be saved, and do not even desire it. For we can cut off our unruly desires when they are newly born and we don't think about it; we allow them to grow up and harden against us so that we make the last evil greater than the first. For, as I often tell you, it is one thing to uproot a blade of grass and another to uproot a great tree.[3]

One of the great old men was at recreation with his

disciples in a place where there were cypresses of different shapes and sizes, some large, some small. And he said to one of his disciples, 'Pull up that cypress over there'. It was a very small one and immediately the disciple pulled it up with one hand. Then the old man showed him another one, larger than the first, and he said, 'Pull up that one.' Working it backwards and forwards with both hands he pulled it up. The old man showed him yet a larger one, and with much more trouble he pulled that up too. Then he showed him an even larger one and with much more labor, straining backwards and forwards and sweating profusely, he finally lifted that one too. Then the old man showed him a still larger one, but for all his energy and sweating he could not pull it up. And when the old man saw that he could not pull it up, he turned to another brother [and told him] to get up and help him, but even the two of them together could not pull it up. Then the old man said to all the brothers. 'So it is with our evil desires: insofar as they are small to start with, we can, if we want to, cut them off with ease. If we neglect them as mere trifles they harden, and the more they harden, the more labor is needed to get rid of them. But if they grow to any degree of maturity inside us, we shall no longer be able to remove them from ourselves no matter how we labor unless we have the help of the saints interceding for us with God.' No doubt you see the force of what the saints have to say. And the prophet in the psalm says something similar, 'O miserable daughter of Babylon; blessed is he who repays you as you repaid us; blessed is he who dashes your little ones to the ground.' [4]

But let us search out the meaning of this saying in detail. 'Babylon' means confusion. For Babel has the same meaning as Shechem. [5] 'Daughter of Babylon' means enmity [or the enemy]. First the soul is put to confusion and so it produces sin; but he calls sin miserable, because sin (and I have spoken of this elsewhere) has no existence or substance of its own but is brought into existence through our own carelessness; and again through our correction it is destroyed and loses its existence. Therefore, he says, as though a holy man were speaking to sin, 'Blessed is he who pays back to you what you have repaid us.' Let us learn what we have given, what we have received, and what we should desire to give back again. We have given our desire and we received back sin. This text calls 'happy' the man who gives back this evil and by this 'giving back' he means no longer doing it. Then he adds, 'Happy the man who takes your little ones and dashes them against a rock'—as if he would say: Happy the man who seized the things generated from you, 'the enemy,' i.e. the evil thoughts, not giving them a chance to grow strong in him and constrain him to evil deeds, but immediately, while they are still in their infancy, before they are fed and grow strong against him, flings them down on the rock, which is Christ.[6] In other words he utterly destroys them by taking refuge in Christ.

You see how our elders and the Holy Scripture agree in calling 'happy' those who struggle to cut off those passionate reactions when they are new-born, before they experience their pain or their bitterness. Let us be zealous that we may obtain mercy; let us cut off a small thing that we may find great peace. The fathers used to tell us how we should purify ourselves bit by bit, that is, by examining ourselves carefully every evening about how we have passed the day, and again at dawn about how we have passed the night and by asking forgiveness from God, if need be, for any faults we have committed. We really need to scrutinize our conduct every six hours and see in what way we have sinned, since we sin so much and are so forgetful. And we should say to ourselves, 'Have I said anything to irritate my brother? Have I seen my brother do certain things and judged him harshly or despised him or spoken evil of him? Have I asked the cellarer for something, and when I did not receive it murmured against him? Have I spoken ungraciously or had an argument? Have I abused the cook or criticized him or when I did not like the food murmured against him? For if a man murmurs against anyone it is a fault.' Or again, 'did the

M.C. [7] or another of the brothers correct me, and I would not accept it, but contradicted him?' In some such way we ought to scrutinize ourselves and find out how we have passed the day. Similarly we ought to examine how we passed the night. 'Did I get up willingly for vigils?' Or, 'Did I take slight notice of the waker or murmur against him?' For we ought to recognize that the person who wakes us up for Vigils does us a favor and procures great benefits for us over our sins, and to receive the [divine] light. Ought we not then to be grateful to hold that our very salvation is all but due to him? Truly we ought to.

I will tell you something marvellous that I heard about a great old man gifted with spiritual insight.[8]   Standing one day in church, as the brethren were starting the psalmody, he saw someone coming out of the sanctuary dressed in shining garments and holding a small vessel full of holy oil and a small stone cylinder. And he moistened the stone in the vessel and went round to every one of the brothers and set the seal on each of them. Some of the places which were empty were signed and some were passed by. Again they were about to be dismissed [after completing the office] when he saw the same splendid figure come from the sanctuary and repeat the same action. Filled with wonder the holy father cast himself at the feet of this mysterious visitor and begged him to tell the meaning of his actions, and who he was. And the resplendent visitor told him, 'I am an angel of God, and am ordered to this assembly to place this seal on those found in the church from the beginning of the psalmody, and those who remained until the dismissal, because of their earnestness and zeal and by their own free and deliberate choice.' And the old man asked, 'And why did you sign the place of those who were not to be found here?' To this the holy angel replied, 'All those who were zealous and had the generous intention of being there but were absent through some violent sickness and with the abba's blessing, or those who were engaged in fulfilling a command given them under obedience—all these, although absent, received the sign since by their right intentions they were there; but those who were able to be there and through their carelessness were absent, I was commanded not to sign, since they had made themselves unworthy of it.' There you are! You see what a great gift the waker obtains for his brother by waking him up for the regular vigils! Take care then, brothers, not to be deprived of the imprint made by the holy angel. But if it should happen that someone forgets and another reminds him, he ought not to be vexed but, profiting by the good done him, give thanks to the one who reminds him, whoever he is.

When I was with the community in the cenobium, the abba, on the advice of the Seniors, put me in charge of the guesthouse. I was just recovering from a severe illness. Strangers would arrive and I would spend the evening with them or there would be cameleers and I attended to their needs; after that I would go to bed but I was often awakened for some other emergency. In those circumstances I had usually snatched very little sleep before it was time for vigils, and the waker would come to call me. What with the work and my weakness and the intermittent fevers that attacked me, I was in a bad way and hardly knew what I was doing, and I would reply like one in a dream, 'God love you and reward you, father, you called and I am coming' and as he went away I fell asleep again. But I used to be very annoyed that I had delayed getting up for church. Since it was not convenient to the waker to remain with me, I asked two of the brethren [for help]—one to wake me up for the office in church, the other to stop me from going to sleep during the office. Believe me, brothers, I was devoted to them as though my very salvation depended on them. I very nearly worshipped them. You ought to be equally well disposed to those who wake you up for Vigils, for the canonical hours, and for every good work.

So everyone, as I was telling you, ought to examine how he passed the day and the night—whether he stood for the psalmody with disciplined mind or was captivated at prayer by extraneous thoughts, or whether he kept his mind fixed on the divine readings.   Whether or not he gave up the psalmody and being puffed up left the church and went out-side. If he examines himself on every point and takes care to repent of every fault and correct it, he begins to diminish the evil. And if he used to commit nine faults, he commits eight, and so with God's help he cuts them off in a short time and does not allow his evil inclinations to harden.   For there is great danger for the man who falls into the habit of indulging his evil inclinations, because as we said, such a man, even if he desires it, is not able alone to cast off his evil inclination unless he has help from some of the saints.

Do you want me to narrate the facts about a certain brother who got into the habit of indulging one of his passions? Listen to a story worthy to weep over.   When I was in the cenobium, I don't know how it happened, but the brethren simply deluded themselves into entrusting me with their secret thoughts.   The abba agreed and with the consent and approval of the seniors, he commanded me to carry out this service. One day, therefore, there came to me one of the brothers who said, 'Forgive me and pray for me, because I steal and eat [outside the proper time].' I said to him, 'Why is this? Do you get hungry all the time?' And he told me, 'Yes, I don't get enough at the brothers' table and I cannot ask for more.' So I said, 'Why don't you go to the abba and tell him about it?' He replied, 'I am ashamed to.' So I said, 'Would you like me to go for you?' He said, 'I leave it to you, father.' I went and told the abba, and he said to me, 'Do what charity commands and devise the best means of curing him.' Then I took him to the cellarer, and said to him, 'Do an act of charity and at whatever time this brother comes to you, give him as much food as he wants and do not hinder him in any way.' When the cellarer heard this, he said to me, 'I will do exactly as you have commanded.' This worked all right for a few days before the brother came to me and said, 'Forgive me, father, because I have begun stealing again.' I said to him, 'Why? Did the cellarer not give you whatever you wanted?' 'Yes!' he replied, 'he supplied whatever I asked for but I was filled with shame before him!' Then I said, 'Are you not ashamed before me?' He said, 'No.' So I said, 'All right, whatever you want, come and ask me for and you shall have it, but don't steal any more.' At that time I was doing service in the infirmary. So he used to come and get what he wanted from me. After some days he began stealing again and came in great trouble to tell me, 'Look! I'm stealing again.' I said, 'My dear brother, did I not give you everything you wanted?' And he said, 'Yes!' I said, 'Then why do you keep on stealing?' But he said, 'Forgive me, but I don't know why. I simply feel the urge to steal.' Then I said to him, 'If so, what do you do with what you have stolen?' And he said, 'I give it to the donkey.' And I found that he had stolen scraps of bread, dates, figs, onions and anything else he could lay hands on. All this he hid, some under his bed, some in other places. And at last, not knowing what to do with it all, when he saw it was getting rotten, he finally went out and threw it away or gave it to the animals.

You see then what happens when a man gets the habit of giving in to his instinctive urges? Do you see what a miserable affliction it is? He knew it was evil, he knew that he was doing wrong, he was troubled and wept over it, and all the same the unfortunate man was dragged along by his evil habit, which he had made for himself by his previous negligence. It was well said by Abbot Nistheron that if a man is pulled down and carried off by a passion, he becomes a slave of that passion. May the good and merciful God shield us from bad habits lest we also should say (with the Psalmist), 'What use is my blood[9] if I go down into corruption?'[10]

I have told you the different ways a man falls into bad habits. For if a man is angry once, he is not straightway called irascible; nor if a man falls once into fornication is he straightway called a fornicator; nor if a man does one act of mercy is he called a merciful man. But virtue and vice are formed in the soul by repeated actions, and ingrained habits bring peace, or punishment, with them. We speak of virtue bringing rest to the soul and vice bringing punishment—why the difference? Because virtue belongs to the nature we possess; the seeds of virtue are ineradicable. I say, therefore, that insofar as we carry out what is good, we generate for ourselves a habit of virtue—that is, we take up a state proper to our nature, we return to a state of health which belongs to us, as diseased eyes recover their normal reactions to light, or from any other state of weakness, we return to the normal state of health which belongs to our very nature. In the case of vice it is entirely different, by doing repeatedly what is evil we acquire a habit which is foreign to us, something unnatural. We put ourselves, as it were, into a permanent state of pestilential sickness, so that we can no longer be healed without many tears, which have the power to attract Christ's compassion to us. We find the same sort of thing in bodily sickness. There are certain foods which are supposed to generate a certain humor [in the body] which causes melancholy—for example, cabbage and lentils and things like that. By eating such foods once or twice the body generates a certain quantity of the fluid which predisposes to melancholy; but if a man continues feeding on these things for a long time, the body becomes full of this fluid, which promotes fevers which burn up the sufferer and bring on thousands of attendant troubles. So it is with the soul: if a man continues sinning, he gets into a bad condition and it is this which torments him.

However, there is one other thing that you ought to know about this: it sometimes happens that a soul has an ingrained tendency towards one particular passion. If it indulges that passion only once, there is immediate danger that it will turn into a fixed habit. The same thing happens with regard to the body. Suppose a man has a melancholy temperament, generated perhaps by past negligence [with regard to food]; it is all but certain that eating a certain food only once will kindle in him a fit of depression.

There is need therefore of much vigilance and zeal, and a

healthy fear, if we are to avoid falling into bad habits. Believe me, brothers, a man with a single passion set into a habit is destined to punishment. Maybe he will do ten good actions for every one resulting from bad habit, but the latter will prevail over the ten good actions. If an eagle gets out of a snare except for one claw which remains caught in the net, it has lost all its power to escape. Though it is outside the net, is it not half-captive by it? Can the hunter not strike it down whenever he pleases? So it is with the soul: if it has one passion set into a bad habit, the enemy at any moment he pleases strikes it down, for he has the upper hand over the soul though that passion. This is why I am always telling you not to allow a passion to harden into a habit. We must go on fighting and praying God night and day lest we fall into temptation. If we get beaten, as being men we shall, and slip into sin, let us quickly get up again and do penance, weeping in the sight of God's goodness. Let us be on the watch and go on fighting, and God, seeing our good-will, our humility and our contrition, will lend us a hand and extend his mercy to us. Amen.

FOOTNOTES

1. Cf. Ignatius, *Ad Eph.* 7 (SCh 10:74), Origen, *Hom. 13 in Luc.* (PG 13:1831), *In Jer.* (GCS, p. 156), Evagrius, *Ep.* 42 (Frank, p. 595).

2. Apo Nau 265; ROC 1909, p. 369. Cf. PL 73:939A.

3. Cf. Barsanuphius, *Biblos* 552, Chrysostom, *Hom 11 in 1 Cor 5* (PG 61:93).

4. Ps 137:9.

5. Gen 12:6.

6. 1 Cor 10:4.

7. κανονάρχης

8. διορατικοῦ

9. blood = life.

10. Ps 30:9.

XII

ON FEAR OF THE PUNISHMENT TO COME
AND THE NEED FOR ONE DESIRING TO BE SAVED
NEVER TO BE NEGLIGENT ABOUT HIS OWN SALVATION

WHILE I was in trouble with my feet and very weak, some of the brethren came to see me and asked me to tell them something about the cause of my sickness. I think they had a double purpose, first to comfort me by distracting me from my pain and second to set me off talking about something profitable [for the spiritual life]. But my pain did not allow me to do so as I wished then, so now I must obey and speak of these things. For it is a pleasure to talk about affliction when affliction is passed; at sea, when the tempest is raging, everybody is troubled, but when the storm has passed away everybody is happy to talk with everyone else about all that happened. And it is right, brethren, as I am always saying, to lead every single thing back to God and to say that without God nothing happens, but, just as God knows what is good and profitable, so it always happens even if the thing should have from outward appearances its own cause. As, for example, I can say, 'Since I was eating with the guests and was constrained to be with them in order to put them at their ease, my stomach was over-charged and a noxious humor descended to my feet and it was that which caused the pain and swelling'—or some other different causes you can always find if you want to look for them. But it is more accurate and helpful and better in every way to say that God knew that this was profitable to my soul and so it happened, for nothing that God does is not good, but everything is for the best. Therefore, no one ought to be disconsolate about the painful things that come upon him but should lead back all things to God and take rest in his providence. Of course there are some who are so weighed down by their troubles in such circumstances that they are ready to give up their lives and think it a pleasure to die and be free from them. Such men suffer from pusillanimity and ignorance, not knowing the fearful necessity they must encounter after the soul has left the body. It is by God's great love of men that while we are in this world we are ignorant of what happens in the next; we regard what we have to endure here as a great burden, but this is not so. Do you not know that it tells in the book of the Ancients how an exceedingly hard-working brother went to consult one of the seniors and said, 'My soul longs for death'. The senior said to him, 'Then you may run away from your present troubles, but you do not realize that the trouble you propose to undergo is much worse than what you suffer here.'[1] And another brother likewise went to consult a senior and said, 'Why must I endure weariness sitting in my cell?' The senior replied, 'Because you have not seen the point of the rest to be hoped for, nor of the punishment to come. For if you really grasped them, even if your cell were full of worms so that you were buried up to the neck, you would endure it without weariness.'[2]

And we, poor devils, want to be saved while we doze off to sleep and for this reason we grow faint-hearted when trials come upon us. We ought rather to thank God and count ourselves fortunate that we may be really worthy to suffer a little affliction here so that we may find a little rest there. And Evagrius used to say, 'A man who is suffering and prays for a swifter exit from this world is like a man who begs a carpenter to come and break up the bed of a sick man.'[3] For through this body the soul gets away from its own passions and is comforted; it is fed, it drinks, sleeps, meets and associates with friends. When at last it goes out of the body it is alone with its own passions and, in short, it is tormented by them, forever nattering to them and being incensed by the disturbance they cause and being torn to pieces by them so that it is unable to remember God.   For the mere remembrance of God comforts the soul, as it says in the Psalm, 'I was mindful of God and I was made glad',[4] and the passions do not allow this to happen.   Do you want me to give an example to make this clear?   Suppose one of us were shut up in a dark cell with no food or drink for three days without sleeping or meeting anyone, or psalmodizing, or praying, and not even thinking of God. You know what his passions would do to him, and this when he is still in this world—how much more so when the soul goes out of the body and he is delivered up to his passions and is all alone with them. How grievous the agony a man has to suffer from his passions can be perceived from a trial like that [of isolation and powerlessness].

When someone has a fever, what is it that burns him? What sort of fire and what sort of fuel produce that burning heat?   If a man has a body of bad melancholic temperament, is it not the bad temperament which makes him feverish and annoys him and afflicts his life?   So also is the soul under the influence of strong emotions [passions]; the conflict, arising from its own bad habits, punishes it all the time, the memory being always embittered, the mutterings of its passions constantly emerging, always burning it and enraging it.   In addition to these things, who can describe, brothers, that fearsome place where the bodies to be punished serve to inflict such varied and terrible torment to the souls and are not corrupted, that unspeakable fire, the darkness, those harsh chastising spirits and the thousand and one other torments of which Holy Scripture speaks in so many different ways, all proportioned to the evil course of the soul and the evil desires they entertained?   Whereas the saints are received into places full of light and angelic happiness proportionate to their own good conduct, the sinners are received into dark and gloomy places full of horror and petrifying dread, as the

saints tell us. What is more fearful and pitiable than those
places to which the demons were sent? What more bitter
than the punishment to which they were condemned? And
sinners will be punished in the same way with the devils
themselves. As it says, 'Depart into everlasting fire which
was prepared for the devil and his angels.'[5]

St John Chrysostom speaks of something even more to be
feared when he says: even if a river of fire did not engulf you
and fearsome fallen angels surround you, yet when you were
being summoned [to judgment] by name and some were
being approved and made glorious while others were sent
away in dishonor so that they did not see God's glory, would
the shame and ignominy of that punishment and the pain of
being deprived of so great a good not be more bitter than
hell?[6] For then the gnawing of conscience and the memory
of deeds long done would be worse than innumerable and
indescribable torments. For as the Fathers tell us, the souls
of the dead remember everything that happened here—
thoughts, words, desires—and nothing can be forgotten. But,
as it says in the Psalm, 'In that day all their schemes shall be
brought to nothing.'[7] The schemes he speaks of are those of
this world, about houses and possessions, parents and
children, and business transactions. All these things are
destroyed immediately when the soul passes out of the body,
none of all this is remembered or considered. But what he
did against virtue or against his evil passions, he remembers,
and nothing of this is lost. And if a man helped someone or
was helped by someone else, this is remembered as is the
persons concerned, or if he injured someone, or was injured
by someone, all this is remembered. In fact, the soul loses
nothing that it did in this world but remembers everything at
its exit from this body more clearly and distinctly once freed
from the earthliness of the body.

One day we were talking to one of the venerable Ancients
about this, he was saying that after leaving the body the soul
remembers the passions it gave way to and the sins it
committed and the persons with whom it committed them.

But I said to him, 'This is probably not quite exact, but it is probably that it had contracted habits of sin through repeated acts and these it remembers.' And we heatedly debating the point for a long time in our desire to learn the truth, but he was not convinced by my arguments and continued to maintain that the soul remembers each particular sin, its place, and the person it was committed with. If this is really so, the final evil we do ourselves by sinning is even greater than the first. And this is the reason why I am forever saying that you should take care always to cultivate good thoughts: so that you find them again hereafter. Whatever is in a man here is going to leave the earth with him, and going to be with him there. Let us set about freeing ourselves from this dread necessity; let us be very zealous and God will treat us with great mercy. 'For he is the hope of those at the ends of the earth and at sea afar off.'[8] Those at the ends of the earth are those in complete iniquity. Those at sea afar off are those in extreme ignorance; yet Christ is yet the hope even of these.

What we need is a little labor! Let us endure this labor that we may obtain mercy. If someone has some land but neglects it and leaves it untilled, he finds it produces thorns and thistles in proportion to his neglect. When he does come to clean it, the more it is infested with these weeds the more his hands will bleed when he wants to pull up what he allowed to grow in the time of his neglect. It is impossible for a man not to reap what he sows. A man who wants to sow his field must first thoroughly uproot all the weeds. For if one does not pull out the roots properly but cuts off the tops only, they spring up again. If a man wants to be sure that he has pulled up all the roots, after ridding [the field] of briars and all kinds of weeds, he must plough it, and break it up and till it and finally sow it with good seed. For if, after giving it all this careful attention, he allows it to lie fallow, fresh weeds arrive, and finding the soil soft and well-tilled, they will push their roots down deep and grow even stronger and more numerous.

So it is with the soul; first it must cut off all its old tendencies and bad habits. As St Basil says, 'It is no mean contest to overcome one's bad habits, for custom, strengthened by enduring a long time, takes on the force of [second] nature.'[9] Therefore, a man must combat, as I was saying, not only the bad habits, but the unruly passions which cause them and are their roots. And if the roots are not plucked out, the thorns inevitably spring up again. There are certain passions which do not grow strong if one cuts out their causes; an example of these is jealousy, which in itself is nothing, but one of its causes is vainglory. Someone who is eager for praise is jealous of someone who is being praised or given a special honor. Similarly anger has diverse causes but the principal one is love of pleasure. Evagrius reminds us of this when he tells us that one of the holy fathers used to say, 'The reason why I turn away from pleasures is to cut off occasions for getting angry.'[10] And all the fathers used to say that every one of the vices comes from one of three things—love of glory, love of money, and love of pleasure.[11] As I have told you on different occasions, a man must cut off not only his vices but their very causes, and so really put his life in good order through repentance and sorrow for sin, and then begin to sow good seed, i.e. good works. We said about the land, if good seed is not sown, the weeds soon come back and find good soft cultivated land and put down more roots into it. So it is with man: if, after putting his soul in good order and doing penance for his former conduct, he is negligent about doing good works and cultivating virtue, what happened in the Gospel happens to him. When the unclean spirit goes out of a man, he goes about through parched places seeking rest, and not finding any, and he says, 'I will return to the house from which I came out', and coming, he finds it empty—'clearly empty of all virtues'—and swept and garnished. Then he goes and takes seven other devils, worse than himself, and goes in and lives there, and the last state of that man becomes worse than the first.[12] It is impossible for the soul to remain in the same state but it must move along either to what is better or to what is worse. Therefore, everyone who wants to be saved must not only stop doing evil, but also work at what is good, as it says in the psalm, 'Turn away from evil and do good.'[13]   Mark what is says. Not only 'turn from evil', but also 'do good'!   For example: If a man was used to being unjust, he wants not only to stop being unjust but to act with justice continually.   If a man used always to be angry, he wants not only to stop being angry but to cultivate mildness.   If he was bold and insolent, he must not only give it up, but he must act with humility. This is to turn away from evil and to do good. Each of the vices has its contrary virtue.   Pride has humility, avarice has almsgiving; licentiousness, self-discipline; neglect, perseverance; anger has meekness; hatred, love.   In short, I repeat, every vice has its contrary virtue.

I have often repeated all this so that as we cast away virtue and brought in vices in the past, we may now work at throwing out our vices and replacing them with contrary virtues and at making them permanent in our souls, which is the proper place for them.   For by God's gift the virtues belong to the nature we possess.   For truly when God made man he sowed the virtues in him, as it says: 'Let us make man to our own image and likeness'.[14]   To his image, since God made the soul incorruptible and self-determining; to his likeness, which means having similar virtues.   Does the scripture not say: 'Be merciful, as your heavenly Father is merciful'?[15]   And: 'Be holy, for I am holy'?[16]   And again, the Apostle says: 'Be kind to one another!'[17]   In the Psalm: 'The Lord is kind to those who are waiting for him.'[18]   There are more like these, all showing this likeness to God. God gave us the virtues as an endowment of our nature, but he did not endow us with vices.   For they have no essence or existence of their own, but are like darkness which has no substantial existence but is a mere condition of the air—as the great Basil says, a complete absence of light.[19]   So it is with the vices. If the soul departs from virtue through love of pleasures, it puts itself in a state of vice, which is a state of privation of what ought to be there. So we must, as I said about tilling the land, quickly sow the good seed, both for the sake of the land and for the sake of the good fruit to be obtained. The sower must cover up the seed at once and hide it in the earth, for the birds come and snatch it up and destroy it. Having done this he awaits God's mercy until he sends rain and the seed sprouts. For even if the farmer works incessantly weeding, tilling and sowing [his land], unless God sends rain upon the seed, all his labor is in vain. We want to do the same. If we do something good, let us hide it through humility and cast our weakness upon God, praying him to have mercy on our labors lest they prove fruitless. Then again, when the seed has germinated after the rain, if it does not have more rain, it soon withers away and dies. The seed needs rain to germinate and the seedlings need rain for growth, otherwise they will not grow to maturity. We need the mercy of God, and none of us can afford to be negligent. Besides, after the plant grows and forms an ear, there may be locusts or a hailstorm, or something like that, and the grain be destroyed. So it is with the soul. When it has been worked on and cleansed of the vices of which we were speaking and has been zealous for acquiring virtues, it needs the mercy and protection of God lest it be abandoned and perish. As we were saying about the seed: after springing up and growing and forming the ear, it shrivels up and dies unless it gets the rain when it needs it. God leaves a man to himself when he does something foreign to his [spiritual] state—as for example when a man who is cautious indulges in foolhardiness, or a mild man breaks into violence. God does not abandon a foolish man who acts foolishly or a courageous man who is over-courageous as he does a discreet man who is foolhardy or a meek man who acts violently. This is to sin against his own natural temperament and from this comes his abandonment by God. [20]

This is why Saint Basil judges the sin of a god-fearing man differently from that of a careless man. Whenever a man keeps a guard over himself and desires to make progress, he demands that, should he undertake some small good, he do it not out of vainglory or regard for men or with some human advantage in mind, lest the little good that he does be spoiled—just as we were saying about the locust and the hail.

To advert again to the land: even when no harm comes to the crop, but it is preserved until the harvest, the farmer cannot afford to be neglectful. Sometimes it happens that when he has cut his corn and done all the work, a wicked man, out of hatred, puts fire to the stalks. He cannot be free of all anxiety until he has threshed his corn and stored it in his barn. So also the [spiritual] man, when he has been able to avoid all the dangers we have mentioned, must not consider his cares at an end. For it happens repeatedly that after all this the devil finds a way of leading him astray, either through self-righteousness or arrogance or by insinuating thoughts against faith or heretical doctrines and so he not only destroys all his fruits but also turns him away from God. Even if the devil cannot bring him to act wickedly, he may produce one evil thought. For a single thought can turn a man away from God when it is taken in and adhered to. Therefore, if a man has truly made up his mind [to be saved] he ought never to feel completely secure until his last breath. Labor and deep concern and prayer to God about everything is necessary that he may protect us and bring us to safety by his goodness to the glory of his name.

FOOTNOTES

1. MS Bibl. Nat. Paris graec 1598, f. 145r—J.C. Guy.

2. Apo Nau 196; ROC 1908, p. 277.

3. *Cent.* IV, 76; PO 28: 168. Cf. PG 65:908.

4. Ps 77:3. Cf. Gregory Naz., *Orat.* 17; PG 35:968C.

5. Mt 25:41.

6. *Ad Theodorum lapsum*; PG 47:294.

7. Ps 146:4.

8. Ps 65:5.

9. *Reg. fus. tr.* 6; PG 31:925B. Cf. Nilus, *Ep.* 2:239 (PG 79:321C).

10. *Praktikos* 99; PG 40:1252B; CS 4:41.

11. Cf. Apo Poemen (ed. Bousset, p. 148, n. 98**), Ps. Nilus (Evagrius), *De mal. cogit.* 1 (PG 79:1200D), Mark the Hermit, *De lege spirit.* 103-104, 107 (PG 65:917CD).

12. Lk 11:24-7.

13. Ps 37:27.

14. Gen 1:26.

15. Lk 6:36.

16. Lev 11:44.

17. Eph 4:32.

18. Lam 3:25.

19. *Hom. 2 in Hexam.*; PG 29:40C.

20. See *DS* 4:344-57: *Egkataleipsis*.

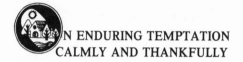

XIII

N ENDURING TEMPTATION CALMLY AND THANKFULLY

ABBOT POEMEN used to say very accurately that the signs of a true monk make their appearance in time of temptation.[1] For a monk, truly setting out to serve Our Lord, must be wise enough to prepare his soul for temptations,[2] lest he at any time become estranged [from the Lord] or be overwhelmed by what comes upon him. And he must believe that nothing happens apart from God's providence. In God's providence everything is absolutely right and whatever happens is for the assistance of the soul. For whatever God does with us, he does out of his love and consideration for us because it is adapted to our needs. And we ought, as the Apostle says, in all things to give thanks for his goodness to us,[3] and never to get het up or become weak-willed about what happens to us, but to accept calmly with lowliness of mind and hope in God whatever comes upon us, firmly convinced, As I said, that whatever God does to us, he does always out of goodness because he loves us, and what he does is always right. Nothing else could be right for us but the way in which he mercifully deals with us.

If a man has a friend and he is absolutely certain that his friend loves him, and if that friend does something to cause him suffering and be troublesome to him, he will be convinced that his friend acts out of love and he will never believe that his friend does it to harm him. How much more ought we to be convinced about God who created us, who drew us out of nothingness to existence and life, and who became a man for our sakes and died for us, and who does everything out of love for us?

It is conceivable that a friend may do something because he loves me and is concerned about me which, in spite of his good intentions, does me harm; this is likely to happen because he does not have complete knowledge and understanding of what my needs and destiny are. But we cannot say the same about God, for he is the fountain of wisdom and he knows everything that is to my advantage, and with this in view he arranges everything that concerns me without counting the cost. Again, about the friend who loves me and is concerned about me and conscientiously looks after my welfare: it can certainly happen in certain circumstances that he thinks I need help and yet he is powerless to help me. Even this we cannot say about God. For to him all things are possible; with God nothing is impossible. God, we know, loves and takes care of what he has fashioned. He is the fountain of wisdom and he knows what to do to promote our welfare and nothing is beyond his power. Hence we must be convinced that all he does, he does for our benefit and we ought to receive it with gratitude, as we said before, as coming from a beneficent and loving Master—and this even if some things are distressing, for all things happen by God's just judgment and he who is merciful does not overlook what is wrong nor does he give life to our tribulations. Often a man in doubt about this will say, 'What if a man in difficult circumstances does something sinful because of the affliction he is suffering? How can he be sure that the affliction happens to him for his own good?'

God does not allow us to be burdened with anything beyond our power of endurance, and therefore, when difficulties come upon us we do not sin unless we are unwilling to endure a little tribulation or to suffer anything unforeseen. As the Apostle says, 'God is faithful and will not allow us to be tempted beyond what we are able [to endure].'4 But we are men who have no patience and no desire for a little labor and [no desire] to brace ourselves to accept anything with humility. Therefore we are crushed [by our difficulties]. The more we run away from temptations, the more they weigh us down and the less are we able to drive them away. Suppose a man for some reason dives into the sea: if he knows the art of swimming, what does he do when a great wave comes along? He ducks under until it goes past and then he goes on swimming unharmed. But if he is determined to set himself against it, it pushes him away and hurls him back a great distance, and when again he begins to swim forward another wave comes upon him, and if again he tries to swim against it, again it forces him back, and he only tires himself out and makes no headway. But if he ducks his head and lowers himself under the wave, As I said, no harm comes to him and he continues to swim as long as he likes. Those who go on doing their work this way when they are in trouble, putting up with their temptations with patience and humility, come through unharmed. But if they get distressed and downcast, seeking the reasons for everything, tormenting themselves and being annoyed with themselves instead of helping themselves, they do themselves harm.

If painful experiences crowd in upon us, we ought not to be disturbed; allowing ourselves to be disturbed by these experiences is sheer ignorance and pride because we are not recognising our own condition and, as the Fathers tell us, we are running away from labor. We make no progress because we have not squarely taken our own measure, we do not persevere in the work we begin, and want to acquire virtue without effort.5 Why should an emotional man find it strange to be disturbed by his emotions? Why should he be overwhelmed if he sometimes gives way to them? If you have them inside yourself why are you disturbed when they break out? You have their seeds in you and yet you ask, why do they spring up and trouble me? Better to have patience and go on struggling with them and beg for God's help. It is impossible for someone struggling against his evil desires not to suffer affliction from them. The agents of the passions, as Abba Sisoes says, are inside you; pay them a deposit and they bring you under their power.[6] By 'agents' [of passions or vices] he means their causes.[7] In so far as we are attached to these and seek fulfilment in them we cannot escape being led captive by evil thoughts, while we are led forcefully—against our intention—to fulfil them because we have already willingly delivered ourselves into their hands. This is what the prophet says about Ephraim, who 'over-powered his adversary',—that is his own conscience—and 'trampled underfoot [right] judgment':[8] that he went in search of Egypt and was taken by force by the Assyrians.'[9] By 'Egypt' the Fathers understand the bodily inclination to be at rest, which teaches us to set our minds on pleasure and soft living. By 'Assyrians' they understand passionate engrossing thoughts which trouble and confuse the mind and fill it with unclean images and carry the unwilling mind forcefully towards sinful acts.

If, therefore a man willingly gives himself up to bodily pleasures, he will of necessity be led unwillingly by the Assyrians and forced to serve Nebuchadnezzar. Knowing this, the prophet was troubled and kept saying to them, 'Do not go down to Egypt.'[10] What are you doing, miserable wretches? Humble yourselves, bow your shoulders and work for yourselves under the King of Babylon and go on occupying the land of your fathers. And again he encouraged them saying, 'Do not be afraid before his face, for we have God with us, to deliver us out of his hands.'[11] Then he prophesied all the affliction that would come upon them if they disobeyed God. For, he said, 'if you go to Egypt you shall be in a wilderness at the mercy of everyone for abuse and cursing.' But they replied, 'We do not want to occupy this land, but we want to go down to Egypt, where we shall not see any more war, or hear the sound of the trumpet and we shall not hunger for bread.'[12] And they went down and willingly became Pharaoh's slaves; soon they were taken by force by the Assyrians and made *their* unwilling slaves.

Fix your attention on what has been said. Before a man gives way to his passions, even if his thoughts mount an assault against him, he is always a free man in his own city and he has God as an ally. If, therefore, he humbles himself before God and bears the yoke of his trial and affliction with thanksgiving, and puts up a little fight, the help of God will deliver him. But if he flees labor and goes after bodily pleasures, then he is necessarily led into the land of the Egyptians and without wishing it becomes their slave. Then the Prophet says [to those people]: 'Pray for the life of Nebuchadnezzar because his life is your salvation.' [13] Nebuchadnezzar stands for someone who does not underrate the value of the affliction that comes to him from temptation, or kick against it, but bears it humbly as something due to him; someone who holds that he is unworthy to be freed from that burden, yes, that his trial should be prolonged and made more severe; someone who, whether or not he understands that the cause is in himself or in his present circumstances, believes that nothing from God is indiscriminate or unjust. Such was the brother who mourned and wept when God removed his temptation and cried, 'Lord, am I unworthy to endure a little affliction?' [14] And again there is the account of the disciple of one of the great old monks who was severely attacked by the spirit of fornication, and the master seeing this said to him, 'Do you want me to beg God to lighten this attack?' But the disciple said, 'Even if I am hard-pressed, I see that there is great fruit coming to me from this labor. Rather ask this of God that he give me endurance!' [15]

You see then how strenuous are those who really want to be saved! This is what it means to bear the yoke with humility and to pray for the life of Nebuchadnezzar. [16] The same thing is implied in saying, 'I see great fruit coming to me from this labor' as 'in the life of Nebuchadnezzar is our salvation'. This the Old Man made clear by saying, 'Today I know that you are in the way to making progress and you will outstrip me.' For when someone struggles manfully against committing sin and begins to fight against the thoughts that attack his mind, he humbles himself and endures a buffeting and yet struggles on—and on this account he is soon cleansed and returns to what is in accord with his nature. [17]

Whereas, as we were saying, from his ignorance and pride a man is overcome when he is beset by his unruly passions, he ought after the humiliation [of falling] all the more correctly to take his own measure and to continue praying until God pours out his mercy upon him. For unless a man is tempted and sees the troubles which uncontrolled passions cause him, he will not at any time fight to be cleansed of them. About this the Psalm says, 'As soon as sinners spring up like grass and workers of iniquity appear, they will be thoroughly destroyed for ever and ever.' [18] 'Sinners springing up like grass' refers to passionate desires, for grass is a feeble thing and has no strength. When passionate thoughts arise in the soul therefore, they are brought to light; this means that the workers of iniquity, viz. the inordinate passions, appear, in order that they can be completely destroyed for ever and ever. For whenever passionate desires reappear in the mind of those who put up a fight, they are utterly and immediately rejected.

Consider now the consequences of this saying. First passionate desires arise in the mind, and then the underlying passion comes to light and they are destroyed. All this applies to contestants [for the heavenly crown]. But we who give way to the sins and are always satisfying our passions, never recognize the passionate desires that spring up, or the underlying passions they reveal, so that we can combat them, but we remain under their sway, in Egypt, in the pitiful brickfields of Pharaoh. And who will give us the clear realization of our bitter slavery so that we may be truly humbled and eager to obtain mercy? When the sons of Israel were in Egypt and enslaved to Pharaoh, they made bricks, and those who made bricks were always underdogs, they

were scorched by the furnaces and bent down to the ground
[by the burden they had to carry]. So it is with the soul if it
is dominated by the devil and goes on acting sinfully; the
devil tramples down the soul's good intentions and causes it
to understand nothing spiritual, but makes its thoughts and
activity revolve about earthly things. Then the Israelites built
for Pharaoh from the bricks they made three strongly fortified
cities, Pithom, Rameses, and On, which is Heliopolis [the city
of the sun].[19]   These represent luxury, avarice and vainglory;
from these all sin is derived. When God raised up Moses to
lead them out of Egypt and deliver them from slavery to
Pharaoh, they were burdened with even greater labors by the
king, and he said to them, 'You are worthless and lazy and
therefore you say, "Let us go and offer sacrifice to the Lord,
our God".'[20]   In like manner, when he knows that God
intends to have mercy on a soul and relieve it of the burden
of its evil passions either by his word or through one of his
servants, the devil aggravates them all the more and attacks
it all more vehemently.

The Fathers, knowing this, strengthened mankind with
their teaching and do not allow us to be a prey to anxiety.
One of them said, 'Have you fallen?   Rise up; and if [it
happens] again and again and again, do the same.'[21]   And
another said, 'The strength of those who really want to
acquire virtue is this: even if they fall they don't get dis-
couraged and give up, but go on, thinking only of starting
again.'[22]   Each of the Fathers quite simply, each in his own
special way, holds out a hand to help those who are in
combat with the enemy and are being attacked by him. For
they take as applying to themselves the words of holy
scripture, 'Shall not the fallen rise again?' or, 'Shall not one
who has turned away from me turn back again?'[23]   'Turn to
me again, my children, and I shall heal you from your
wounds,' says the Lord![24]   And many other like it. When the
hand of the Lord was heavy on Pharoah and his attendants,
they were willing to send away the sons of Israel, and He
said to Moses, 'Go and sacrifice to the Lord your God, but

leave your sheep and oxen behind,'[25] by which are signified to us the thoughts of our minds of which Pharoah wanted to be master, hoping through them to draw back to his service the sons of Israel. But to this Moses replied, 'By no means, but you should also give us victims and holocausts which we may offer to the Lord; our cattle shall also set out with us and we shall not leave one hoof behind.''[26] When Moses did succeed in leading the sons of Israel out of Egypt, he took them across the Red Sea. Although God wanted to lead them to the seventy palm trees and the twelve fountains of water, he led them first to Marah, and the people were in distress since they found nothing to drink as the water was bitter;[27] and from Marah he brought them to the seventy palm trees and the twelve fountains of water. So too the soul, when it stops committing sins and passes by the spiritual [Red] Sea, must first fight laboriously and be much afflicted; then it comes out of affliction into a state of holy rest. 'Through many tribulations we must enter the Kingdom of Heaven.'[28] For tribulations set the mercy of God in motion towards the soul, as the winds bring down the rain. But too much rain coming down on delicate young plants makes them rot and destroys their fruit, a modest amount of wind dries them out and stiffens them—so it is with the soul. Relaxation, freedom from care, and repose make it flabby, but temptations put it on its mettle and unite it to God, as the prophet says, 'Lord, in tribulation we were made mindful of you.'[29] So, as we said, we must not let ourselves be bowled over or become slothful, but stand firm and give thanks in our tribulations, and pray to God with humility at all times, that he may have mercy on our weakness and protect us in all our temptation to the glory of his name.

FOOTNOTES

1. Apo Poemen 13; PG 65: 325B; CS 59:142.
2. Wis 2:1.
3. 1 Th 5:18.
4. 1 Cor 10:13.
5. Apo Nau 297; ROC 1909, p. 379.
6. Apo Sisoes 6; PG 65:393A; CS 59:179.
7. See Ch. IX, XIII, XII.
8. Hos 5:11, 13.
9. Hos 7:11.
10. Jer 42:19.
11. Jer 42:11.
12. Jer 42:13-14.
13. Bar 1:11-12.
14. Apo Nau 192; ROC 1908, p. 276.
15. Apo Nau 170; ROC 1908, p. 55.
16. Cf. Dan 4:25ff.
17. Virtue = natural. See above, p. 180.
18. Ps 92:7.
19. Cf. Ex 1:11.
20. Ex 5:17.
21. Apo Sisoes 38; PG 65:404C; CS 59:184.
22. Apo Moses (PE 1, 28, p. 99) cited by Abba Isaiah, PE 1, 1, p. 8.
23. Jer 8:4.
24. Jer 3:22.
25. Ex 10:24.
26. Ex 10:25-6.
27. Ex 15:24.
28. Acts 14:21.
29. Is 26:16.

XIV

ON THE STRUCTURE AND HARMONY OF THE VIRTUES OF THE SOUL

HOLY SCRIPTURE says of the midwives who kept alive the Israelites' male children, that through the god-fearing midwives they made themselves houses.[1] Does it mean they made visible houses? How can they say they acquired houses through the fear of God when we do the opposite, and learn in time, through fear of God to give up the houses we have?[2] Evidently this does not refer to visible houses but to the house of the soul which each one builds up for himself by keeping God's commandments. Through this Holy Scripture teaches us that the fear of God prepares the soul to keep the commandments, and through the commandments the house of the soul is built up. Let us take hold of them, brothers, and let us fear God, and we shall build houses for ourselves where we shall find shelter in winter weather, in the season of storm-cloud, lightning, and rain; for not to have a home in winter-time is a great hardship.

How the house of the soul is built we can learn from the building of a material house and from the knowledge and care it demands. A man who wants to build a house must see that it is solid and thoroughly safe and he raises it four-square [on a sound foundation]. He does not concentrate on one part and neglect the rest since this is of no use but defeats his aim and makes vain the expense and labor. So it is with the soul:

we must on no account neglect any part of it, but build it up equally and harmoniously. This is what Abba John means when he says, 'I would rather a man acquire a little of each one of the virtues than master one virtue as some have done, persisting in it and practising only that but neglecting the rest.'[3]

They may indeed have a certain pre-eminence in that one virtue and, therefore, not be weighed down by the contrary vice, but they remain caught by their other passions and burdened by them and do not pay attention to them, thinking instead that they have acquired something grand. They are like a man who builds one wall and raises it up as high as he can and, considering the height of the wall, thinks what a great work he has done. He does not know that one good strong wind coming along will blow it down because it stands by itself, nor from only one wall has that man gained a shelter for himself, for he is exposed on the other sides. That is not the way to do it. If a man wants to build a home and make a refuge for himself he must build up all four walls and protect himself all round.

And I will tell you how to do it: First he must lay the foundation, which is faith. Without faith, as the Apostle says, it is impossible to please God.[4] So, according to our comparison, it is impossible to build our [spiritual] house without this foundation [viz. faith]. Is there occasion for obedience? A stone must be laid, obedience. Does a disagreement arise among the brethren? The stone of patience must be laid. Is there need for self-control? That stone too must be laid. So whatever the virtue required, that stone must be laid in the building, and in this way the perimeter of the building rises up. One stone for forebearance, another for mortifying self-will, one for meekness, and so on. In all this, great attention must be paid to perseverance and courage: these are the cornerstones of the building and by them the house is held together and all is united to all so that they do not lean over and fall apart; without these a man will not succeed in perfecting any of the virtues. If a man has no courage in his soul, he will not endure with patience, and if he has no patience he cannot entirely succeed. Therefore, it is said, 'In patience you shall possess your souls.'[5] Similarly, the builder must set his stones in mortar. If he piles up his stones without mortar, the stones come apart and the house falls down. The mortar is humility, which is composed from the earth and lies under the feet of all. Any virtue existing without humility is no virtue at all, as it says in the sayings of the Elders: 'As it is impossible to construct a ship without nails, so there is no hope of being saved without humility.'[6] Whatever a good man does, he must do with humility so that what he does is kept safe. But besides all this, the house needs what are called tie-beams or braces—that is to say discretion—which, besides adding much to its appearance, draws the whole building together.

The roof is charity, which is the completion of virtue as the roof completes the house. After the roof comes the crowning of the dwelling place; and what is this crowning? In the Law it is written, 'If you build yourself a house and make it your dwelling place, put a crown round your house [i.e. railings around the flat roof] lest your children fall from the roof.'[7] The crown is humility.[8] For that is the crown and guardian of all the virtues. As each virtue needs humility for its acquisition—and in that sense we said each stone is laid with the mortar of humility—so also the perfection of all the virtues is humility. The saints, while making progress towards this perfection, came to humility—this is why we are always saying that the man who is getting closer to God looks on himself more and more as a sinner. Who are the children that the Law says must not fall from the roof top? These children are the thoughts generated in our souls, which must be guarded through humility lest they fall out of the house. So it is completed, it has its protecting walls, its roof of virtues; there it is, the house of perfection we are speaking of, complete with its crowning virtue of humility and all that it needs to complete it.

Is there anything left out? Yes! Something remains to be said. What is that? What about the builder of the house? If there is no craftsman there, the house may finally deteriorate and perhaps fall down. The craftsman is one who acts with a knowledge of what he is doing. For a man may work at the virtues and because he acts without knowledge he may destroy his own work or it may be insecure, so that he can not find the way to complete it but lays one brick only to have to take it up again. Another may lay one and take up two. [For example:] A brother comes along and says one word to annoy or offend you. You say nothing and defer to him—you have laid a brick. Then you go off and speak to another brother, and say, 'That blighter so-and-so said this and that to me and I did not say a word, I just bowed to him in deference.' There you are—you have laid one brick and taken up two. Again a man may bow in submission to someone because he desires to be praised; he is humble, with a touch of vainglory—this is to lay one brick and take up another. He who humbles himself 'with knowledge' convinces himself that he has failed, and acknowledges that he has been at fault. This is what it means to humble oneself 'with knowledge'. One practises silence but not with knowledge; such a man holds that he acts virtuously, but he does nothing of the kind. The man who keeps silence with knowledge is the man who is convinced that he is unworthy to speak, as the Fathers used to say,[9] and this is silence 'with knowledge'. Again a man may over-estimate himself because he thinks he is doing a great thing and is humble, and he does not know that he possesses nothing, because he does not act with knowledge. To esteem himself correctly, with knowledge, is to be convinced that he is nothing and unworthy to be counted among men, as Abbot Moses said of himself, 'Dirty ash heap, not a man, why do you come among men?'[10] Another man serves the sick so to win a reward; in this he does not act with knowledge. If something painful happens to him he quickly cuts himself off from his good work and does not anticipate completing it since he is not acting with knowledge. A man who ministers with knowledge ministers because he is moved by sympathy [for the sufferer], because his heart is moved with pity. If anything happens externally that troubles him, or if the sick man is cantankerous with him, a man who aims at expressing this pity will bear it without being put out, because he sticks to his own intention and knows that the sick man is doing him more good than he is the sick man. You must believe that a man who ministers to the sick with knowledge is relieved of many evil tendencies and the battles they cause. For I know a brother who was fighting hard against persistent evil desires and because he ministered, with knowledge, to a man suffering from dysentery he was freed from that battle. Evagrius says of one of the famous Elders that he freed one of his disciples who was being regularly overcome by such shameful thoughts at night by ordering him to fast and minister to the sick, and they faded away. When he was asked about this incident he used to say there way nothing like works of mercy for extinguishing these evil impulses. [11] Again, if a man practises great mortification from vainglory or in the opinion that he is practising great virtue, he is not acting with knowledge. Because of this he begins to despise his neighbor and to think that he himself is really something; he is not only laying one brick and taking up two, but also shaking the building and putting the whole wall in danger by judging his neighbor. He who practises bodily mortification with knowledge does not think he is being marvellously virtuous nor does he desire to be praised as an ascetic but he maintains that through his mortification he acquires moral vigor, and through this he comes to humility. As the Fathers say, 'The road to humility is labor, bodily labor, with knowledge,' etc. [12] In short, in the case of every virtue, a man must work to acquire it and to practise it automatically. He is then a good and skillful craftsman capable of building his house in safety.

The man who desires, with God's help, to come to such an enviable state must not say the virtues are too great for

him or that they cannot be reached. For this is either failing
to hope in God's help or shrinking from something good.
Whatever virtues you desire you have only to practise and
you will see that you have in yourself power to succeed. See
what it says: 'Love your neighbor as yourself.'[13] Because
you are conscious of how far you are from virtue, do not be a
coward and ask, 'How can I love my neighbor as myself?
How can I pay attention to his troubles as to my own,
especially those hidden in his heart which I cannot see or
even know: How can I consider them my own?' Do not
excuse your slothfulness with thoughts like these, do not
consider virtues excessively difficult or unattainable, but
make at least a little effort and have confidence in God. Show
him your enthusiasm and zeal and you will see the help he
brings towards your success.

Take an example: Suppose there are two ladders, one
going upwards to heaven and the other leading down to hell.
You are standing on the earth between the two ladders. You
would not reason it all out and say, 'How can I fly from the
earth and be once and for all on the top of the ladder?' This
is impossible and God does not ask it of us, but he does ask
that we meanwhile keep from going downwards and do not
harm our neighbor nor offend him, nor calumniate him, nor
rail at him or demean him. And so at last we begin to do a
little good and are of help to him in speech, and bear with
him, and if he needs something give it him freely, so we go
up one rung at a time until finally, with God's help, we reach
the top of the ladder. For through this repeated coming to
your neighbor's rescue, you come to long for what is advantageous for him as well as advantageous for yourself and
what is profitable to him as well as profitable to yourself.
This is 'to love your neighbor as yourself'. If we seek we
shall find; and if we ask God, he will enlighten us, for it says
in the Gospel, 'Ask and it shall be given to you, seek and you
shall find, knock and it shall be opened to you.'[14] 'Ask', it
says, that we may call for aid through prayer; 'seek', that is,
search out how virtue may be reached, what brings it about,

what we ought to do in order to possess it. 'Seek and you
shall find' means to inquire every day in this way into everything. To 'knock' is to carry out the commandments. Every
one knocks at the door with his hands; our hands are given to
us that we may do something. We need, therefore, not only
to ask, but to seek diligently and know what to do as the
Apostle says, 'Perfectly prepared for every good work'. [15]
What does 'perfectly prepared' mean? When a man wants to
build a ship, he first of all prepares everything he needs
down to the smallest nail, the pitch and the caulking. So it is
when a woman sets up the loom to weave a piece of cloth;
everything has to be prepared to the last thread. This is
what is meant by being prefectly prepared—to have everything that is needed ready at hand for the work.

So, therefore, that we may be ready for every good work,
let us make all our preparations to do the will of God 'with
knowledge'—what he desires and in a way that pleases him.
What is it the Apostle means by saying, 'The will of God is
good and well-pleasing and perfect'? [16] Everything that
happens, happens with God's permission or approval, as it
says in the Prophet, 'I, the Lord, make the light and create
darkness,' [17] and again, 'There is no evil in the city which
the Lord did not make'. [18] He speaks of evil here in the
sense of the consequences of evil and the troubles that are
brought upon us for our correction because of the evil we do,
such evils as famine, earthquakes, droughts, diseases, and
wars. All this happens to us, not according to God's
pleasure, but by his permission, with his permission they
come upon us for our profit. God does not, therefore, want
us to desire them or to approve of them. For example: 'It is
God's will, in that he allows it, that the city be ruined.' Since
it is God's will that it be ruined, does he want us to set fire to
it and burn it, or take a pickaxe and smash it down? Or it is
God's will that someone be afflicted or sick; does he wish us
then to afflict the person or to say that since it is God's will
that he is sick we shall not take pity on him? No! God does
not want this; he does not want us to serve him that way. He

wants us to desire the good that he intends [as a result of this affliction], that which happens according to his good pleasure, as we said, all that is done in accord with the command-ments: to love one another, to bear one another's burdens, to give alms and the like. That is the good that God wills. But what is well-pleasing? If someone does something good, it is always good, but sometimes it is not well-pleasing. And I will tell you why not. It may happen that someone finds a poor orphan girl who is very beautiful. Delighted with her beauty, he takes her in and brings her up because he thinks the poor orphan is beautiful   And that is the will of God—something good; it is not, however, well-pleasing [to God]. The thing is well-pleasing to God not when a man acts mercifully on account of some human consideration but because the act is good in itself and because he acts sincerely out of compassion. That is truly well-pleasing to God! The thing is perfect when a man gives alms without meanness or reluctance, without despising the recipient but with eagerness according to his ability, of deliberate choice, giving as freely as if he were receiving, doing a kindness as graciously as if a kindness were being shown to him—then it is perfect. And so a man is well-pleasing to God, doing his will, as the Apostle says, the good, the well-pleasing and the perfect thing. This is to act with knowledge.

If you want to know the special good and grace attached to alms-giving and how great it is, consider that it is able to take away sins. As the Prophet says: 'The ransom of a man is his own riches,' [19] and in another place it says, 'By alms-giving redeem your sins.' [20]   Our Lord himself says, 'Be merciful as your heavenly Father is merciful.' [21]   He does not say, 'Practice fasting as your heavenly Father fasts,' nor does he say, 'Be without possessions as your heavenly Father is without possessions'. What *does* he say? 'Be merciful as your heavenly Father is merciful.' This is the virtue which emulates God in a special way; it is characteristic of him. It is, therefore, necessary to pursue this aim always and to act with knowledge. There are great differences of intention in giving alms. One person gives alms to bring a blessing on his neighborhood and God blesses his neighborhood. Another gives alms on account of his ship, and God saves his ship. Another, for his children, and God saves and protects them; another to be praised and God lets him be praised; God sets aside no one, but grants to each one what he desires so long as it does not harm his soul. But they all give up their reward and lay up no treasure for themselves with God, since the aim they set themselves was not something for the profit of their souls. If you acted to bring a blessing on your country and God blessed your country, if for the sake of your children and God protected your children, if you wanted to acquire a good name and God made you famous, what more does God owe you? He has already given you the reward for what you did. There is another man who gives alms to be delivered from future punishment and he does something for the good of his soul, and he acts according to God's will except that he does not do quite *all* that God wishes, for he is still in a state of servility. The slave does not do the will of his master of his own free will, but because he is afraid of being beaten. So too this man acts to be freed from punishment and God frees him from it. Another gives alms in the hope of [heavenly] reward. This is a higher motive than the first but even this is not quite up to what God wants. He has not yet the sentiments of a son but, as a hired man, does what his master wants in order to receive his wages and to gain his living. This man acts for the sake of gain.

In doing good we have to pass through three different states, as St Gregory says. Of these we have spoken to you elsewhere:[22] Either we do good because we are afraid of punishment, and we are in the state of servility; or to earn a reward, then we are in the state of hirelings; or for the sake of the good itself, then we are in the state of sonship. A son does not do his father's will out of fear, or because he wants to earn a reward, but because he wants to be of service, to honor his father and to make him happy. And, therefore, we ought to give alms in this way because it is a noble thing to do, having compassion on one another as if caring for our own affairs; and so treating another as we are treated by Him; giving to others as we receive. This is to give alms with knowledge and in this way we are found to be in the state of sonship, as we said. No one can say, 'I am poor and hence I have no means of giving alms.' For even if you cannot give as the rich gave their gifts into the temple treasury, give two farthings as the poor widow did, and from you God will consider it a greater gift than the gifts of the rich. And if you do not have as much as two farthings? You still have power to give alms, you can take pity on the sick and give alms by ministering to them. And if you cannot do even this? You can comfort your brother by your words. Express your pity for him in words and take heed of the one who said, 'A good word is better than the best of gifts'.[23] Suppose you cannot even help him by words; you can still, even when he is incensed against you, take pity on him and bear with him in the time of his fury, seeing that he is being dealt with spitefully by the common enemy and, instead of making a sharp remark and adding to his fury, keep silent and so have pity on him and his soul, thus dragging him away from the enemy. Even if he offends against you, you can have mercy on him and forgive his offence against you, so that you may receive forgiveness from God. For it says, 'Forgive and it shall be forgiven you.'[24] And you shall be found to have mercy on your brother's soul by pardoning him his offence against you. God made us a gift of the power, if we wish to use it, of forgiving one another the sins committed against us, so that if we do not have the means of coming to the aid of their bodies, we may come to the aid of their souls. And what act of mercy is as great as having mercy on a soul? As the soul is more honorable than the body, so doing a work of mercy for the soul is greater than a corporal work of mercy. So, you see, no one can say he does not have the power to do works of mercy. Everyone according to his ability and the condition of his soul has the power to be merciful; he must only take great care to do whatever good he does with knowledge, as we have said, for each of the virtues. For we say that a man acting with knowledge, is capable of building his own house safely. About this the Gospel says, 'A wise man builds his house on a rock', [25] and nothing can overturn it. May God, who is a lover of men, grant you may hear, and what you hear do, that these words do not become your condemnation on the day of judgment, so that to him be glory for all ages. Amen.

FOOTNOTES

1. Cf. Ex 1:21.
2. Cf. Mt 19:29.
3. Apo John the Dwarf 34; PG 65:216A; CS 59:79.
4. Heb 11:6.
5. Lk 21:10.
6. Apo Syncletica; MS Berol. 1624. Cf. Vita Syncl. 56; PG 28:1521B.
7. Deut 22:8.
8. Cf. Ps Nilus, *De octo. spir. malit.* 19; PG 79:1164C.
9. Apo Nau 321, ROC 1912, p. 208.
10. Apo Moses 4; PG 65: 284B; CS 59:118.
11. *Praktikos* 91; PG 40:1249B; CS 4:39.
12. Apo Nau 323, ROC 1912, pp. 208-9.
13. Lev 19:18, Rm 13:9.
14. Mt 7:7, Lk 11:9.
15. 2 Tim 3:17. Cf. 2 Cor 9:8.
16. Rm 12:2.
17. Is 14:7.
18. Amos 3:6.
19. Prov 13:8.
20. Dan 4:24.
21. Lk 6:36.
22. Ch. IV.
23. Qo 18:17.
24. Lk 6:37.
25. Mt 7:24.

Part Two

THE PASCHAL MYSTERY

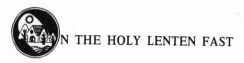

XV

N THE HOLY LENTEN FAST

IN THE LAW, God laid down that the sons of Israel should each year give tithes of all they possessed, and if they did so they were blessed in all their works.[1]   The holy apostles, knowing this to be for the help and advancement of our souls, resolved to fulfil it in a better and higher way, namely, for us to deliver up a tithe of the very days of our lives as if to consecrate them to God, so that we may be blessed in all our works, and each year to be unburdened of the whole year's sins. They elected to consecrate out of the three hundred and sixty-five days of the year, seven weeks of fasting,[2] and so they ordained; but our Fathers, in their time, thought it advisable to add another week, both to train and better prepare themselves to enter on the labor of fasting and to honor with their fasting the holy number of forty days which Our Lord fasted.   The eight weeks, subtracting Saturdays and Sundays, makes forty days, but we honor Holy Saturday with a fast because it is a very holy day and the only Saturday fast of the year.

The seven weeks, without Saturdays, gives thirty-five days, and if finally we add the half of the brilliant and light-giving night,[3] this makes thirty-six and a half, which is exactly a tenth of three hundred and sixty-five. For thirty is the tenth of three hundred, six is the tenth of sixty, and the

215

tenth of five is one half.   Here then, as we said, are the
thirty-six and a half days, the very tithing of the whole year
as one might say, which the holy apostles consecrated to
penance for the cleansing of our sins of the whole year.[4]
Whoever, therefore, keeps careful guard over himself, as is
fitting during these holy days, will be rewarded with
blessings, brothers, even if it happens that, being a man, he
has sinned either through weakness or carelessness.   You
see, God gave us these holy days so that by diligence in
abstinence, in the spirit of humility and repentance, a man
may be cleansed of the sins of the whole year and the soul
relieved of its burden.   Purified he goes forward to the holy
day of the Resurrection, and being made a new man through
the change of heart induced by the fast, he can take his part
in the Holy Mysteries and remain in spiritual joy and
happiness, feasting with God the whole fifty days.   Paschal
time, as has been said, is the resurrection of the soul and the
sign of this is that we do not kneel in church during the
whole season up to Pentecost.[5]

Everyone who wants to purify himself of the sins of the
whole year during these days must first of all restrain himself
from the pleasure of eating.   For the pleasure of eating, as
the Fathers say, caused all man's evil.   Likewise he must take
care not to break the fast without great necessity or to look
for pleasurable things to eat, or weigh himself down by
eating and drinking until he is full.

There are two kinds of gluttony.   There is the kind which
concerns taste: a man does not want to eat a lot but he
wants it to be appetizing.   It follows that such a person eats
the food that pleases him and is defeated by the pleasure of
it.   He keeps the food in his mouth, rolling it round and
round, and has not the heart to swallow it because he enjoys
the taste. This is called fastidiousness.[6]   Another man is
concerned about satisfying himself.   He doesn't ask for fancy
food nor does he care especially about whether the taste is
nice or not, he only wants to eat and fill his stomach. This is
gluttony.[7]   I will tell you how it gets this name: *margainein*

means to rage furiously, to be mad; according to the profane, *margos* is the name given to the man who rages furiously or is mad. When this disease or mania for packing his belly full of food comes upon a man, therefore, it is called *gastro-margia*, the madness of the stomach, whereas *lairmargia* is the madness of the palate. These must be guarded against and abandoned seriously by the man who desires to be cleansed of his sins. They accord not with the needs of the body, but with its vicious inclinations, and if they are tolerated, they lead a man into sin. As is the case with legitimate marital union and fornication, the practice is the same but the object is different. In the one case, there is copulation in order to raise a family, in the other, to satisfy a desire for pleasure. The same is true with feeding: in one case it is a question of the body's needs and in the other of eating for pleasure. The intention is what makes it a sin. A man eats to satisfy a need when he lays down how much he will take each day and, if what he has determined on overloads him, takes a little less, or if he is not overloaded and his body is weakened, adds a little. And so he estimates exactly his need, and he bases his conclusion not on pleasure but on preserving the strength of his body. And what he takes he receives with prayer, deeming himself unworthy of that comfort and he is not on the look out to see if others, as is likely, because of special need or necessity are given special attention, lest he himself hankers for that comfort or think it a trivial thing for the soul to be at rest.

One day when I was in the monastery, I went to see one of the seniors—and there were many great men among the seniors there. I discovered that his disciple sat down to eat with him, and in private I said to the young man, 'You know, brother, these seniors whom you see eating and taking a little recreation are like men who had deep purses and kept at work, always putting something into them until they filled them up. And after sealing them up they went on working some more and amassed another thousand crowns, so as to have something to draw on in time of need, and so they preserved what was sealed up in the purse. And so it is with these [seniors], they persevered in their labors, always storing up treasures for themselves, and after sealing up the treasure they worked a little more, and they hold these treasures in reserve for times of sickness and old age so they have something to draw on, and still preserve the treasures they have stored up. But we haven't even a purse to draw on!

As I was saying, therefore, we ought, even if we take food out of necessity, to consider ourselves unworthy of any kind of special relief or even of monastic life itself—and not take food purely for pleasure, and in this way food will not bring our condemnation.

Enough about sobriety in eating. We must not only keep a sharp watch over our diet, but keep away from all other kinds of sin so that as our stomach keeps fast, so also may our tongue as we abstain from calumny, from deceit, from idle talk, from railing and anger and all other vices which arise from the tongue.

So also let our eyes keep fast. No looking for trivialities, no letting the eyes wander freely, no impudent lying in wait for people to talk to. The same with the hands and feet, to prevent them from doing anything evil. Fasting in this way, as St Basil says,[8] is an acceptable fast and, leaving behind all the evil to which our senses are inclined, we may come to the holy day of the Resurrection,[9] renewed and clean and worthy to share in the holy mysteries, as we have already said.

First we go out to meet Our Lord and receive him with palms and olive branches and we seat him on the colt and come with him into the Holy City.[10] What does this mean: sitting on a colt? He is seated on a colt that he may convert the soul (which, as the prophet says,[11] has become irrational and is compared to senseless beasts) into an image of God, and subject it to his own divinity.[12] What does it mean: going to meet him with palms and olive branches? When someone marches out to war against an adversary and returns victorious, all his own people go before him with palm branches to mark his victory. The palm-branch is the symbol of victory. Again, when one man is injured by another, he desires to approach an authority who can vindicate him. He carries an olive branch and calls out, asking to be heard and helped. The olive branch is the symbol of mercy [pity]. [13] Therefore, we go out to meet our Master Christ, with palms because he is victorious—for he conquered our enemy—and with olive branches—for we are asking his mercy. May we, by asking, conquer through him and be found carrying the emblems of his victory, not only the victory by which he won for us, but also the victory which we also won through him by the prayers of all the saints. Amen.

FOOTNOTES

1. Cf. Num 18.
2. a five day week: Saturday and Sunday were excepted—tr.
3. Easter vigil.
4. Cf. Cassian, *Conf.* 21:25.
5. Cf. canon 20 of the Council of Nicaea.
6. λαιμαργία
7. γαστριμαργία
8. *De jejunio hom.* II.7; PG 31:196D. Cf. *In Is.* 31; PG 30:180D.
9. Easter.
10. Cf. Mk 11:1-8, Jn 12:13.
11. Ps 49:20, Qo 3:19.
12. Cf. Origen (PG 13:130D), Gregory Nyssa (PG 44:813, 820-21).
13. Cf. Ps. Athanasius, *Sermo in ramos palmarum* (PG 26:1313A).

XVI

COMMENTARY ON AN EASTER HYMN
OF ST GREGORY NAZIANZEN

St Gregory's Hymn for Easter[1]

This is the Day of Resurrection.
Let us offer God its first-fruits—which is ourselves.
Let us, as his most precious children, return
* to the likeness [of God],*
What is verily his likeness in us.
Let us reverence our worth.
Let us honor our Exemplar.
Let us come to understand the power
* of the 'mystery' wherein Christ died.*

AS USUAL, I am happy to say a few words about the song we sing, so that you will not be too taken up with the melody, but that your minds will be in harmony with the meaning of the words. What were we singing just now? 'This is the Day of Resurrection. Let us offer God its first-fruits, which is ourselves'.

The Israelites of old, coming together for their festivals, according to the Law offered God gifts such as incense, burnt offerings, first-fruits, and the like. St Gregory invites us too to celebrate this feast in God's honor as they did, and exhorts us to do so by saying, 'This is the day of Resurrection', a day to replace all their holy feasts, a day of divine assembly, the day of Christ's Passover'. What is this 'Passover' of Christ? The Israelites kept the Passover when they came out of Egypt. Easter, the Passover which we are now keeping and which the Saint commends to our celebration, is enacted in the soul, which comes out of the spiritual Egypt, that is, from sin. When the soul passes over from sin to virtue, then it celebrates the Passover of the Lord. As Evagrius says: 'The Passover of the Lord is the passage away from evil'.[2]

Today, Easter Day, is therefore the 'Passover' of Christ, a day of brilliant festival, the day of Resurrection, the day of his nailing sin to the Cross, of his dying and being raised to life—all for our sakes. Let us offer ourselves as sacrificial gifts and holocausts to the Lord, who has no desire for sense-less animals. 'You did not desire irrational sacrifices and offerings, and are not pleased with burnt offerings of sheep and cattle.'[3] And in Isaiah, the Lord says: 'What do I care for the multitude of your sacrifices?'[4] But the Lamb of God was sacrified for us, according to the Apostle who says, 'Christ our Paschal Lamb is sacrificed for us',[5] to take away the sin of the world,[6] and has become 'a curse for our sake' according to the Scriptures: 'Cursed be the man who hangs upon a tree' in order to 'redeem us from the curse of the Law'.[7] That we may receive from him 'the position of sons',[8] we ought on our part at some time to offer him a gift that will please him. And what sort of gift ought we offer to Christ in order to please him on the day of his Resurrection, if he does not desire the sacrifice of senseless animals?

The Saint in his teaching tells us the answer, for after saying, 'It is the Day of Resurrection', he adds, 'Let us offer up its first-fruits, which is ourselves.' The Apostle too instructs us: 'Offer up your own bodies as a living sacrifice, holy and well-pleasing to God, the worship that your reason dictates.'[9]

How then ought we to make an offering of our bodies as a living sacrifice to God? 'By no longer following our physical desires and our own ideas,'[10] but 'walking in the spirit and not fulfilling the desires of the flesh'.[11]   'For this is to mortify our earthly members.'[12]   This is what is meant by a living sacrifice, holy and well-pleasing to God.

But why a *living* sacrifice?   Because an animal destined for sacrifice, by the very fact that it becomes a sacrificial victim, dies.   But the saints who offer themselves to God, offer themselves alive, every day—as David says, 'For your sake we are put to death all the day long, we are considered as sheep for the slaughter'.[13]   St Gregory says, 'Let us offer ourselves as first-fruits [of the Resurrection]', that is, let us sacrifice ourselves, let us die to ourselves all the day long, as did all the saints, for the sake of Christ our God.   How did they put themselves to death?   By not loving the world or what is in the world[14]—as it says in the Catholic Epistles, 'By rejecting the lust of the flesh, the lust of the eyes and the pride of life',[15] that is, the love of pleasures, the love of money and of vainglory, and taking up the Cross and following Christ and crucifying the world to themselves and themselves to the world.[16]   About this the Apostle says, 'Those who belong to Christ have crucified the flesh with its passions and desires.'[17]   This is how the saints put themselves to death.

But how did they offer themselves up?   By not living for themselves, but reducing themselves to servitude to God's commandments and putting away their own will for the sake of the command and love of God and their neighbor.   As Saint Peter says, 'Behold we have given up everything and followed you.'[18]   He had no possessions, riches or gold or silver, he only had his net and that was very old, as said St John Chrysostom.[19]   But, as he also said, he did give up all his own aspirations, all desire of having the things of this world, and it is clear that had he had riches or power, he would have despised them and taken up his cross to follow Christ according to the word, 'I live, yet no longer I, but now Christ lives in me.'[20]   This is how the saints offered themselves up, putting themselves to death, as we were saying, in regard to all their passionate desires and doing their own will and living solely for Christ and his commandments.

So then for us!   Let us offer ourselves as St Gregory teaches us. For he wants us to be 'God's most precious children'.   Truly man is, of all visible creatures, the most precious.   All other things the Creator brought into being by his word alone, saying, 'Let it be'—and there it was; 'Let there be the earth' and it was made, 'let there be the waters' and so forth. [21]   But man he fashioned and formed with his own hands; and he established all the rest of creation for the service and comfort of man whom he set up as ruler and let him enjoy all the delights of paradise. [22]   And what is even more astonishing!   When man fell from there through his own fault, God called him back again through the blood of his only begotten Son, so that of all the visible creatures man should be the most precious.   And not only the most precious, but also 'the most closely related', for he said, 'let us make man to *our own* image and likeness', [23] and again, 'God created man in his own image and likeness and breathed into his person the breath of life'. [24]

Our Lord himself, having made himself a home among us, took up the person of a man, the body of a man, the mind of a man—in short, he became a man in everything except sin. He became our neighbor as a man, as it were, made himself the same as us men.   This was beautifully and graciously expressed by the saint in saying that man was the most precious and nearly related to God.   Then he adds, even more clearly, 'Let us return to him the likeness he has patterned after his own.'   How can we do that?   Let us learn from the Apostle who says, 'Let us purify ourselves from all defilement both of flesh and of spirit'. [25]   Let us make clean and clear the likeness as we received it.   Let us separate from it the dirt of sin, so that it may appear in all its beauty through the virtues.

David, in his prayer about this beauty [power] says, Lord, by your will, give reality to my beauty'. [26]   Let us therefore, purify our own likeness [to God].   God wants this from us, as he gave it 'not having spot or wrinkle, or any such blemish'.[27] 'Let us return to his likeness that likeness he has patterned after his own. Let us honor our worth.' Let us try to understand something of the great good by which we have been honored; let us try to understand something of the likeness to which we were created. Let us not despise the great gifts he has given us for no other reason than his goodness, not for any worth of ours. Let us be convinced that we are made to the image of the God who made us. 'Let us honor our Exemplar.' Let us not wantonly insult the Exemplar to which we were created. What man intending to paint the Emperor would be bold enough to lay on mouldy colors in his picture, and so dishonor the Emperor, and be punished? Would not all the colors he used be precious and brilliant and worthy of the imperial portrait? Sometimes even gold leaf is used in pictures of emperors; and great care is taken to portray as accurately as possible the royal robes he is wearing, so that anyone seeing the portrait may grasp the whole character of the emperor and may consider that he all but saw the emperor himself, the very exemplar [from which it was painted]. Likewise, we should not dishonor our model. We were created to the image and likeness of God, so let us make that likeness clean and precise, worthy of our Exemplar. If the man who dishonors the portrait of the emperor—a visible being of our own race though he is—is punished, what ought we to suffer for despising the likeness of God in us and not, as St Gregory says, 'returning to his likeness what is verily his likeness in us'? Let us, therefore, give honor to our Exemplar.

'Let us come to understand the power of the mystery wherein Christ died.'

The power of the mystery of Christ lies in this: By sin have effaced what belongs to his likeness in us and so we were put to death, as the Apostle says, 'by our sins and our transgressions'.[28]   God, having made us like himself and having compassion on his own creation and his own likeness, became man for our sakes and himself accepted death in our stead in order to lead us, who were dead, back again to the life from which we had fallen away.

When he mounted the holy cross, he nailed to the cross that sin for which we were thrown out of Paradise, and 'led captivity captive' as it is written. [29]

What does it mean: 'leading captivity captive'? In consequence of the fall of Adam, our enemy captured us and held us in his power. From then on the souls of men, on leaving the body, went to hades, because they were shut out from paradise. Christ, therefore, when he was lifted high on the holy and life-giving cross, snatched us by his own blood from the captivity by which the enemy had enslaved us through our fall. In other words, he seized us again from the hand of the enemy and, as it were, made us his own captives by defeating and casting down the one who had captured us before. This is the reason why he is said to have 'led captivity captive'.

This is the power of the mystery; this is why Christ died for us: to lead us, who, as the saint says, were dead back to life. We were, therefore, snatched from hades through the loving kindness of Christ, and now it is within our power to go back into paradise. Our enemy no longer has tyrannical power over us as he did at first; no longer does he hold us as his slaves.

The one thing is, brothers, we must be attentive and keep ourselves from sin in every one of our actions. For, as I have said many times before, every sinful action we take puts us once again under the power of the enemy, since of our own free will we cast ourselves down [before him] and enslave ourselves [to him]. For is it not a shameful thing and a great misery, if—after Christ has delivered us from hell through his blood and after we know this to be true—we go back again and cast ourselves into hell? Are we not worthy of worse and more pitiable punishment?

May God, who loves us, have pity on us and give us the childlike simplicity to understand this and help ourselves, that we may find a little mercy [waiting for us] on the day of judgment.

FOOTNOTES

1. Discovered by S. Petrides in an Easter homily of St Gregory and reconstructed in *Byzantinische Zeitschrift* (1904) 421-3.

2. *Sent. aux moines*, 40; TUGL 39:156 (PG 40:1279).

3. Heb 10:5-6, Ps 40:6.

4. Is 1:11.

5. 1 Cor 5:7.

6. Cf. Jn 1:29.

7. Gal 3:13.

8. Gal 4:5.

9. Rm 12:1.

10. Eph 2:3.

11. Gal 5:16.

12. Col 3:5.

13. Ps 44:22.

14. 1 Jn 2:15.

15. 1 Jn 2:16.

16. Cf. Mt 16:24.

17. Gal 5:24.

18. Mt 19:27.

19. *Hom. 7 in Rom*; PG 60:452. Cf. Cassian, *Conf.* 30.

20. Gal 2:20.

21. Cf. Jn 1, 3, 1, 10.

22. Cf. Jn 2.

23. Jn 1:26.

24. Jn 2:17.

25. 2 Cor 7:1.

26. Ps 29:8 (LXX).

27. Eph 5:27.

28. Eph 2:1.

29. Eph 4:8, Ps 68:18.

XVII

COMMENTARY ON ST GREGORY'S HYMN
SUNG IN HONOR OF THE MARTYRS

The Poem[1]

Victims yet living!
Holocausts who reason!
Martyrs to Christ,
God's perfect oblations.

Sheep who know God, and
Whom God most dearly knows,
By wolves can your sheepfold
never be invaded.

Be our ambassadors
by waters of repose.
That we may be with you,
with you in fold.

IT IS A good thing, brothers, to sing something from the god-bearing Fathers,[2] because in every way they were most solicitous always to teach everything that works together for the illumination of our souls. In these hymns, in the words they pronounced, we see always before us something to be learned of the significance of the feast we

227

are celebrating, whether it is a feast of Our Master or of the Holy Martyrs, of the Fathers or any other notable holy day. We ought, therefore, while singing with childlike simplicity, to fix our minds on the meaning of the holy words, so that not only our mouths [sing] but, as the Book of the Ancients says,[3] our hearts sing in unison with our mouths.

We learned from the former hymn something about the power and significance of Easter. Let us now see what St Gregory wants us to learn about the martyrs. He says in the hymn which we have just addressed to them, 'Victims yet living! Holocausts who reason.' What are these 'victims' who continue to live? A victim is anything that is purified for sacrifice to God—for example, sheep or cattle or something similar. Why, then, does he speak about the holy martyrs as 'Victims yet living'? Because when a sheep is offered in sacrifice it has its throat cut and *dies*: then it is dismembered, cut into pieces, and offered up to God. But the holy martyrs, while still alive, were hacked, they were flayed; their flesh was torn; they were tortured and dismembered. The public executioners cut off their hands and feet, tore out their tongues and eyes; their ribs were so badly torn that their entrails were laid open to view. All that, I tell you, they endured with patience, having life and spirit yet in them. For this reason they are called 'Victims yet living!' But why 'holocausts'? It is one thing to be a 'victim', another a 'holocaust'. Sometimes the whole sheep was not offered, but only the prime offering—as it says in the Law, 'The right thigh, the lobe of the liver, the two kidneys and all similar parts'.[4] Those who were making the oblation presented these parts; such was the prime offering, itself considered a sacrifice.

It was a 'holocaust' when they presented a whole sheep or a whole ox or any other whole oblation and burnt the whole to cinders, as it says in Leviticus 'complete with the head and the intestines.'[5] It even happened sometimes that they burnt the skin and the dung.[6] In short, the whole blessed lot was reduced to ashes. That is what they called a holocaust. This is the way that the sons of Israel performed their sacrifices and their holocausts in accordance with the Law. These sacrifices and holocausts were symbols of the souls of those who desired to be saved and to offer themselves to God, and I am telling you a little of what the Fathers have said about them, so that when you are quite clear about them, you may elevate your minds a little and enrich your souls.

They say the right arm is strength and the hands are received for action [practical work], as we said elsewhere. The right arm, therefore, is the strength of the hands. So they offered the power of the right hand, that is the practice of good works, for they received the right hand for the sake of the good.[7] And the other things that are specified, such as the lobe of the liver and the two kidneys and the fat from them, the thigh and the fat of the hams, the heart and the breast and such like, all these are symbols also. All these things, as the Apostle says, happened in figure and are written for our instruction.[8] How? I will explain. The soul, St Gregory says, has three parts. One is the seat of attraction (desires, appetites);[9] another is the seat of repulsion (anger, passion); the third, the seat of reason (intelligence). Suppose they offer the liver? The Fathers take this to mean the seat of attraction (desires, appetites). The lobe of the liver is its summit. Therefore, they were offering up the finest part of the organ of attraction, that is the prime portion of it, the most noble and valuable part of it. By this they signified that nothing was to be loved before God! Of all desirable things nothing is to be considered more precious than the desire for God. For as we said, they offered to God the most valuable portion.

The kidneys with the fat surrounding them, or the thigh and the fat on the limbs signify the same thing by analogy. The symbol for the vehement passions [anger, hatred] is the heart, for there, they say, is the life-power. This is what St Basil means when he says, 'Rage is the boiling up and violent movement of the blood around the heart.'[10]

The breast is the symbol for the reasoning power, for the

Fathers saw this meaning in the breast. For this reason, they say, Moses clad Aaron with the high priestly robe upon the breast of which was the *logion* [rational],[11] according to God's decree.[12]

All these things, as we said, are symbols of the soul by actions[13] purifying itself, with God's help, until it returns to what accords with its true nature. Evagrius says that the rational soul works according to its nature 'when it gives itself up to virtue, and its own vehement natural powers fight to obtain it, and power of reason is set upon the contemplation of created beings.'[14]   When, therefore, they brought forward a sheep or an ox or something of the kind for sacrifice, they took from the oblation these parts and laid them on the altar before the Lord, and it was called a sacrifice. But it was a holocaust when they offered up the whole of the slaughtered victim and burnt it to ashes, as we said above, so that the sacrifice was entire, complete and perfect. This is the symbol of the perfect, of those who say, 'Behold we have given up everything and followed you'.[15] To this degree of perfection Our Lord invited the one who said to him, 'I have kept all these things from my youth'. For Jesus replied, 'Yet one thing remains'.[16]   What was that? 'Take up your cross and follow me.'[17]   The holy martyrs offered up their whole selves to God in this way, and not only themselves but all that was theirs and everything that had to do with them. 'We ourselves are one thing', St Basil says, 'what is ours is another and what has something to do with us is another.'[18]   This is exactly what I am saying to you, but in another way. *We*, then, are mind and soul, *ours* is the body, *what has to do with us* is possessions and the rest of material things. The saints offered themselves up to God, with all their heart, with all their soul and all their strength, as it is written: 'You shall love the Lord your God with all your heart and all your soul and all your mind'.[19]   They despised not only children and wives and glory and riches and all the rest of their surroundings, but also their own bodies and for they they are called holocausts, rational holocausts because man is a rational animal and 'a perfect sacrifice to God'.

Next St Gregory says, 'God-knowing sheep, whom God most dearly knows.' Knowing God! But how? As the Lord himself taught us when he said, 'My sheep hear my voice and I know mine and they know me'.[20] Why does he say, 'My sheep hear my voice'? It is just another way of saying, 'They obey my words, they keep my commandments; for this reason they know me [by experience]'. Obeying the commandments the saints draw near to God; the more they draw near to God, the better they know him and are known by him—for God knows everything, hidden things, even things that do not exist. And so St Gregory says of the saints that they are known to God, because, as I was saying, through the commandments they come close to him, they know him by experience and are known by him. The more a man turns away, the greater the distance he puts between himself and God, the less he is said to know of him and the less he is known to him; whereas if he comes close to [God] he is said to know him and be known by him. Accordingly, God is said not to know sinners because they keep him at a distance. Therefore, our Lord himself says to such as these, 'Amen, I say to you, I do not know you.'[21] Wherefore, as I have said many times, insofar as they possessed the virtues, through keeping the commandments, the saints advanced towards God, and the more they advanced the better they knew God and were known by him.

'To wolves is your sheepfold inaccessible.' Sheepfold is what we call the enclosure into which the shepherd leads the sheep to protect them, so that they are not devoured by wolves or stolen by robbers. But if the sheepfold, in any of its parts, is delapidated, it will be vulnerable and readily a prey to the cunning plots of wolves and robbers. The sheepfold of the saints is made safe on all sides and permanently guarded. As the Lord says, 'In there thieves do not break through and steal, neither are they able to do any harm by their cunning.'[22] Let us pray, therefore, brothers, that we may be kept in that fold with them and find a corner in that blessed place where they are nourished and may share their repose. For if we do not first reach their state [of perfection] we shall not be worthy to be with them in glory, but we can avoid being thrown out of paradise if we live soberly.   As St Clement says, 'If a man be not crowned [with martyrdom] let him take care not to be far distant from those who are.'[23] In the royal palace there are great and illustrious appointments—for example, the council, the patricians, the generals, the governors, the marshals, for these all hold highly paid positions.   There are also others in the palace who serve for very small salaries, and they too are said to serve the King and reside inside the palace but do not have the same honor given to them as the others.   But all the same they are inside.   It falls out that, little by little, by their work, they succeed to something of the honor and glory of the great and illustrious.   So may we, by our diligence, escape all sinful actions so that at least we may be delivered from hell. And so we can, by the loving kindness of Christ, attain our entry into paradise itself by the prayers of all the saints.   Amen!

FOOTNOTES

1. Reconstructed by S. Perides, *Byzantinische Zeitschrift* (1904) 425-7.
2. αγιων Θεοφόρων
3. Apo Elias 6: PG 65:184; CS 59:61.
4. Lev 3:4.
5. Lev 8:24, cf. 4:11.
6. Cf. Lev 8:17.
7. Cf. Cassian, *Conf.* 12:5.
8. 1 Cor 10:11.
9. PG 37:1382. Cf. Evagrius, *Praktikos* (PG 40:1236).
10. In Is.; PG 30:424.
11. AV: 'breastplate of righteousness'; JB 'pectoral of judgement'.
12. Ex 28:15.
13. πρακτικῆς: the practice of asceticism.
14. *Praktikos* 1:58; PG 40:1233-36; CS 59.
15. Mt 19:27.
16. Lk 18:21-22.
17. Mt 16:24.
18. *Hom. in illud: Attende tibi ipsi;* PG 31:204.
19. Mt 22:37.
20. Jn 10:14 & 27.
21. Mt 25:12.
22. Mt 6:20.
23. 2 Clement 7; PG 1:337B.

Part Three

DIALOGUE AND REPLIES

MAXIMS

XVIII

F THE RELATIONS BETWEEN THE PRESIDENT
AND HIS DISCIPLES IN MONASTERIES

How the President should conduct himself towards the
brethren, and how they should subject themselves to him.

I F YOU ARE put in charge of the brethren, in your care of
them be strict in thought and merciful in action, teach
them the way to live both by word and by deed but
especially by your deeds, because example is more
stimulating than words. If you are strong in body, mould
them by bodily works; if you are weak in body, by the fruits
of the spirit (which the Apostle enumerates[1]) which emanate
from a noble state of soul, in love, patience, joy, peace,
constancy, goodness, faith, meekness and control of all the
passions. If a fault occurs, do not be too anxious, but explain
the disorder and the harm that comes from these faults. And
if there is need to rebuke, take into account the person to
whom rebuke is due, and choose a suitable time. Do not be
exacting about small faults or anxious about your own rights,
do not correct too severely, for this is burdensome and piling
up corrections leads to insensitivity and contempt and not to
orderly government. Rather, with humility take counsel with
the brother. Speaking like this is more effective and more
persuasive and keeps your neighbor calm. At a time of disturbance, when the brother is resisting you, control your

tongue lest you say anything simply to vent your anger and do not allow yourself to curse him in your heart but remember that he is your brother, a member of Christ and made to God's likeness, and he has been used spitefully by the common enemy. and so be compassionate towards him, lest the devil, having led him captive through the onslaught of passion, should condemn him to death through the remembrance of old injuries and through our inattentiveness a soul should be lost for whom Christ died. Remember that you will also lie under the same condemnation for anger. And because of your own weakness, have sympathy with your brother and give thanks that you have found a starting place for forgiveness, that you may be forgiven by God for your many and greater faults. For 'if you forgive it shall be forgiven you'.[2] Do you perhaps think that your brother is harmed by your long-suffering? But the Apostle exhorts us to slay evil by good, not good by evil.[3]

Our Fathers are in the habit of saying that if someone rebukes another when he is burning with anger, he is merely fulfilling his own evil inclination, and no wise man would destroy his own house to build up his neighbor's. While the disturbance lasts, put a curb on your heart and pray in this way: 'O Merciful God and lover of souls who created us out of nothing to communicate your own goodness to us and, when we fled away from your commandments, called us back through the bloody sacrifice of your Son, our Savior, come now to the help of our weakness, and as you once calmed the waves of the sea, so now put an end to the rage in our hearts. Do not at one time do away with two of your sons, condemned to death by sin, and do not say, "What use is there in my blood, in my going down to death?"[4] or, "Amen, I say to you, I do not know you",[5] because our lamps are gone out for want of oil.' After this prayer, when your heart has calmed down, you will then be able with an understanding heart to correct and convince according to the Apostle's exhortations,[6] and to do it with sympathy so as to heal a weak member and set him on the right path. Then the brother will accept the correction with confidence and blame himself severely, and through your peace you will bring peace to his heart. Never separate yourself from the holy example of Christ, who said, 'Learn of me for I am meek and humble of heart'.[7]. First make a point of acquiring a peaceful state of soul, so that correction is given not out of pretended righteousness or for the pleasure of rebuking, but as a duty performed for the sake of love and cleanness of heart. Building up your brother in this way, you shall hear a voice saying to you, 'If you extract what is precious from what is unclean, you shall be compared to my own voice.'[8]

If you are in a state of obedience to another, never believe your own heart; for it is blinded by its long-standing habitual preoccupations. Do not determine your way of life in anything by your own judgment. Do not make rules about anything for yourself without inquiring and taking counsel. Do not think that your own thoughts and resolutions are more profitable and more virtuous than those of your director, do not make yourself the examiner of his works, and so be often mistaken in your judgements. For it is the craft of the evil one to prevent submission with faith in every circumstance and, through faith, a state of certain security. It bars you also from obedience with tranquility, and from travelling without danger, or wandering from the road laid down by the Fathers. Do yourself violence in all things and cut off your own will, and, by the grace of Christ living in you, you will become so habituated to cutting off self-will that you do it without constraint or trouble as naturally as you do your own will. Then no longer will you want certain things to happen, but what is happening will be the thing you want and you will be at peace with all. This, however, applies to the things which are not contrary to the commandments of God or of the Fathers. Strive to find in everything something to blame yourself for, hold fast to indifference in knowledge and believe that everything that concerns us, even the most trivial thing, happens through God's providence, and you will bear anything that comes upon you without being troubled. Believe that disgrace and contempt is a healing remedy against the arrogance of your soul, and pray earnestly for those who, as true healers, abuse you. Believe that he who hates disgrace hates humility, and he who flees from those who provoke him flees from meekness. Do not desire to know the evils of your neighbor and do not entertain suspicions about him, but if suspicious thoughts burst out of your own wickedness, take care to mould them into noble thoughts, and in all things give thanks in accord with God's goodness and holy love. Before everything let all of us keep a guard on our own conscience in all things, both with regard to God and our neighbor and in regard to material things. Before we say or do anything, let us determine if it is in accord with God's will. And praying with this intention let us speak or act, at the same time casting our powerlessness before God, and in this way his goodness will come upon us in everything we do.

FOOTNOTES

1. Gal 5:22-3.
2. Lk 6:37.
3. Rom 12:21.
4. Ps 30:9.
5. Mt 25:13.
6. Gal 6:1.
7. Mt 11:29.
8. Jer 15:29.

XIX

DIALOGUE WITH THE CELLARER

ABBOT. You do not want to fall into anger and to remember injuries, do you? Do not have an all-in attachment to material things and do not lay claim for yourself to anything whatever, or despise even the least thing. But whatever is asked of you, give it gladly. If through negligence or levity anything is broken or lost, don't get upset about it. You ought to act in this way not from contempt for the monastery and its goods—for you have a debt to take care of them with all your ability and zeal—but because you want to be undisturbed and tranquil in mind, always referring what has happened to God as much as possible. This you should be able to do if you manage things not as if they belonged to yourself, but as things dedicated to God and only entrusted to you. This is the way, as I said, not to be too attached to things and not to be led to despise them. If you do not have this as your aim, you will get angry and never be at peace. Being upset yourself, you will upset others.

CELLARER. My mind delights in what you say and I want to act this way, but how is it that whenever I am attending to these affairs I do not find myself capable of doing so?

REPLY. Because you do not have these things clearly in your mind all the time. If you want to have these ideas before you at the moment you need to use them, go over them in your mind all the time and set your heart on them, and I am convinced that, by God's grace, you will make progress. Combine prayer with your good intentions. Take great care of the sick, in the first place to gain an understanding sympathy with the sick, but also so that, should you fall sick, God will raise up someone to look after you. 'For with what measure you mete, it shall be meted out to you again.'[1]

If you make a practice of doing things conscientiously, to the best of your ability and understanding, and you are told you have slipped up in something you did this way, you ought to see, and be fully convinced, that you do not yet know how to do it and ought not to be overcome or troubled, but accept the fact with joy. For by the criticism of your confrères, what is wanting will always be put right, or what is well done will be more firmly established. Be keen to make progress so that even if troubles arise, either bodily or spiritual, you can bear them with patience, without being troubled or cast down. Even if you are told off for doing something you did not do, do not be frightened or enraged, but bow your head before your accuser and say humbly, 'Forgive me, and pray for me', and keep silent about it, as the Fathers used to tell us. But if you are asked about whether the thing is true or not, still bow your head with humility and say honestly how the thing stands. And after speaking again, bow down humbly and say, 'Forgive me and say a prayer for me!'

CELLARER. What shall I do if I am not in that state of mind when I encounter the brethren?

REPLY. Obviously you cannot always be in the same amiable frame of mind when you meet the brethren, but you can take care not to be scandalized at anyone, or to condemn anyone, or abuse anyone, or by word or deed or movement set on anyone of the brethren who refuses to help you. But rather in everything edify him, without desiring to be rewarded by word or deed, or becoming vain about your work. Procure for yourself freedom in your way of life and your speech even in trivial matters. Be convinced that if a man is interiorly fighting and is troubled by some impassioned thought and publishes it abroad, he gives it more strength against himself, giving it power to fight against him and trouble him more. But if he faces it squarely and contests it and stirs up contrary thoughts, as I often tell you, he weakens that passionate thought and it becomes unable to fight against him and trouble him. And fighting in this way, little by little, and with the help of God, he overcomes the passion itself. May God protect us by the prayers of all the saints. Amen.

CELLARER. [Evidently not concerned exclusively with his office] Why does Abbot Poemen say that three things are fundamental: To fear the Lord, to pray to the Lord; and to do good to your neighbor?

ABBOT. The Old Man says, 'Fear the Lord,' because the fear of God in itself leads on to every virtue. 'The fear of God is the beginning of wisdom.'[2] Also, without the fear of God no one would acquire any virtue or do any good whatever, for it is 'by the fear of God that everyone turns away from evil'.[3] He says then, 'Pray to God', because a man cannot gain victory or do any good, even if he fears God and keenly desires to do so, unless he has God's help. It is absolutely necessary that his own zeal and God's help be continually working together. A man needs therefore to pray about everything, and to beg God's help and cooperation in everything he does.

Finally 'to do good to one's neighbor'. This is love. A man who fears the Lord and prays to God only helps himself. But only through loving our neighbor is all virtue made perfect. This is why the Old Man adds 'to do good to our neighbor'. For even if a man fears God and even if he continually prays to God he still has the debt of being useful to his neighbor and being good to him; for this is an essential part of love, which is, as the Apostle says, the perfection of the virtues.[4]

FOOTNOTES

1. Mt 7:2.
2. Ps 111:10.
3. Prov 16:6.
4. Cf: Rom 13:10, 1 Cor 13:13.

XX

REPLY TO CERTAIN HERMITS WHO ASKED HIM
ABOUT HOLDING MEETINGS

THE FATHERS tell us that to sit alone in the cell is one half and to consort with the elders is the other half. The significance of this saying is this: both in the cell and outside it there is an equal need for discretion and for a man to know why he ought to be quiet in his cell and why he ought to consort with the seniors and his brethren. For if a man is discreet about his way of life, he is earnest about what he is doing, as the Fathers say. And whenever he sits at home in his cell, he prays, he studies, he does some manual work, he pits himself against the power of his thoughts. Again, when from time to time he goes to a meeting, he comes to understand and look into his [spiritual] condition and to see whether he receives help from the encounter with others, and if he is able to return in safety to his cell. And if he has been harmed he learns his own weakness and learns that he has by no means gained the full benefit from his time of retirement, and he turns back humbled to his cell, lamenting and repenting and asking God to protect him against his own weakness and stupidity. So at last he sits in silence, attentive to his spiritual life.

When he comes again into the company of men, he sees for himself if he remains worsted in the same way as before or in other ways, and so he goes back to his cell and does the

244

same things, lamenting and doing penance, praying God to improve his spiritual state. The solitude of his cell should lift him up and the company of men test him. And so the Fathers speak truly when they say that to sit in the solitude of the cell is one half, and to sit with the elders is the other half.

You, therefore, when you set out to meet one another, ought to know why you leave your cells and not continually be going out at any time. The man who makes a journey without purpose, as the Fathers say, labors in vain. A man setting out to do something ought always to have a clear object in view and to know why he does it. What aim then ought we to have when we come to meet one another? First of all, love, for it is said, 'When you see your brother you see the Lord, your God.' Secondly, to listen to the word of God, for in the assembly the word of God is always more moving. For often one man does not understand [until] another one asks questions. And in addition to this, to learn to understand one's own spiritual state (as we said before). Let us, for example, suppose a man comes along to eat with those who have just celebrated the Eucharist, with the purpose of understanding himself and looking into his own conduct. If he is offered pleasant food and it pleases him, can he master himself and not partake of it? Is he careful not to over-reach his brother and take more than his share? And what if the food is already divided into portions? Is he eager to get a large portion for himself and leave a smaller portion to his brother? There are times when a man is not ashamed to stretch out his hand and place the smaller portion before his brother and put the larger one before himself. What is the good of knowing the difference between the larger and smaller portion? The difference between this is after all very little. Why should such a trivial thing cause you to over-reach your brother and do what is wrong? Again, let him consider whether he can abstain from taking enormous meals. Similarly, if there are many dishes, must he partake of *all* of them and so overeat? Is he on his guard about speaking too freely?   Does he take a dim view of the brother who is honored more than himself, or does he take it amiss that someone is more at peace than himself?   If he sees a brother conversing freely with another and doing a lot of talking, does he sometimes refrain from joining him?   Does he dismiss him from his mind without judging him, but rather seek the company of someone more disciplined, as was said about Abbot Anthony, namely, that when he was visiting the brethren, whatever good he saw in each he set about to acquire for himself.   From one he picked up self-control, from another humility, from another hard work, from another serenity.   And so he was found to have in himself the good that he found in each of the others.

This then is what we ought to do and why we ought to come together, and when we return to our cell let us examine ourselves and learn where we have been helped and what good we have received.   As soon as we find we have been protected, let us give thanks to God who has preserved us unharmed, but if we have done wrong, let us do penance and grieve over our own weakness.   For if a man comes to harm, he owes it to his own feeble condition, since nobody did him any harm.   But if we do any harm [to anyone else] through our own feeble state, we also do harm to ourselves.   We can, if we intend it, gain some benefit or suffer some loss, as I am always telling you.   And that you may understand how true this is, I give you an example: A certain man happened one night to be in a certain place.   I won't call him a monk, but someone from the town.   Three men passed by him.   One thought he was waiting for a street walker; another thought he was a thief; and the third thought he had been invited by a friend to meet him at a neighboring house and they were going off somewhere to say some prayers.   You see, all three men saw the same man in the same place and, similarly, each one thought his own thoughts about him.   One thought one thing, another another, and the third something else, each one according to his own state [of mind].   There are bodies which are melancholic and produce unhealthy body fluids;

every food they take in they turn into unhealthy vital juices, even if the food itself is good and wholesome. The cause of this ill-health does not come from the food but from the body which is, as they say, distempered. Of necessity it works on the digestion and changes the food [for the worse].

So it goes also with the soul [which is] a prey to bad habits. It is harmed by every occurrence; even if a thing is in itself useful, that soul is still harmed by it. Suppose I have a pot of honey and someone adds a little absinth, does that little bit not spoil the flavor of the lot and make it bitter all through? This is what we do when we throw out a little of our own bitterness and sully the good [name] of our neighbor by looking at him through the window of our own bad dispositions.

Those who have habitually good dispositions are like a man whose bodily temperament is so healthy that even if he should eat something harmful it turns into health-giving body fluids and the unsuitable food does not harm him. Since, as we were saying, his body is in a healthy state, by the digestive processes it extracts what is nourishing in the same way as we mentioned about the first [kind of body] which through its distempered condition changes good food into harmful body fluids. I give you an example that you may do the same: The body of a sow has an exceedingly well-tempered constitution; its food is acorns, date-stones and mud. So well-tempered is its bodily constitution that it turns food like that into healthy nourishment. So also if we have habitually good dispositions and are in a healthy [spiritual] state, we can extract spiritual benefit from any occurrence, even if the occurrence itself is not particularly helpful. As the Book of Proverbs truly says, 'He who scrutinizes attentively shall obtain mercy',[1] and elsewhere, 'Everything goes against a senseless man'.[2]

I heard about a certain brother who, if he saw that his cell was uncared for and disorderly when he went to consult any of the brethren, used to say to himself, 'Happy indeed is this brother! How free from care about many things, or rather, about all earthly things, and he so fixes his whole mind on high so that he has no leisure to put his cell in order.' And again, if he came on another and saw his cell in good order, clean, beautiful, he used to say to himself, 'The soul of this brother must be as clean and well-kept as his cell, for the good state of his soul must be represented by the good state of his cell.' He never said about anyone, 'This man is uncouth or that one is vainglorious', but on account of his own habitual good disposition he took edification from each of them.

May God, who is so good, give us these good dispositions, that we also may gain some benefits from every single person, and never think badly of our neighbor. And even if our own condition makes us think, or suddenly suspect, something evil of our neighbor, let us quickly change our thoughts into something kind and beautiful. For not to see evil in our brother generates, with God's help, that goodness which is well-pleasing to God, to whom be glory and honor for ever and ever. Amen.

FOOTNOTES

1. Prov 28:13.
2. Prov 14:4 (LXX)

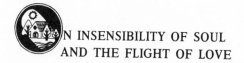

XXI

N INSENSIBILITY OF SOUL
AND THE FLIGHT OF LOVE

A S FOR INSENSIBILITY of soul, brother, you need continual reading of the divine writings combined with the heart-rending words of the god-fearing Fathers, also the memory of the fearful judgments of God, the separation of soul and body, and the fearful power to be let loose on those who have practised wickedness in this short and fretful life. Think that you are already about to stand before the fearsome and impartial judgment seat of Christ to be examined not only about your deeds, but about your words and thoughts also, before God and all his angels and the whole of creation. Remember continuously that judgment which the fearsome and just judge will pronounce on all who stand on his left: 'Depart from me, you cursed, into the everlasting fire, which was prepared for the devil and his angels.'[1] It is a good thing also to call to mind the great troubles and disasters that befall men, for only with trouble and toil will a hardened and insensitive soul be brought back from this evil state to its own proper state of perceptiveness.

The weakening of love towards your brothers comes from dwelling on suspicious thoughts and trusting in your own heart, and not wanting to suffer what divine providence arranges for you. Do you want to be helped by God about this? Do not be predisposed to believe your own suspicions.

Strive with all your might to be humbled for the sake of your brethren. For their sake, cut off your own will. If anyone insults you or otherwise troubles you, pray for him, as the Father says, as for one who does you a great benefit in curing you of your love for pleasure. From this your violent passions will be lessened. The Fathers say that genuine love is the curb of the passions, and, before all, it entreats God to give you sobriety and a clear understanding to know what is his will, what is good and well-pleasing to him and perfect, and the power of being constant in the performance of every good work.[2]

FOOTNOTES

1. Mt 25:41.
2. Rm 12:2.

XXII

MAXIMS ON THE SPIRITUAL LIFE

ABBOT DOROTHEOS used to say:
1. It is impossible for a man who sticks to his own judgment and his own idea to submit himself and promote the good of his neighbor.
2. Because we all have passions we ought not to have complete faith in our own [goodness of] heart, for a crooked rule makes the crooked straight and the straight crooked.
3. It is no great thing not to judge, and to be sympathetic to someone who is in trouble and falls down before you, but it is a great thing not to judge or to strike back when someone, on account of his own passions, speaks against you and to disagree when someone else is honored more than you are.
4. If a man does not despise all material things, all glory, all bodily rest, and all claim to righteousness, he cannot cut off his own will, or be delivered from anger and sorrow, or bring tranquillity to his neighbor.
5. Do not ask for love from your neighbor, for if you ask he does not respond you will be troubled. Instead, show your love for your neighbor and you will be at rest, and so you will bring your neighbor to love.
6. If a man is doing something according to God, trial of

some kind will come upon him, for trial and temptation either precede or follow all good. Neither is it sure the thing is happening according to God, unless it is proved so by trials and temptations.

7. Nothing is so conducive to unity as rejoicing about the same things and holding to the same purpose.

8. Not to despise the favor of any of your neighbors is humility; it ought to be accepted with thanksgiving even if it is small and of little moment.

9. If it is my duty to get something done, I prefer it to be done with my neighbor's advice, even if I do not agree with him and it goes wrong, rather than to be guided by my own opinion and have it turn out right.

10. It is a good thing on every occasion to prepare for ourselves a little less than we need, for it is not good for us to be completely satisfied in everything.

11. In all things that come upon me I never desire to run around in quest of human wisdom, but I always act with the small power I have on whatever it is, and at the same time leave the whole thing to God.

12. He who does not hold to his own will always has what he will; for externally he does not get his own way but whatever happens, no matter what it is, gives him quiet satisfaction and he discovers for himself that he has what he will. For he does not want things to happen as he wishes; he wants things to have happened as they happen.

13. It is not right to correct a brother at the moment when he is doing something wrong, or at any other time for the sake of getting back our own.

14. Love according to God is more powerful than natural affection.

15. No evil! Not even for a joke! A man may do something for a joke, but in the end he is trapped in it against his will.

16. A man ought to want to be freed from vice not because he wants to escape its affliction, but because he

detests it, according to Scripture. ['I hated them with a perfect hate; they have become my enemies.'[1]]

17. It is impossible for a man to be angry with anyone unless his heart is first lifted up against him, unless he despises him and esteems himself superior to him.

18. If, when a man is rebuked or corrected, he is roused to anger, it is a sign that he freely gives way to his passions. Bearing a rebuke or correction without being put out is a sign that a man does not give way to his passion through weakness or ignorance.

19. I know of no falling away of a monk which did not come from his reliance on his own sentiments. Nothing is more pitiful, nothing more disasterous than to be one's own [spiritual] director.

20. As shadows accompany the bodies that cast them, so temptations accompany the fulfilment of the commandments.

21. He who hates irritating people, hates gentleness. He who runs away from distressing people, runs away to rest in Christ.

FOOTNOTE

1. Ps 139:22.

INDEX

Abasement (*see also* Humility)   87

Abstinence (*see also* Fasting)   216

Angel(s)   133, 136, 162, 176, 177, 185, 249

Anger (*see also* Rage)   80, 95, 96, 149, 151, 153, 187, 229, 238

Arrogance (*see also* Self-righteousness)   81, 82, 83, 166, 167, 190, 240

Baptism   79, 80, 83

Body, the   102, 153, 165, 172, 180, 183, 185,
                                                   210, 217, 221, 230, 237, 246, 247, 249

   one body   138

Cell (*see also* Cenobium, Monastery)   89, 117, 137, 161, 183,
                                                        184, 244, 245, 247, 248

Cenobium (*see also* Cell, Monastery)   126, 127, 138, 157, 158, 159, 177, 178

Change of heart (*see also* Conversion)   82

Charity (*see also* Love)   178, 203

Christ   83, 84, 88, 110, 117, 132, 143, 154, 173, 175, 180,
                         186, 220, 221, 223, 224, 225, 227, 232, 238, 239, 249, 253

   Doctor of souls   173

   Jesus   230

   King of kings   86

   Lamb of God   221

   Only begotten son   79

   Our God   222

   Our King   86

   Our Lord   143, 192

   The Lord   80, 231

   Our Master   80, 86, 104, 135, 219, 228

   Our Savior   238

   Paschal Lamb   221

   Truth   162

Commandments of God   78, 79, 81, 83, 84, 88, 99, 100, 104, 114, 119,
                           120, 134, 144, 145, 149, 152, 201, 207, 208, 223, 231, 239

Communion, Holy (*see also* Eucharist)   158, 159

Conscience   80, 104ff., 112, 116, 117, 120, 137, 142, 147, 185, 195, 240

Contemplation   77

Contempt (*see also* Judgment) 81, 114, (124), 135, 237, 241

Conversion (*see also* Change of heart) 78, 136

Counsel 122-9, 237, 239

Death 78, 82, 85, 87, 113, 120, 124, 131, 161, 173, 183, 222, 224, 238

Devil (*see also* Enemy) 95, 96, 123, 124, 125, 126, 127, 134, 149, 154, 156, 157, 158, 159, 162, 190, 198, 238, 239, 249

Director (*see also* Counsel, Spiritual Father) 125, 126, 239, 253

Discipline 78

Disobedience 80, 102

Emotions (*see also* Passions) 77, 115, 127, 150, 184, 194

Enemy (*see also* Devil) 77, 94, 95, 124, 126, 152, 198, 210, 225, 238

Eucharist (*see also* Communion, Holy) 145

Evil 79, 83, 112, 125, 131, 137, 149, 151, 152, 165, 169, 173, 178, 179, 186, 188, 207, 243

Experience 99, 113, 127, 172, 194

Faith 94, 144, 190, 202, 237, 251

Fasting (*see also* Abstinence) 97, 122, 205, 208, 215, 216, 218

Fear of God 94, 109-121, 128, 142, 144, 145, 160, 161, 181, 201, 243

Forbearance 141, (161), 202

Gluttony 216, 217, (245)

God

   passim

   Being with God 109

   Resting with God 112

   United with God 111, 138

   Will of 123, 129, 139, 207, 208, 240

Grace 87, 90, 96, 127, 239

Habits, good and evil 106, 131, 156, 161, 168, 170, 178, 179, 180, 181, 186, 187, 247

Habit, monastic 86-8

Heart 83, 115, 118, 127, 129, 135, 138, 141, 144, 150, 153, 154, 165, 205, 228, 229, 238, 239, 251, 253

Humility (*see also* Abasement) 81, 82, 83, 90, 91, 94, 95, 99, 100, 101, 102, 115, 117, 120, 128, 145, 150, 154, 161, 162, 166, 168, 173, 181, 188, 189, 194, 196, 199, 203, 205, 216, 237, 242, 246, 252

   Humility and physical labor 101, (244)

Indifference (*apatheia*) 88, 239

Intelligence 229

Joy 113, 127, 128, 129, 216, 237

Judgment(s) 124, 126, 131-6, 157

  Judgment of God 100, 129, 133, 135, 193

  Judgment Day 154, 211, 225

  Judgment Seat 249

  Own judgment 129, 239

Knowledge 126, 147, 152, 169, 170, 193, 201, 204, 205, 207, 208, 210, 211, 234

Love (*see also* Charity) 109, 110, 113, 115, 117, 118, 120, 136, 137, 139, 144, 145, 154, 183, 188, 192, 193, 206, 208, 222, 237, 239, 240, 243, 245, 249, 250, 251, 252

Man, created by God 77, 104, 223 *et passim*

  Image and likeness of God 77, 188, 218, 220, 223, 224

  Rational animal 231

Material things (85), 86, 106, 241, 251

Mind 84, 100, 127, 138, 150, 160, 195, 230, 242

Monastery (*see also* Cell, Cenobium) 85, 97, 127, 140, 164, 166, 217, 241

Mortification(s) 84, 87, 88, 202, 205

Nature, Law of 77, 104

Neglect (*see also* Negligence) 119, 166, 172, 174, 186, 188, 202

Negligence (*see also* Neglect) 107, 173, 179, 180, 241

Neighbor(s) 106, 107, 112, 119, 120, 131, 132, 133, 135, 136, 137, 138, 139, 144, 157, 161, 167, 205, 206, 209, 222, 223, 238, 240, 243, 248, 251, 252

Obedience 81, 89, 90, 91, 92, 122, 127, 176, 202, 239

Ordination 91

Paradise 77, 81, 82, 223

Passion(s) (*see also* Emotion) 77, 80, 81, 83, 85, 88, 96, 114, 149, 154, 167, 168, 169, 170, 178, 179, 180, 181, 183, 184, 187, 195, 196, 197, 222, 229, 237, 243, 250, 251, 253

Peace of mind/soul 83, 91, 92, 96, 113, 127, 129, 141, 142, 150, 153, 160, 175, 180, 237, 241

Pleasure(s) 85, 152, 195

  Love of 77, 80, 102, 160, 173, 187, 188, 222

Poverty 84, 85, 161

Prayer(s) 77, 101, 106, 115, 128, 145, 150, 154, 157, 177, 190, 217, 223, 242, 243, 246

Pride   80, 81, 101, 188, 197

   Of monastic life   97-8

   Two kinds   96-8

Punishment   84, 96, 109, 111, 113, 133, 141, 168, 180, 181, 183, 209, 225

Rage (*see also* Anger)   149, 150, 217

Rancor   149-54

Reading(s)   164, 178, 249

Resentment   153

Rest (*see also* Peace of mind)   81, 82, 127, 141, 143, 144, 187, 199

Salvation   91, 163, 176, 177, 196

Scripture(s)   77, 79, 91, 109, 110, 129, 175, 184, 188, 201, 253

Self-accusation   83, 140-41, 143

Self-control   94, 95, 106, 171, 173, 202, 246

Self-discipline   (141), 188

Self-elevation   81

Self-examination   157

Self-glorification   99

Self-indulgence   114

Self-justification   83

Self-preference   81

Self-righteousness   123, 124, 190

Self-satisfaction   129

Self-will   82, 83, 87, 88, 89, 119, 123, 124, 125, 101

   Own will   123, 124, 145, 209, 222, 239, 250, 251

Senses   79

Sense perceptions   77

Simplicity   100, 118, 135, 225

Sin(s)   77, 79, 80, 81, 90, 132, 133, 135, 136, 143, 144, 168, 172, 174,
             181, 185, 186, 193, 197, 198, 208, 216, 217, 221, 223, 224, 225, 238

   Forgiveness of   80

Solitary life   84-5, 245

Soul(s)   79, 83, 96, 99, 100, 102, 111, 113, 114, 125,
                          127, 131, 133, 134, 135, 142, 143, 157, 158, 161,
                          166, 167, 172, 174, 180, 181, 183, 184, 185, 187,
                          188, 189, 192, 197, 199, 201, 203, 209, 210, 215,
                          217, 225, 227, 229, 230, 237, 240, 247, 248, 249

Spiritual father (*see also* Director)   90, 91, 125

Spiritual insight 91, 176

Suspicion(s) 95, 157, 158, 159, 160, 249

Temptation(s) 96, 102, 115, 125, 126, 142, 146, 181, 192-9, 251, 253

Tithes 215, 216

Tranquility 81, 82, 88, 89, 128, 153, 239, 251

Vainglory 80, 87, 96, 160, 167, 168, 169, 170, 173, 187, 190, 198, 204, 205, 248

Vice(s) 114, 116, 167, 179, 180, 202, 252

Vigil(s) 95, 97, 122, 160, 176, 177

Virginity 84, 85

Virtue(s) 83, 85, 88, 89, 90, 91, 95, 96, 100, 101, 111, 141, 144, 146, 161, 162, 163, 164, 165, 166, 167, 179, 180, 187, 188, 194, 198, 202, 203, 204, 205, 206, 208, 211, 231, 243